LOGIC GAMES FOR THE LSAT

LEARNINGEXPRESS®

NEW YORK

Library of Congress Cataloging-in-Publication Data
Logic Games for the LSAT.
 p. cm.
 ISBN-13: 978-1-57685-779-3 (pbk.)
 ISBN-10: 1-57685-779-4 (pbk)
 1. Law School Admission Test—Study guides. 2. Law schools—United States—Entrance examina-
tions—Study guides. 3. Logic—Problems, exercises, etc. I. LearningExpress (Organization)
 KF285.Z9L645 2011
 340.076—dc22
                                2011006976

Printed in the United States of America

9 8 7 6 5 4 3 2 1

First Edition

ISBN 978-1-57685-779-3

For more information or to place an order, contact LearningExpress at:
  2 Rector Street
  26th Floor
  New York, NY 10006

Or visit us at:
  www.learnatest.com

CONTENTS

Introduction v

Chapter 1: LSAT Logic, Game Types, and General Strategies 1

Chapter 2: The LearningExpress Test Preparation System 21

Chapter 3: Sequencing Games Review 39

Chapter 4: Selection Games Review 71

Chapter 5: Distribution Games Review 101

Chapter 6: Matching Games Review 129

Chapter 7: Hybrid Games Review 167

Chapter 8: Practice Test 1 195

Chapter 9: Practice Test 2 227

INTRODUCTION ▶

The Law School Admission Test (LSAT) is the standardized test used by American Bar Association–approved law schools in assessing and admitting law school applicants. If you're planning to go to law school in the United States, taking the LSAT is a must. The test includes five 35-minute multiple-choice sections followed by a 35-minute writing sample. It's a long test; including breaks, distribution and collection of tests, and other test-day procedures, it lasts over four hours.

The LSAT is administered by the Law School Admission Council (LSAC), a nonprofit corporation that assists law schools and applicants with nearly every aspect of the admissions process, from the LSAT to letters of recommendation. (LSAC will be responsible for collecting your application information if you sign up for their Law School Data Assembly Service.) LSAC usually administers the test four times a year, in February, June, September or October, and December. For law school admission in the fall, you're often required to take the LSAT by the previous December, but applicants who are on the ball often the take one of the earlier June or September/October tests—that is, a year or more before they intend to enroll in law school.

The LSAT is administered at one of many test centers worldwide. Make sure to register early (at www.lsac.org) to ensure that you get your choice of testing locations, as they have limited availability and are filled on a first-come, first-served basis.

What's on the LSAT

According to LSAC, the purpose of the LSAT is to "measure skills that are considered essential for success in law school: the reading and comprehension of complex texts with accuracy and insight; the organization and management of information and the ability to draw reasonable inferences from it; the ability to think critically; and the analysis and evaluation of the reasoning and arguments of others."[1]

---

1 See "What the Test Measures" at www.lsac.org/JD/LSAT/about-the-LSAT.asp

Essentially, the LSAT tests reading comprehension, information management and analysis, and argument analysis. These areas correspond to the three sections on the LSAT. LSAC calls these sections Reading Comprehension, Analytical Reasoning, and Logical Reasoning. Among test-takers and test prep literature, the Analytical Reasoning section is known as the *logic games* section, and the Logical Reasoning section is known as the *arguments* section.

The five multiple-choice sections are broken down as follows, but can appear on the actual test in any order (except for the Writing Sample, which is always last):

- One Reading Comprehension section
- One Analytical Reasoning (i.e., logic games) section
- Two Logical Reasoning (i.e., arguments) sections
- One experimental section—an unscored section resembling one of these section-types for the sake of future LSAT test creation (you won't know which is the experimental section)
- Writing Sample

The sequence of sections and breaks at a typical LSAT administration might be as follows:

1. Analytical Reasoning (35 minutes)
2. Logical Reasoning (35 minutes)
3. Reading Comprehension (35 minutes)
4. Break (10–15 minutes)
5. Analytical Reasoning, experimental (35 minutes)
6. Logical Reasoning (35 minutes)
7. Break (5 minutes)
8. Writing Sample (35 minutes)

So what are these section types all about anyway?

Reading Comprehension

The Reading Comprehension section on the LSAT should be familiar to you already, as it is essentially a spiced-up version of similar sections on the SAT and the ACT. You are given four passages on various subjects in the natural sciences, social sciences, and humanities, each accompanied by five to eight questions (for a total of 26 to 28 questions). These questions test your ability to quickly absorb essential information from the passage, understand and interpret the passage, and reason about the ideas presented. You could be asked about the author's attitude, details in the passage, implications of statements made, main ideas, the function of various parts of the passage, or a host of other questions designed to test your level of comprehension. The passages are generally 55–60 lines—about what you're used to on standardized tests you took in high school—but they are more complex than those on the SAT and ACT, drawn from sources ranging from *Scientific American* to the *ABA Journal*, and seemingly chosen to make you sweat.

Logical Reasoning

The Logical Reasoning section of the LSAT may not look like anything you've seen on other standardized tests you have taken. Nonetheless, it tests your ability to carefully read and analyze arguments—skills that the LSAC deems essential for success in law school. Beyond that, it is the only scored section that appears twice on the LSAT. The sorts of ideas and skills tested in this section are truly the bread and butter of legal education and practice: as LSAC puts it, the skills of "drawing well-supported conclusions, reasoning by analogy, determining how additional evidence affects an argument, applying principles or rules, and identifying argument flaws."[1]

A Logical Reasoning section consists of 20–25 short passages, each followed by one or two questions (for a total of 24 to 26 questions). The passages, if followed by one question, are usually three to four sentences long, and comprise an argument of some sort—that is, a presentation of a viewpoint or thesis along with supporting claims (although often not explicitly so). If followed by two questions, the passages will usually consist of two short opposing arguments, often presented as an argument followed by a rebuttal. The vast majority of questions are based on a single argument, rather than the argument-rebuttal format.

The questions test precisely the concepts LSAC says they will. They will include asking you to provide missing assumptions in the argument, identify logical flaws, identify statements that would undermine or strengthen an argument, and sometimes even complete an argument (when a part has been left out of a passage).

Analytical Reasoning (i.e., Logic Games)

The Analytical Reasoning section will be the least familiar section to the majority of test-takers. It consists of four logic games, each accompanied by five to seven questions, for a total of 22 to 24 questions. Each game consists of a setup paragraph, which provide the general parameters of the game, followed by a set of conditions. For example:

> **1.** Over the course of seven days, exactly seven different Shakespeare plays will be presented in a theater.
>   **a.** Othello must follow *Romeo and Juliet*
>   **b.** If *Hamlet* is shown on Wednesday, *Macbeth* won't be shown on any subsequent day
>   **c.** Either *The Taming of the Shrew* or *Hamlet* must be shown on Wednesday
>   **d.** *A Midsummer Night's Dream* will be shown on Saturday

Following this game setup, a series of questions are presented that test your ability to understand the mechanics of the game and work with new information presented. For example, one question might ask: if *The Taming of the Shrew* is not shown at all, which play cannot be shown on Friday? A likely answer will be *Macbeth*, since if *The Taming of the Shrew* is not shown, *Hamlet* must be shown on Wednesday, and if *Hamlet* is shown on Wednesday, *Macbeth* can't be shown on any later day.

Logic games are designed to present information concerning relationships among entities and then test your ability to both manage the information and reason logically about those relationships. The relationships can be spatial, temporal, or logical, and the entities can be persons, places, or things. The example here concerns temporal relationships between things (e.g., that *Othello* follows *Romeo and Juliet*).

When in the midst of trying to solve a particularly cumbersome or difficult logic game, LSAT test-takers often find themselves wondering how on earth this could be relevant to law school. LSAC says these highly

---

1 See "What the Test Measures" at www.lsac.org/JD/LSAT/about-the-LSAT.asp

unusual mental exercises "reflect the kinds of complex analyses that a law student performs in the course of legal problem solving."[1] Now, this may or may not be true—and many have difficulty seeing how it could be—but in the end, that's beside the point. LSAC thinks logic games are important, and until you finish the last question on the LSAT, it's in your interest to think they're important, too!

Altogether, the three section types on the LSAT will call on your powers of rigorous analytical reasoning. This book will help you to master the art of manipulating rules and conditions and to develop expertise with the logic games section of the LSAT.

How the LSAT Is Scored

Four of the five multiple-choice sections are scored, and they will have a considerable impact on your law school application. The writing sample is not scored, but it is sent to law schools along with your application.

The Raw Score
While you will end up answering between 120 and 130 questions (including those on the experimental section) on any given LSAT administration, the four scored multiple-choice sections comprise only 100 to 101 questions. There is no penalty for wrong answers, and each question is weighted equally. Your raw score is simply the number of questions (of the 100 to 101 scored questions) you answer correctly.

The Scaled Score
Your raw score out of 100 or 101 is translated into a scaled score between 120 and 180. This occurs through a statistical process called *equating*, which attempts to correct for minor differences in difficulty between tests. Every LSAT question is pretested (partially through the experimental sections), and data collected from these tests enable equating. The original test that the score is equated against was given in June 1991, and the process effectively ensures that you are competing for your scaled score against a much larger pool of LSAT takers from various test administrations. So don't worry if all the geniuses you know are taking the test on your test date, and the test seemed harder than your practice LSATs—that won't prevent you from getting your best score.

On the high end, a 180 doesn't necessarily reflect a perfect raw score. You can miss up to three questions and often still get a 180. On the low end, to get past a 120, you generally need to get 14 to 17 questions right. Beyond that, for every three raw points you get (every three questions answered correctly), your scaled score will generally go up about two points—but that is a rough rule and varies from test to test.

The Percentile Rank
The score report LSAC sends you will include your percentile rank, which indicates the percent of test-takers over a recent three-year period with scaled scores lower than your scaled score. So if you got a scaled score of 166 and your reported percentile rank is 93%, it means that 93% of all LSAT test-takers over some specified period of time scored lower than 166. Each LSAT will have a table, slightly different from test to test that correlates each

---

1 See "What the Test Measures" at www.lsac.org/JD/LSAT/about-the-LSAT.asp

scaled score to a percentile rank; for example, a score of 180 put you in the 99.9th percentile, while a score of 151 put you in the 50th percentile. To score better than 90% of test-takers, you need to get around a 164 or 165.

In the extreme upper and lower ranges, differences in raw and scaled scores don't translate to major percentile rank changes: someone who misses one question to get a 180 might be in the 99.9th percentile, while someone who misses 11 questions to get a 173 might be in the 99.0th percentile. But in the middle of the field—for the majority of law school applicants—LSAT percentile ranks can be very sensitive to changes in raw and scaled scores, and test-takers would be wise to keep this in mind as they look for motivation to keep practicing. Say someone misses 40 questions to get a score of 153 and a rank in the 59th percentile. Another person might miss 30 questions, and get a score of 159 and a rank in the 79th percentile. That is a 20-point percentile difference!

The following table gives a sense of the approximate relationship between raw scores, scaled scores, and percentile ranks. Please note that this is merely an example meant to illustrate how LSAT score correlations generally work—actual score correlations will vary from test to test.

RAW SCORE (how many questions you answered correctly)	SCALED SCORE (your actual LSAT score, reported to law schools)	PERCENTILE RANK (the percent of test-takers during a recent three-year period with a lower scaled score)
101	180	99.9
90	173	99.0
80	166	94.0
70	159	79.0
60	153	59.0
50	147	36.0
40	141	17.0
30	134	5.5
20	125	0.5
0–15	120	0.0

The LSAT is constructed so that the majority of test-takers won't finish every section and every problem. Keep this in mind both as you consider this table and as you practice for the test. To maximize your scaled score and percentile rank, you are better off ensuring that you correctly answer as many questions as you can, rather than rushing through the test attempting to answer every question and ultimately getting fewer correct answers. If you only get to 3/4 of the questions on the test, answer 4/5 of those correctly, and randomly guess on the rest, you are looking at raw score of about 65, which might translate to a scaled score of about 156 and percentile ranking of about 70. If you manage to correctly answer all of those carefully analyzed questions, your decision to focus energies on that select set will result in a raw score of about 80, which might translate to a scaled score of about 166 and percentile rank of about 94!

How the LSAT Is Used

Virtually every law school uses the LSAT as a major factor in the assessment of their applicant pool. According to validity studies conducted by LSAC, the LSAT is a statistically significant numerical predictor of performance in law school (better than undergraduate GPA alone).[1] The median statistical correlation between LSAT scores and first-year performance is 0.33 (a value of 0 indicates a random relationship, and a value of 1 indicates perfect correlation). The idea is that the LSAT directly tests a large portion of the skills necessary for success in the first year of law school and beyond. But that claim is largely speculative, and is exceedingly difficult to validate. Students should realize that although the test is a predictor (statistically speaking), it might not be a very strong one—and more importantly, that the LSAC validity study results certainly don't mean that the test will predict your performance in law school, let alone your success in a legal career. LSAC itself wisely notes that the LSAT is not a perfect predictor, especially because it varies from one school to another in its predictive ability.

The LSAT and undergraduate GPA together provide a slightly better predictor of first-year grades than either one taken alone (with a median statistical correlation of 0.46). For this reason, and for the sake of convenience, many law schools combine the GPA and LSAT into one *index score* with which they rank their applicants. Law schools often devise their own formulas for calculating this index score, based on the relative importance they attach to the LSAT score versus GPA. Applications are sorted for further review based on this index. However, the same caveats apply to the index, so no deterministic conclusions about the future performance of any individual in law school or the legal profession should be made based on that measure!

How to Use This Book

This book is designed to help you master the art and science of logic games. The Analytical Reasoning (logic games) section of the LSAT is one of the most unusual standardized test sections out there, and most test-takers will be unfamiliar and unpracticed with the skills it requires. Fortunately, there are a limited number of principles behind both the mechanics of the games and the proper approach to the games, which when studied and practiced, will make the Analytical Reasoning section just as approachable and tractable as any other section. There are a limited number of game types, question types, and specific strategies and skills tested—and once you learn them you will become a confident logic gamer.

This book breaks down the LSAT logic games into five types—sequencing games, selection games, distribution games, matching games, and hybrid games—with a chapter devoted to each. Each chapter breaks down the essential components of that game type, and provides specific tips and strategies for mastering it.

First, familiarize yourself with the LearningExpress Test Preparation System in Chapter 2. There, you will find suggested schedules for working through the rest of the book. Make sure to read the general strategies in Chapter 1. Beyond that, you will be advised that if you have the time, you should work through each chapter sequentially, carefully reading the tips and strategies at the beginning of the chapter, working through each practice game and the answer explanations to understand how the strategies should be applied to each, and making sure to apply them to each new practice game as you go along. If you are crunched for time, you will be advised

---

1 See www.lsac.org/jd/pdfs/LSAT-Score-Predictors-of-Performance.pdf

to start by taking one of the practice tests at the end of the book to assess which games you need the most help with. Then go to those chapters, and work through the tips, strategies, and practice games. Either way, make sure to take both practice tests, at least one of which you should do after working through the strategy chapters, to see your progress!

When working through practice games, whether in the strategy chapters or on the practice tests, make sure to mix timed and untimed trials. There are eight practice problems in each chapter, so consider doing four games untimed, and then four games in a row with a 35-minute total time limit (since you will have to do four games in 35 minutes on the actual LSAT). The untimed games will help you to practice the thought processes and diagramming techniques recommended, and to carefully and deliberately apply the tips and strategies you have learned. The timed games will help you practice efficiency with those processes and learn to quickly and efficiently apply the proper techniques. Over time, this approach will build speed, efficiency, and accuracy.

After every practice game or group of four games, make sure to review the detailed answer explanations, even for answers you got right. Your main concern, especially in the initial practice games for each game type, is to ensure that you are tackling the game and questions with the right thought processes and approaches, and reasoning in a sound, logical manner. This comes from reviewing the answer explanations, comparing your approach to that presented in the explanation, and (if needed) determining how you can improve your approach the next time around. Don't get into a logic game rut: stay active and engaged with the practice and explanations by reflecting on what your thought processes were when working through a practice game, and constantly strive to amend those processes so that you won't miss similar question types, deductions, or connections in the future. The book is carefully designed to help you master logic games, but your success in doing so depends on how much you put into it!

LSAT Logic, Game Types, and General Strategies

C H A P T E R

1

LSAT logic games are ultimately about logical reasoning. They require general logical reasoning, such as realizing that if A comes before B, then B cannot be first in a sequence and A cannot be last in a sequence. This kind of logical reasoning is ubiquitous in logic games.

Logic games also require that we translate sentences into formal logical constructions using "logical connectives" (in particular, "and," "or," "not," and "if-then"), and that we manipulate the resulting constructions. This kind of logical reasoning is more complex and may be unfamiliar to many students.

Know Your LSAT Formal Logic

In the following discussion, we describe how statements are formed using logical connectives and how to reason with such statements. Our building blocks are two "simple" statements, which we call statement "A" and statement "B." "A" and "B" can stand for any declarative statement, but on the LSAT, these statements will often be bits of concrete information presented in the logic game setup, such as "Abigail is in the morning section" or "Brian is in the morning section."

Conjunctions ("A and B")

A conjunction uses the word "and." It means that both statements are true. If you're told that A and B are true, then the conjunction is "A and B."

An example would be "Abigail and Brian are both in the morning section."

Disjunctions ("A or B")

A disjunction uses the connective "or." It means that either one or the other statement is true, or both are true. The disjunction "A or B" means that either A or B is true, or both are true. An example is the statement "Either Abigail or Brian is in the morning section." Note that this disjunction is inclusive—both A and B can be true. An exclusive disjunction is where only one statement, not both, can be true.

Negations ("not A")

You can also negate a single statement with the connective "not" (it's called a connective even though it operates on just one statement, rather than connecting two statements). This is very straightforward: if you want to say that A is not true, you say "not A." It can be symbolized with an equal sign with a line through it: $\neq A$

Note that if we negate the negation of statement A—that is, if we say "not A" is not true—we end up with "not (not A)," which is the same things as just saying "A." Think about it this way: if you say that it is not true that A is not true, you are really saying that A is true. A double negative in English grammar works the same way. If you say that you are not unhappy, that means you are happy.

Negating Conjunctions and Disjunctions ("not (A and B)," "not (A or B)")

We have considered the connectives "and," "or," and "not." Before turning to the other connectives, we must take a look at how to apply connectives to one another—in particular, how to negate conjunctions and disjunctions.

First, keep in mind that what results from using a connective on any statement is itself a new statement, which can be a part of yet another statement using a connective. So if we create the conjunction "A and B," this new statement "A and B" can be negated to create "not (A and B)."

What does "not (A and B)" mean? It means that it's not the case that both A is true and B is true. In other words, one of the two statements (or both) must be false. Using the previous example, the statement "not (A and B)" tells us that either Abigail is not in the morning section or Brian is not in the morning section, or neither are in the morning section. Notice that you can also say "either A is not the case or B is not the case." This is simply the disjunction "not A or not B."

In fact, these two statements are equivalent: *not (A and B) = not A or not B.*

Saying A and B can't both be true ("not (A and B)") is the same as saying at least one isn't true ("not A or not B").

It is important to use parentheses to avoid confusion. For example, "not (A and B)" isn't the same statement as "not A and B." The first one, "not (A and B)," says that A and B can't both be true, so B could be true, as long as A is not true. The second one, "not A and B," says "A is not true" and "B is true." These two are clearly not equivalent statements.

So far we have seen how to negate a conjunction "A and B." What about negating the disjunction "A or B"? The disjunction "A or B" tells us that at least one statement is true. So "not (A or B)" means neither statement is true. This is the same as both not A and not B are true ("not A and not B").

Therefore, these two statements are equivalent: *not (A or B) = not A and not B*.

Saying that it can't be true and that at least one statement is true is the same as saying that both A is not true and B is not true.

Conditionals ("if A, then B")

The most important logical concept on the LSAT is the conditional statement, which takes the form "if A, then B." It is symbolized with an arrow: A → B.

This conditional means that if statement A is true, then statement B is true. Before we can understand how to work with conditional statements, it's worth pausing to figure out what this means exactly in the *logical* sense, which is similar to, but slightly different from the everyday sense.

The Logical Meaning of Conditionals

When people make "if A, then B" statements in everyday English speech, they usually have some sort of causal connection between A and B in mind. A common example of an everyday English "if-then" statement is "if it is raining, then I will bring my umbrella." The idea is that a causal connection exists between the first part of the statement and the second part—you bring your umbrella *because* it is raining. However, this statement is false when it is raining but I do not bring my umbrella, because the causal connection clearly does not hold (the rain did not cause me to bring my umbrella). Therefore, we do not have a clear understanding of the circumstances that make the conditional statement true. For example, is the conditional statement true when I bring my umbrella even though it is not raining? Further, this example doesn't address the confusion students often feel when they encounter if-then statements on the LSAT that do not have a clear causal connection, like "if car A has a spoiler, then car B has performance tires." What does car A's spoiler have to do with car B's performance tires? How is that the same as me bringing an umbrella because it is raining?

In short, in the logical meaning of conditionals, there is no causal connection between A and B. It simply means that when A is true, B is also true. Think of it as "if A is true, then B must be true." We don't know why the truth of A guarantees the truth of B (why car A having a spoiler guarantees that car B has performance tires), but from a logical perspective (which is the *only* perspective of the LSAT logic games!), we don't care. All we care about is that fact: when car A has a spoiler, car B must have performance tires.

Further, the conditional statement must be true in all circumstances except when A is true and B is false. So, a conditional statement is true when A is true and B is true, when A is false and B is true, and when A is false and B is false.

This answers our question about what happens when it isn't raining, but I bring my umbrella anyway: What happens is that the statement is true. You might wonder how this could be.

Remember that there is no causal connection in the strictly logical "if-then" statement. Even still, you might have issues with conditionals that are true whenever A is false but B is true—that's ok, but for the purpose of the LSAT, you need to accept it. Why does this even matter for the LSAT? Well, let's take a look at an example. Suppose that a logic game gives us the following set of restrictions:

> If Brian is in the afternoon section, then Charles is in the evening section.
> If Danielle is in the morning section, then Elizabeth is also in the morning section.

Now suppose that in the course of trying to answer a question, we want to check whether the following is acceptable for Brian and Elizabeth, without even knowing where Charles and Danielle are assigned.

> *Morning:* *Elizabeth*
> *Afternoon:*
> *Evening:* *Brian*

We need to see whether this assignment violates either of our two restrictions. Given our understanding of the logic of conditionals, we can quickly check the assignment against each of the conditional statements—and as long as either the first part of the conditional statement is false or the second part of the conditional statement is true (or both), we know that that conditional statement is true (that is, the restriction is not violated).

For the first conditional statement, we see that the *first* part of the conditional (that Brian is in the afternoon section) is *false* (because according to this assignment, Brian is in the evening section). So the conditional statement as a whole must be true (regardless of whether Charles ends up in the evening section or not).

If you're still having trouble with the logic of conditionals, another way to think about this is that since Brian is not in the afternoon section, the first restriction can't be violated because the first restriction "does not apply" to this scenario—it would only apply if Brian were in fact in the afternoon section (which would then require Charles to be in the evening section).

For the second conditional statement, the *second* part (that that Elizabeth is in the morning section) is *true*, so (again) the conditional statement as a whole must be true (regardless of whether Danielle ends up in the morning section or not). Since Elizabeth is in the morning section, the second restriction can't be violated because the only way for it to be violated would be for the first part to be true (Danielle in the morning section) and the second part false (Elizabeth *not* in the morning section). Since both restrictions are true with this (partial) assignment of students to sections—that is, since neither restriction is violated—this would be an acceptable assignment. The point here is that checking to see whether the conditional restrictions are violated becomes a relatively straightforward matter once you understand the logic of conditionals.

The Basic Operation of Conditionals

To make sure we understand the basics of how conditionals work, let's use another logic game example. Suppose that a game gives us the following set of restrictions (each a conditional statement):

> If book A is selected for the reading list, then book B is selected for the reading list.
> If book B is selected for the reading list, then book C is selected for the reading list.
> If book D is selected for the reading list, then book E is selected for the reading list.

Now, we can symbolize these conditional statements in the following manner. First, let

> A = A is selected
> B = B is selected
> C = C is selected
> D = D is selected
> E = E is selected

Then, we can rewrite the conditional statements as:

> If A, then B
> If B, then C
> If D, then E

Or we can rewrite them as:

> A → B
> B → C
> D → E

Suppose we have a question which begins, "if A is selected for the reading list…". What deductions can be made from this information?

Well, we know that "A → B"—if A is true, then B must be true—and we know that A is true (A is selected), so we can deduce that B is true as well (B is selected). And we know that "B → C"—if B is true, then C must be true—and we know that B is true, so we can deduce that C is true as well. This is the most basic way in which conditional statements operate.

Now, suppose we are considering a reading list and trying to figure out whether it is acceptable given the set of restrictions for the game. Suppose A, B, C, and D are selected for the list, but E is not selected. To figure out whether that reading list is acceptable, we need to see whether it violates any of the three conditional statements (the three restrictions).

The first statement (A → B) is true (not violated) because B is true (B is selected). The second statement (B → C) is true (not violated) because C is true (C is selected). But the third statement (D → E) is *not* true (the restriction is violated) because while D is true (D is selected), E is not true (E is not selected). That is, this reading list, which includes only A, B, C, and D, makes the conditional statement "D → E" false.

COMMON MISTAKES WITH CONDITIONALS

Finally, an important word of caution concerning two common mistakes students make with conditionals. Suppose we have a question which begins, "if book B is selected for the reading list…". What deductions can be made from this information? Many students are tempted to try to apply the conditional statement "A → B" to conclude that since B is selected, A must have been selected. **This is a mistake!**

The conditional statement "A → B" means that if A is true, B must be true. But that does *not* mean that if B is true, then A must be true! It might be that B is true even though A is not true—we just don't know. A likely reason that students sometimes make this mistake is that they rely on the causal sense of the conditional, like when the rain causes me to bring my umbrella. However, "if I bring my umbrella, then it must be raining" is flawed logical reasoning. The *only* information conveyed by the statement "if A, then B" is that if A is true, then B must be true. To reiterate, knowing that book B is selected for the reading list doesn't give us any information about whether book A is selected, despite the fact that we know that "if A is selected, then B is selected."

Suppose we have a question that begins, "If book A is *not* selected for the reading list…". What deductions can be made from this information? Many students are tempted to conclude that B is also not selected. **This is also a mistake!**

Again, the conditional statement that "if A, then B" does not mean that B is true *only* when A is true! In other words, knowing that book A is not selected for the reading list doesn't give us any information about book B.

To make sure that you avoid these common mistakes, keep in mind that "if A, then B" does not mean "if B, then A," and does not mean "if not A, then not B."

Conditionals as Disjunctions

Recall that we said that a conditional statement (such as "if A, then B") is true when either A is false or B is true, or both are true. Notice that we can write this as a disjunction: either not A or B. In fact, these two statements are equivalent:

If A, then B = not A or B

Or, using the arrow symbol: $A \rightarrow B = not\ A\ or\ B$

It is especially useful to keep in mind that conditionals can be written as disjunctions because occasionally the LSAT will give you a restriction that looks like this:

If book A is not selected for the reading list, book B is selected.

We can translate this as: $(\neq A) \rightarrow B$

But we know that this is equivalent to the disjunction: $\neq (\neq A)\ or\ B$

And we know that "not (not A)" is the same thing as A, so we end up with "A or B."

So the conditional "$(\neq A) \rightarrow B$" is really the disguised disjunction "A or B," and that's sometimes helpful to know in a logic game.

The Wording of Conditional Statements

The wording of conditional statements is usually fairly straightforward. However, sometimes "if A, then B" is worded "B, if A." Using the reading list example, the conditional could be worded "book B is selected for the reading list if book A is selected for the reading list."

Sometimes you might encounter the phrase "only if." If you see a statement "A only if B," just rewrite this to as "If A, then B." To understand this, think of them as both saying that if A is true, then B must be true (the *only* circumstances in which A is true are those in which B is also true). For example, the condition "book A is selected only if book B is selected" could be reworded "If book A is selected, then book B is selected."

You might also sometimes encounter the word "unless." This has a special meaning in a strictly logical sense. "Unless" means "if not." So if you see the statement "A unless B," just rewrite this as "A if not B," or "if not B, then A," or "$(\neq B) \rightarrow A$)."

For example, the condition "book A is selected unless book B is selected" can be reworded as "book A is selected if book B is not selected" or "if book B is not selected, then book A is selected."

Note that this does not mean that if book B is selected, book A is not selected! This is often confusing for students who might think that the wording of "A unless B" intuitively means that A is true except when B is true, in which case A is false. It's an interesting interpretation, but you need to forget it. The word "unless" has a specific logical meaning ("if not"), which you just need to accept for the LSAT. You can blame logicians for giving "unless" a less-than-intuitive logical meaning.

Contrapositives

Every conditional statement has an equivalent "contrapositive" form. The conditional (if-then) statement and its contrapositive say exactly the same thing, only in different words.

The contrapositive is: *If not B, then not A.*

Pause here, and memorize this. The procedure for producing the contrapositive form of any conditional statement is to flip the order of the two parts of the statement and negate each part: from "A → B" to "≠ B → ≠ A."

How does the contrapositive follow from the original conditional? Suppose B is not true. Well then, A couldn't be true because according the original statement, if A were in fact true, B would have to be true. It might help to make this a bit more concrete. Suppose I have the conditional statement: "if book A is selected for the reading list, then book B is also selected for the reading list." Now, suppose I know that book B is not selected for the reading list. Then I know that book A couldn't possibly have been selected for the reading list, since if it were, book B would also have to be selected. In other words, the following conditional is true: "if book B is not selected for the reading list, then book A is not selected for the reading list."

The contrapositive is equivalent to the original conditional, regardless of any implied causal connection: "if A, then B" and "if not B, then not A" is the same thing, even if A and B have nothing to do with one another.

Basically, any time you see a statement of the form "if A, then B" (in symbols, "A → B"), you should immediately write down the equivalent (but seemingly different) piece of information that "if not B, then not A" (in symbols, "≠ B → ≠ A"). As we will see, this contrapositive form of the original statement will often allow for connections and deductions that you otherwise might have missed.

Because contrapositives are so important to the LSAT, let's take a look at some more complex examples where we use the rules for negating disjunctions and conjunctions.

Conditional:	If A, then B.
Contrapositive:	If not B, then not A.
Example of Conditional:	If book A is selected, then book B is selected.
Corresponding Contrapositive:	If book B is not selected, then book A is not selected.
Comments:	This is the simple, basic form of the contrapositive. Apply this general form when dealing with more complex constructions.

Conditional:	If A, then (B and C).
Contrapositive:	If not (B and C), then not A.
Equivalent Contrapositive:	If not B or not C, then not A.
Example of Conditional:	If book A is selected, then books B and C are selected.

Corresponding Contrapositive:	If either book B is not selected or book C is not selected, then book A will not be selected.
Comments:	We have negated a conjunction ("B and C") in producing this contrapositive.

Conditional:	If A, then (B or C).
Contrapositive:	If not (B or C), then not A.
Equivalent Contrapositive:	If not B and not C, then not A.
Example of Conditional:	If book A is selected, then either book B is selected or book C is selected.
Corresponding Contrapositive:	If neither book B nor book C is selected, then book A is not selected.
Comments:	We have negated a disjunction ("B or C") in producing this contrapositive.

Conditional:	If A and B, then C.
Contrapositive:	If not C, then not (A and B).
Equivalent Contrapositive:	If not C, then not A or not B.
Example of Conditional:	If book A and book B are both selected for the reading list, then book C will also be selected.
Corresponding Contrapositive:	If book C is not selected for the reading list, then either book A will not be selected or book B will not be selected.
Comments:	We have negated a conjunction ("A and B") in producing this contrapositive.

Conditional:	If A or B, then C.
Contrapositive:	If not C, then not (A or B).
Equivalent Contrapositive:	If not C, then not A and not B.
Example of Conditional:	If either book A or book B is selected, then book C is selected.
Corresponding Contrapositive:	If book C is not selected, then book A is not selected and book B is not selected.
Comments:	We have negated a disjunction ("A or B") in producing this contrapositive.

Conditional:	If not A, then B.
Contrapositive:	If not B, then A.
Example of Conditional:	If book A is not selected, then book B is selected.
Corresponding Contrapositive:	If book B is not selected, then book A is selected.

Comments:	We have negated a negation in producing this contrapositive; we negated "not A" to produce "A." Also, note that if we use the disjunctive form of this conditional, we get "either not (not A) or B," which is the same as "either A or B."
Conditional:	If A, then not B.
Contrapositive:	If B, then not A.
Example of Conditional:	If book A is selected, then book B is not selected.
Corresponding Contrapositive:	If book B is selected, then book A is not selected.
Comments:	We have negated a negation in producing this contrapositive; we negated "not B" to produce "B."
Conditional:	If not B, then not A.
Contrapositive:	If A, then B.
Example of Conditional:	If book B is not selected, then book A is not selected.
Corresponding Contrapositive:	If book A is selected, then book B is selected.
Comments:	We have negated two negations in producing this contrapositive; we negated "not A" to produce "A" and negated "not B" to produce "B." Note that this example just shows the equivalence of the basic conditional and its contrapositive—that is, that "if A, then B" is the same thing as "if not B, then not A."

These are just a few examples of conditionals and their contrapositives, and they are meant to illustrate how to negate the two parts of a conditional statement and flip them to produce the contrapositive. Keep in mind that you can produce a contrapositive for *any* conditional, no matter the form given to you in an LSAT game. For example, suppose you are given a conditional of the form: "If A, then B and not C."

> Negate the second part to produce: *B and not C = not B or not (not C) = not B or C*
> And negate the first part to produce: *not A*
> Now switch the first and second parts to produce the contrapositive: *If not B or C, then not A*
> In other words, if either B is not true or C is true, then A is not true.

Biconditionals

A biconditional statement can be understood as a conjunction of two conditional statements. The statement "if A then B, and if B then A" is a biconditional statement. If the LSAT uses the phrase "if and only if," then it is giving you a biconditional statement. For example, if you are told "book A is selected if and only if book B is selected," you are being given a biconditional, which is the equivalent of "If book A is selected, then book B is selected, and if book B is selected, then book A is selected." You can see this by breaking down the statement "A if and only if B" into two parts:

A if B	and	*A only if B*

Which is equivalent to:

If B, then A	and	*If A, then B*

One thing to note about a biconditional statement such as "A if and only if B" is that it is true in exactly two circumstances: when statements A and B are both true, and when statements A and B are both false. If one of the two statements is true and the other is false, then at least one of the two conditional statements (*If A, then B* or *If B, then A*) will be false, making the whole biconditional statement false.

Also note that you can symbolize a biconditional statement with a double-arrow: A $\leftrightarrow$ B.

Know Your Logic Game Types

Before you can understand strategies for engaging your adversary, it helps to know your adversary. In this section, we briefly describe the five types of logic games: sequencing, distribution, selection, matching, and hybrid games.

Sequencing Games

The sequencing game is a staple of the Analytical Reasoning section. In a sequencing game, you are given a set of entities that must be put in a sequential order. The entities can be persons, places, or things, and the order can be on a spatial, temporal, or some other metric level. For example, it may be a list of cities (the entities) that are to be visited on a trip (temporal order). Or it may be a set of friends (the entities) who are to be seated around a table (spatial order). Or it may be a list of television shows (the entities) which are to be ranked according to popularity (a nonspatial/nontemporal metric).

A typical sequencing game will present a set of conditions that will determine what the sequence must, can, and can't look like. For example, concerning a list of cities to be visited on a trip, the game might specify that Boston must be visited after New York, that Chicago must be the second stop, and that if New York is visited after Chicago, Seattle can't be the last city visited.

Distribution Games

In a distribution game, you are given a group of entities that are to be distributed into two or more subgroups. The entities can be persons, places, or things, and the division into subgroups can be based on just about any characteristic of those entities. For example, it may be a set of eight movies that are to be classified into drama, comedy, and thriller genres. Or it may be a set of ten books that are to be placed onto three different shelves. Or it may be a group of college students who are to be split into three sections.

A typical distribution game will present a set of conditions that will determine how the distribution must, can, or can't occur. For example, concerning college students who are to be split into sections, the game might specify that Anne is only available for the first and third section times, that Barbara must be in the second section, and that Carlos and Anne cannot be in the same section.

It's helpful to note that distribution games are sometimes called "grouping" games. Some distribution games can be treated as selection games. This is covered in depth in Chapter 5.

Selection Games

In a selection game, you are given a group of entities from which some are to be selected. The entities can be persons, places, or things, and the selection can be based on just about any characteristic of those entities. For example, it may be a group of astronauts to be selected for a space flight. Or it may be a set of novels to be selected for a reading list. Or it may be a list of philosophy lectures that a student must choose to attend.

A typical selection game will present a set of conditions that will determine how the selection must, can, or can't occur. For example, concerning choosing from a list of lectures, the game might specify that the student must attend the Aristotle lecture; that if the Kant lecture is attended, the Mill lecture will not be attended; and that the Hume lecture and Mill lecture meet at the same time.

The selection game can be thought of as a special case of the distribution game: you are given a group of entities that are to be distributed into two subgroups; the "in" subgroup and the "out" subgroup. For this reason, many of the strategies specific to distribution games will also apply to selection games and, keep in mind, some distribution games can in fact be treated as selection games.

Matching Games

In a matching game, you are given a group of entities that are to be matched with another group of entities or with some set of characteristics. The entities can be persons, places, or things, and the characteristics can be anything from shape to color to location. For example, it may be pilots (one group of entities) who must fly (another group of entities). Or it may be supermarket clerks (one group of entities) who must operate checkout aisles (another group of entities). Or it may be a league of soccer teams (a group of entities) that must be assigned a different jersey color (a set of characteristics).

A typical matching game will present a set of conditions that will determine how the matching must, can, or can't occur. For example, concerning the assignment of pilots to routes, the game might specify that Diane cannot fly to Sydney, Gerald will fly either to New York or Boston, and if Francis takes the flight to New York, Edgar will fly to Tokyo.

Hybrid Games

The Analytical Reasoning section will often present logic games that combine two or more of the four game types just discussed: sequencing, distribution, selection, and matching. These games are generally more complex than games that represent just one type. A hybrid game might, for example, present a group of people who are to attend a baseball game. They are to sit in two rows and are to sit in a particular sequence of numbered seats in each row. This game combines a distribution element (of the attendees into one of two rows) and a sequencing element (of attendees into a sequence within each row). The types of conditions will be similar to those in simple game types, but may involve two condition types in a single condition; for example, if Ingrid sits in the front row, Jackie must sit adjacent to Kevin (combining a distribution condition and a sequencing condition).

Keep in mind, even though we go into detail with these explanations, it's not so important to know the names of the game types. The most important thing is to be confident in how you approach the games.

Know Your Logic Game Strategies

The general strategies for approaching logic games can be ordered into a five-step technique:

1. Order Your Battles
2. Distill/Collate the Information and Rules
3. Digest the Game
4. Order and Answer the Questions
5. Keep Your Head

1) Order Your Battles

All questions are equally weighted, and the four games in an Analytical Reasoning section do not come in any strict order of difficulty, so you should consider "ordering your battles" before jumping in. Take a brief look at each game and rank them by how approachable each looks. Which game looks familiar based on your practice? Which game or game type are you best at, based on your experience with practice games?

Hybrid games are often more complex than single question type games. Games that don't have one-to-one mapping of entities to entities, sequence slots, or characteristics are usually more difficult. For example, a game in which five dishes will be served over seven days—such that some dishes will have to make a second or third appearance and some dishes may not be served at all—will be more difficult than a game in which seven dishes appear exactly once over the course of seven days.

Look at the list of conditions as well. A lack of restrictive and concrete conditions will be relatively more difficult. Also keep an eye out for the type of questions asked in a game—questions that make additional suppositions (e.g., if Diane operates aisle three, who cannot operate aisle five?) are generally easier and more straightforward than other questions. These are just some of the general characteristics that might affect a game's difficulty level, but as you go through practice games, you should gain a better sense of what makes a logic game easier or harder for you.

Once you get a better sense of the things that make a game more or less attractive, you'll have to tinker with your ordering strategy and develop your sense for ordering through practice.

Based on your assessment of difficulty, you may wish to do the easiest game first to relieve stress during the section and boost your confidence, and leave the hardest for last—by then, you will have gotten the logic juices flowing, and if you don't get to it, you will have maximized your raw points by not sinking your time into the most difficult game.

However, how you order the games may depend on whether you generally finish all four logic games or not. For example, completing an Analytical Reasoning section in time then saving the hardest game for last may not be the best strategy, since you will be fatigued by that point. If, on the other hand, you usually complete only three of the four games, then doing the three easiest first is probably the right strategy. You will have to experiment with ordering your battles to figure out what the best strategy is for you.

Whatever your strategy, be flexible. It might turn out that in some instances, you may not want to skim all four games in a section and order them before turning to any of the questions. For example, you might read the first game, see that it has only a few supposition questions and is your weakest game type, and skip to the second game. You might then see that the second game has only a moderate number of supposition questions, is your best game type, is structurally similar to a game you've practiced, and contains a lot of highly restrictive or concrete clues. At this point, you might decide to jump in here while the game prompt is fresh in your head. You would answer the questions for the second game and finally return to your difficulty-assessment phase for the next two games.

Just make sure you don't spend too much time ordering your battles. If after a lot of practice, you still have trouble quickly assessing the games, then consider picking an order ahead of time and sticking to it.

2) Distill/Collate the Information and Rules

According to LSAC, logic games are designed to "measure the ability to understand a structure of relationships and to draw logical conclusions about that structure. . . .You are asked to reason deductively from a set of statements and rules or principles that describe relationships among persons, things, or events."[1] Logic games are essentially about logical relationships, and logical relationships are generally more easily understood and manipulated in a symbolic, visual form, rather than in a verbal form (either written or in your head). So, to minimize the time spent referring to the mess of words presented in game setup, you need to gather your information symbolically and visually in one place. If you properly symbolize and diagram the information you're reading, the game will become understandable and amenable to manipulation. Its once-hidden mechanics will become transparent, and you'll start playing the game rather than letting the game play you.

There are three elements here: the symbolic, the visual, and being in one place.

Symbolization

You want to distill the information in the setup using shorthand and logical symbols. Let's take an example mini-game, matching pilots to flights.

Let's suppose the setup tells you that there are five pilots: Diane, Gerald, Francis, Edgar, and Chris. And suppose there are five flights: to New York, Boston, Sydney, Tokyo, and London. The first thing to do is write out a list of shorthand symbols for the entities involved. You might separate the two entity types by using lowercase versus uppercase symbols: c, d, e, f, g for the pilots and N, B, S, T, L for the flights.

Next, turn to the conditions. One condition is that "if Francis takes the flight to New York, Edgar will pilot the flight to Tokyo." The verbal form of this condition is cumbersome, so you might distill this as $f = N \rightarrow e = T$, where the arrow sign indicates an if-then statement, and the equal sign indicates the piloting of a flight (or in general, the matching of entities from two groups—in this case, pilots and flights).

This is just one example of symbolizing a rule based on a conditional statement. We will encounter many different kinds of rules in this book, and ways to symbolize them. The conditional rule deserves special attention, however, because whenever you symbolize a conditional statement, you should *always* symbolize its contrapositive. As we will see below, this will allow you to make deductions you might have otherwise missed. With this example, the symbolization of the contrapositive would be:

$$e \neq T \rightarrow f \neq N$$

Throughout this book, we present suggestions for shorthand symbolizations, but you can develop your own shorthand as you go along. Just remember two very important things: 1) make sure shorthand is unambiguous,

---

1 See "What the Test Measures" at http://www.lsac.org/JD/LSAT/about-the-LSAT.asp

so that you are not making mistakes on account of bad shorthand, and 2) keep it consistent, so you aren't getting confused on test day.

Also, make sure to take each symbolized piece of information and check it against the original to ensure that you aren't misreading the symbolization and that you haven't overlooked any information.

Visualization (Diagramming)

Logic games almost always require a diagram. In subsequent chapters, we will see the kinds of diagrams that are best suited for each game. In general, sequencing games require slots in sequential order, matching games require a grid, and distribution and selection games require columns, lists of entities, or slots. As you practice, you will become better at figuring out what kind of diagram to use. This is probably the most crucial element of approaching any logic game, because the diagram is meant to visually capture and clarify the basic underlying mechanism of the game, giving you a crucial crutch for otherwise very difficult mental calculations. So, pay close attention to both the use of diagrams in this book and what sorts of diagrams work best for you as you practice.

Whatever you do, as with the symbolization, be careful! A slight misreading or misrepresentation of information can have disastrous results for your gaming ability.

Suppose you have a game setup that says "one of seven possible movies is shown each day of a cable channel's movie week, from Wednesday to Tuesday." You might immediately diagram a series of seven slots in sequential order, and congratulate yourself for noting that the setup didn't say that movies can't be shown twice (you won't make the mistake of assuming each movie is show exactly once!). But as you're diagramming, you proceed to label the slots Monday through Sunday, from left to right, forgetting that this movie week starts on Wednesday and ends on Tuesday. But one of the conditions is that *The Matrix* will be shown sometime before *Terminator*, and *Terminator* will be shown on Thursday, which means *The Matrix* must be shown on Wednesday. Missing this crucial piece of information, you get stuck on every question you try, since they all assume you realize that no matter what, *The Matrix* is shown on Wednesday. As you review the symbolized conditions you've collected next to the diagram, you don't realize that the root of the problem is in the diagram itself! So, take the time you need to collect and represent carefully the information given to you.

Once you have the diagram in place, start filling it in, both in this Distill/Collate the Information and Rules phase, and in the Digest the Game phase (following). As you encounter or deduce concrete bits of information (e.g., that Diane does not pilot the flight to Sydney), write them into your diagram to the extent possible (e.g., cross out the box representing the intersection of Diane and Sydney on your matching grid.) Even less concrete bits of information and conditions can sometimes be drawn into the diagram; for example, the information provided by the condition that Gerald will either pilot the flight to New York or Boston can be entered into the diagram by crossing out every box representing the intersection of Gerald with various cities, except for the intersections with New York and Boston.

As we consider each game type in turn, we will see further ways of incorporating rules into the diagrams specific to those games.

All in One Place

Make sure that the symbolic forms of the conditions and setup information, the list of entity and characteristic symbols, and the diagram all appear in one place on your scratch paper. This will be your central place of reference as you work through the questions, and you would be surprised by what jumps out at you when you see pieces of information encoded next to one another. Also, make sure to write down any bit of information that isn't blatantly obvious so that you don't have to rely on memory—it's easy to forget details from the game setup when stressed and under time constraints.

The techniques for distilling and collating the information and rules are highly recommended. But you should use some practice games and tests to tinker and try out different shorthand and diagramming techniques, then settle on your own brand of symbolization and visualization. Afterwards, practice that technique so it becomes like a second language to you.

3) Digest the Game

On some tests, it makes sense to jump straight to the questions; for example, on some Reading Comprehension sections, savvy test-takers will read the questions first, so they can look for specific things as they read the passage. This is obviously not the case with the Analytical Reasoning section of the LSAT—we have discussed the necessity of symbolizing and diagramming the game setup and conditions, but that's just the start. It's usually worth investing a bit more time in understanding the mechanics of the game before engaging the questions. Taking the time to digest the game will pay off once you start on the questions.

How do you do this? First and foremost, you need to make deductions or inferences from the information and conditions presented to you. Look for links between stated game conditions, which usually means looking for entities involved in two or more conditions. Sometimes, the best you can do is just keep in mind the fact that there is some sort of immediate link between two conditions. But you will often be able to generate new conditions or inferences from what's presented. There are a number of ways to make deductions in logic games, but for the sake of illustration, here's a simple example, based on chains of if-then statements.

If-Then Statement Chains

Suppose the game conditions for the game matching pilots to flights (discussed previously) include the following:

> *Diane does not fly to Sydney.*
> *Gerald will fly either to New York or Boston.*
> *If Francis flies to New York, Edgar will fly to Tokyo.*
> *If Edgar flies to Tokyo, Chris does not fly to London.*

Now look at the last two conditions. They are conditional statements (if-then statements), with an element in common: Edgar flying to Tokyo. So you can make a new deduction that "f Francis flies to New York, Chris does not fly to London" (since Edgar must fly to Tokyo).

You might symbolize the last two given conditions as:

$$f = N \rightarrow e = T$$
$$e = T \rightarrow c \neq L$$

And then you could symbolize the new deduction as:

$$f = N \rightarrow c \neq L$$

Or, if you feel comfortable doing so, you might cross out the two given conditions and just write in a chain of symbolized if-then statements to concisely capture all the information given and deduced here in one line:

$$f = N \rightarrow e = T \rightarrow not \ c = L$$

Sometimes it's possible to make a number of different if-then chains. In these cases, it often makes more sense to just note the possible connections between the if-then statements and write out the chains as needed when you get to the questions, rather than write out all the possible chains ahead of time.

Considering Contrapositives

Further, make sure that you always consider the *contrapositive* of any if-then statement. The contrapositive form of the original statement might allow for connections and deductions that you otherwise might not have seen. Let's look at an example.

Suppose that an additional condition to those presented previously for the game matching pilots to flights is that "if Edgar does not fly to Tokyo, then Francis does not fly to Sydney."

As stated, this condition does not seem to yield any new deductions. But now consider the contrapositive: *If it's not the case that Francis does not pilot the flight to Sydney, then it's not the case that Edgar does not pilot the flight to Tokyo.* The double negatives are a bit confusing, so restate the contrapositive without them: *If Francis flies to Sydney, Edgar flies to Tokyo.* This is much simpler, and now we have another inference chain that can be deduced: *If Francis flies to Sydney, then Chris does not fly to London (since Edgar must fly to Tokyo).*

In symbols:

$$f = S \rightarrow c \neq L$$

Or, the full chain:

$$f = S \rightarrow e = T \rightarrow c \neq L$$

Let's consider a second example in which the contrapositive would prove useful. Suppose that we encounter the following question: *If Chris flies to London, then each of the following statements could be true EXCEPT:*

We start by looking for any conditional statements that start with Chris flying to London, to see if we can make any deductions. Unfortunately, there aren't any and so it seems we are stuck: although Chris and London appear in the last conditional, they appear in the form of Chris not flying to London. But if we had written down the contrapositive forms, we would have noticed that the contrapositive of the last conditional statement is that *if Chris flies to London, then Edgar does not fly to Tokyo.*

Bingo. We can now deduce that when Chris flies to London (according to the supposition of this question), Edgar does not fly to Tokyo. In fact, we can deduce even more. The contrapositive of the third conditional is *if Edgar does not fly to Tokyo, then Francis does not fly to New York.*

So we have yet another inference that could be made—since Edgar does not fly to Tokyo, Francis does not fly to New York.

These are concrete bits of information that can provide answers. If one of the choices is "Francis flies to New York," we have found our answer. But without the contrapositive forms, we would be lost.

So always consider the contrapositive forms of the given conditional rules when digesting a game!

General Connections

There are hosts of other ways to generate new conditions or inferences from what's presented that don't just rely on if-then statement chains or contrapositives. When looking for links between conditions of the pilots/flights game, you might notice that the second and third conditions have an element in common—New York. Once you notice this, you might realize that if Francis takes the flight to New York, not only will Edgar fly to Tokyo (as stated), but also Gerald will fly to Boston (since he must fly either to New York or Boston, and New York is taken). You might symbolize this realization as:

$$f = N \rightarrow g = B$$

There are many other kinds of deductions specific to different game types that LSAT authors often require of the test taker. We will discuss these in subsequent chapters so you can be on the lookout for those deductions as you tackle any logic game.

Using Scenarios

One important strategy for digesting a game is to see if you can sketch out the various possibilities for the game. But only do this if you can quickly come up with two or three scenarios that exhaust the possibilities inherent in the game, and that provide a decent amount of concrete information (or at least a lot of information that differs between the two scenarios).

Let's consider a mini-logic game to illustrate (we will learn about selection games and how to diagram them in Chapter 4, but for now we'll keep it simple enough to understand the general mechanics of creating scenarios). Suppose we need to select four items from a group of six items—A, B, C, D, E, and F—and we are given the following rules:

> If A is not selected, B is selected.
> If A is selected, both C and D are selected.
> If E is not selected, B is not selected.

You might notice that whether A is selected makes a big difference to the how the selection goes, and that we can divide the game into two scenarios: one where A is selected, and in another where A is not:

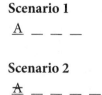

Scenario 1

A _ _ _

Scenario 2

A̶ _ _ _ _

In Scenario 1, since A is selected, C and D must be selected. In Scenario 2, since A is not selected, B must be selected, and since B is selected, E must be selected. All of sudden, we have an information-rich set of scenarios that are exhaustive.

Scenario 1

<u>A</u> <u>C</u> <u>D</u> __

Scenario 2

<u>A̶</u> <u>B</u> <u>E</u> __ __

This kind of scenario list might be useful for answering the questions in the game. And notice that the list completely captures the information in the first two rules, so that as you tackle the questions, you can just pay attention to the scenarios and the third rule. You could make further deductions that fully incorporate the third rule by realizing that B cannot be selected in Scenario 1, since if it were, E would have to be selected, leading to five entities selected.

If you can quickly create an exhaustive list of two to three scenarios, you will have a clear, visual representation of how the logic game works and what the possibilities there are. You will not have to do much more diagramming or deduction-making since you can simply check question stems or answer choices against your scenarios. In general, look for rules that severely restrict or drive the mechanics of a game, and that allow for at least two possible scenarios. And look for disjunctions (such as "either A is selected or B is selected," or "X is either first or second") that set off a chain of deductions (e.g., if we also have the rule that "if A is selected, then C and D are selected," or if we also have the rule that "if X is second, then Y and Z are the last two.") When faced with a logic game, knowing when to create scenarios and when to avoid them is ultimately a judgment call. It is largely a matter of practice.

Knowing When to Move On

Your objective in the digesting phase of any logic game is to gain a solid understanding of its particular mechanics.

But the warning that applies in creating scenarios also applies to the digestion phase in general. Investing time upfront is valuable, but only to a certain degree. If you can make deductions quickly, it might pay off to do them up front; but if they generally take a bit longer for you, cut off the initial deduction process earlier and just make deductions as the questions require (besides, tackling the questions themselves will help you understand the game as well, especially "Test-the-Rules" questions, discussed below).

As you practice, you will both gain efficiency with initial deductions/diagramming and gain a better sense of when you are starting to waste time on this phase and need to move on to the questions.

4) Order and Answer the Questions

Now that you've wrestled with the mechanics of the game, it's finally time to turn to the questions. The time you've invested should pay off now. As you turn to the questions, remember that they are all weighted equally and appear in no strict order of difficulty. So briefly look for the easiest questions and plan to answer them first. Your assessment of which questions are easiest will partly depend on all your practice. As you do practice logic games, take note of which question types are naturally easy for you, and which require more concentration.

Test-the-Rules Questions

Often a logic game will include a question that requires only the simple application of each given condition individually. Every one of the wrong answer choices will violate a rule, while the correct answer choice won't violate any rule. These questions are great to tackle first, for two reasons. First, they are relatively easy; you don't have to do any complicated deductions or game-playing, you just have to check each answer choice against the rules. And second, they force you to review the game conditions once more, a process that helps you to crystallize the rules in your head even further and digest the game in preparation for the subsequent questions. These questions are often the first questions in a set.

When approaching a "Test-the-Rules" question, you could either take each answer choice in turn and check to see if it violates any of the rules, or take each rule in turn and see which answer choices violate it. The second method is often more efficient, partly because sometimes a rule will rule out more than one answer choice.

Supposition Questions

Questions that give additional suppositions are usually easier than the rest because they set into motion a chain of deductions or inferences (not necessarily straightforward if-then inferences) that lead to the correct answer. It's like getting an additional condition in the condition set, which allows for even more deductions and concrete bits of information. Here's an example based on the game matching pilots to flights:

1. If Francis flies to New York, which of the following MUST be true?
   a. Edgar will fly to London
   b. Chris will fly to Sydney
   c. Diane will fly to Sydney
   d. Gerald will fly to Boston
   e. Gerald will fly to Tokyo

The supposition that Francis flies to New York adds an additional bit of information to the game, which when added to the second condition (that Gerald flies either to New York or Boston) immediately yields a new concrete bit of information—that Gerald *must* fly to Boston. It's a very simple example, but it illustrates what a supposition question looks like, and why, in general, they are relatively easy questions to tackle.

In addition, supposition questions often generate acceptable scenarios that can help with other questions. For example, sometimes you may be given a question that reads:

2. Each of the following statements could be true EXCEPT:

If you don't immediately know which answer choice can't be true, then at the very least you can use the scenario generated by a supposition question to rule out statements that are true in that scenario.

As usual, keep in mind that however you attack the question, do not spend too much time trying to figure out which questions to do first. Figuring that out should be a relatively quick process based on skills you have developed through practice, so that you are not wasting valuable time that could be spent actually answering a question.

5) Keep Your Head

Although you should be able to master the Analytical Reasoning section after working through this book, logic games require intense focus, concentration, and mental application. Don't let it get to you. After you've circled the answer choices for all the questions accompanying a given game, transfer that block of answers to your score sheet. That way you don't find out at the end of the section that you misaligned your answers and now have just two minutes to transfer 20 answers. And before moving to the next game, take a brief mental break: 15 seconds of deep breaths to clear your head.

If you approach the Analytical Reasoning section with these five steps and strategies in mind, you will have half the battle won. The other half involves deploying the tips and strategies specific to each game, which will be covered in Chapters 3 through 7.

Develop Your Own General Strategy and Be Ready To Adapt

The strategies and rules presented here are not to be followed blindly. As you practice, change the five steps and strategies around if you need to. For example, if you find yourself always finishing the games in the allotted time for a given section, but missing a few here or there, consider skipping the Order Your Battles phase to save some time.

Sometimes the LSAT will give you a game that isn't readily amenable to the diagramming or general techniques discussed here, or even the specific diagramming methods you have developed on your own. At this point, one of a number of things could happen: 1) you digest the game and perceive its structural similarity to other games you have solved or diagrammed, 2) you realize it really is different from what you've seen and needs a different type of diagram you must develop on the spot, or 3) you realize the game really is different but needs to be solved without a diagram (this is rare, but it happens).

Know What to Do If You Get Stuck

Don't be a deer in the Logic Game headlights! If you get stuck, overcome your paralysis by doing any one of a number of things: re-read the setup and conditions to make sure you didn't miss anything, double- or triple-check that your symbolizations are accurate, and try to find any deductions or connections you may have missed. If you keep engaging the game, you have a much better chance of figuring out what you're missing.

Realize That There Are Objectively Correct Answers

When choosing answers in Logical Reasoning and Reading Comprehension passages, students are often advised to choose the best answer from a set of answers of which more than one might arguably be correct. Not so with logic games, which are more like the math in this respect. There is one true right answer and the other answers are provably wrong. There is no arguing and no ambiguity.

This confidence means two things. First, you can save precious time on this exam. You don't have to weigh the merits of different answer choices and check every answer choice; as soon you know an answer is right, move on with confidence. Second, you can maximize the impact of process of elimination; when you eliminate an answer, you can do so with complete confidence.

Process of Elimination will be discussed in more detail in Chapter 2.

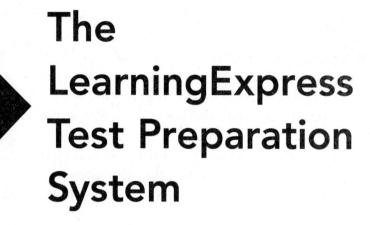

CHAPTER 2

The LearningExpress Test Preparation System

Taking any test can be tough, let alone one that tests unfamiliar logic game skills, but don't let the LSAT scare you! If you prepare ahead of time, you can achieve a top score. The LearningExpress Test Preparation System, developed exclusively for LearningExpress by leading test experts, gives you the discipline and attitude you need to be a winner.

First, the bad news: Getting ready for any test takes work. If you plan on entering law or another career that benefits from a legal education, you will either be required to or be strongly encouraged to take the LSAT. The LSAT has three sections, but this book focuses on the logic games, which many find to be the most difficult material on the test. By honing your logic game skills and mastering that section of the test, you will take your first step toward achieving the career of your dreams. However, there are all sorts of pitfalls that can prevent you from doing your best on exams in general, whether logic-based or not.

Here are some obstacles that can stand in the way of your success:

- Being unfamiliar with the format of the exam
- Being paralyzed by test anxiety
- Leaving your preparation to the last minute
- Not preparing at all
- Not knowing vital test-taking skills like:
  - How to pace yourself through the exam
  - How to use the process of elimination
  - When to guess

- Not being in tip-top mental and physical shape
- Forgetting to eat breakfast and having to take the test on an empty stomach
- Forgetting a sweater or jacket and shivering through the exam

What's the common denominator in all these test-taking pitfalls? One word: *control.* Who's in control, you or the exam?

Now the good news: The LearningExpress Test Preparation System puts *you* in control. In just nine easy-to-follow steps, you will learn everything you need to know to make sure you are in charge of your preparation and performance on the exam. *Other* test-takers may let the test get the better of them; *other* test-takers may be unprepared or out of shape, but not *you.* You will have taken all the steps you need to take to maximize your score.

Here's how the LearningExpress Test Preparation System works: Nine easy steps lead you through everything you need to know and do to get ready to master your exam. Each of the steps listed below gives you tips and activities to help you prepare for any exam. It's important that you follow the advice and do the activities, or you won't be getting the full benefit of the system. Each step gives you an approximate time estimate.

Step 1.	Get Information	30 minutes
Step 2.	Conquer Test Anxiety	20 minutes
Step 3.	Make a Plan	50 minutes
Step 4.	Learn to Manage Your Time	10 minutes
Step 5.	Learn to Use the Process of Elimination	20 minutes
Step 6.	Know When to Guess	20 minutes
Step 7.	Reach Your Peak Performance Zone	10 minutes
Step 8.	Get Your Act Together	10 minutes
Step 9.	Do It!	10 minutes
Total time for complete system		180 minutes—3 hours

Estimate that working through the entire system will take you approximately three hours, though it's perfectly okay if you work faster or slower than the time estimates say. If you can take a whole afternoon or evening, you can work through the entire LearningExpress Test Preparation System in one sitting. Otherwise, you can break it up and do just one or two steps a day for the next several days. It's up to you—remember, *you're* in control.

Step 1: Get Information

Time to complete: 30 minutes
Activities: Read the Introduction.
If you haven't already done so, stop here and read the introduction of this book. There you'll learn all about the LSAT, such as the length of the test, the number and type of questions, and the way that the test is scored.

Knowledge is power. The first step in the LearningExpress Test Preparation System is finding out everything you can about the types of logic game and questions that you will encounter on the exam. The introduction will give general information about the LSAT. Chapter 1 will give you a general idea of how each of the five types of logic games (sequencing, selection, distribution, matching, and hybrid) work, as well as important general strategies, but the chapters dedicated to each type will go into depth, providing very specific game-solving techniques, as well as practice games and detailed solutions which show how to use the recommended techniques.

Ideally, after completing the LearningExpress Test Preparation System, you will begin to apply the test-taking strategies you learn as you work through the practice games in these chapters game-type specific chapters (Chapters 3 through 7). You can see how well your training paid off in the practice tests at the end of the book, which are also accompanied by detailed game solutions against which you can compare your approach.

Step 2: Conquer Test Anxiety

Time to complete: 20 minutes
Activity: Take the Test Stress Test
Having complete information about the exam is the first step in getting control of the exam. Next, you have to overcome one of the biggest obstacles to test success: test anxiety. Test anxiety not only impairs your performance on the exam, but it can even keep you from preparing!

In Step 2, you'll learn stress management techniques that will help you succeed on your exam. Learn these strategies now, and practice them as you work through the practice games in this book, so they'll be second nature to you by exam day.

Combating Test Anxiety

The first thing you need to know is that a little test anxiety is a good thing. Everyone gets nervous before a big exam—and if that nervousness motivates you to prepare thoroughly, so much the better. It's said that Sir Laurence Olivier, one of the world's most celebrated actors, was ill before every performance. His stage fright didn't impair his performance; in fact, it probably gave him a little extra edge—just the kind of edge you need to do well, whether on a stage or in an exam room.

On page 25 is the Test Stress Test. Stop here and answer the questions on that page to find out whether your level of test anxiety is something you should worry about.

Stress Management before the Test

If you feel your level of anxiety getting the best of you in the weeks before the test, here is what you need to do to bring the level down again:

- **Get prepared.** There's nothing like knowing what to expect. Being prepared will put you in control of test anxiety. That's why you're reading this book. Use it faithfully, and remind yourself that you're better prepared than most of the people taking the test.
- **Practice self-confidence.** A positive attitude is a great way to combat test anxiety. This is no time to be humble or shy. Stand in front of the mirror and say to your reflection, "I'm prepared. I'm full of self-confidence. I'm going to ace this test. I know I can do it." Say it into a recorder and play it back once a day. If you hear it often enough, you'll believe it.
- **Fight negative messages.** Every time someone starts telling you how hard the exam is, start telling them

your self-confidence messages above. If you are the one telling yourself that you don't do well on exams and you just can't do this, don't listen. Turn on your recorder and listen to your self-confidence messages.

- **Visualize.** Imagine yourself reporting for your first day on the job. Visualizing success can help make it happen—and it reminds you why you're preparing for the exam so diligently.
- **Exercise.** Physical activity helps calm down your body and focus your mind. Besides, being in good physical shape can actually help you do well on the exam. Go for a run, lift weights, go swimming—and do it regularly.

Stress Management on Test Day

There are several ways you can bring down your level of test anxiety on test day. To find a comfort level, experiment with the following exercises in the weeks before the test, and use the ones that work best for you.

- **Breathe deeply.** Take a deep breath while you count to five. Hold it for a count of one, then let it out on a count of five. Repeat several times.
- **Move your body.** Try rolling your head in a circle. Rotate your shoulders. Shake your hands from the wrist. Many people find these movements very relaxing.
- **Visualize again.** Think of the place where you are most relaxed: lying on the beach in the sun, walking through the park, or sipping a cup of hot tea. Now close your eyes and imagine you're actually there. If you practice in advance, you'll find that you need only a few seconds of this exercise to experience a significant increase in your sense of well-being.

When anxiety threatens to overwhelm you right there during the exam, there are still things you can do to manage your stress level:

- **Repeat your self-confidence messages.** You should have them memorized by now. Say them quietly to yourself, and believe them!
- **Visualize one more time.** This time, visualize yourself moving smoothly and quickly through the test answering every question right and finishing just before time is up. Like most visualization techniques, this one works best if you've practiced it ahead of time.
- **Find an easy question.** Skim over the questions until you find an easy question, and then answer it. Filling in even one circle gets you into the test-taking groove.
- **Take a mental break.** Everyone loses concentration once in a while during a long test. It's normal, so you shouldn't worry about it. Instead, accept what has happened. Say to yourself, "Hey, I lost it there for a minute. My brain is taking a break." Put down your pencil, close your eyes, and do some deep breathing for a few seconds. Then you're ready to go back to work.

Try these techniques ahead of time, and see if they work for you!

Test Stress Test

You only need to worry about test anxiety if it is extreme enough to impair your performance. The following questionnaire will provide a diagnosis of your level of test anxiety. In the blank before each statement, write the number that most accurately describes your experience.

0 = never
1 = once or twice
2 = sometimes
3 = often

___ I have gotten so nervous before an exam that I simply put down the books and didn't study for it.

___ I have experienced disabling physical symptoms such as vomiting and severe headaches because I was nervous about an exam.

___ I have simply not showed up for an exam because I was scared to take it.

___ I have experienced dizziness and disorientation while taking an exam.

___ I have had trouble filling in the circles because my hands were shaking too hard.

___ I have failed an exam because I was too nervous to complete it.

___ Total: Add up the numbers in the blanks above.

Your Test Stress Score

Here are the steps you should take, depending on your score. If you scored:

- **0–3:** Your level of test anxiety is nothing to worry about; it's probably just enough to give you the motivation to excel.
- **3–6:** Your test anxiety may be enough to impair your performance, and you should practice the stress management techniques listed in this section to try to bring your test anxiety down to a more manageable level.
- **6+:** Your level of test anxiety is a serious concern. In addition to practicing the stress management techniques listed in this section, you may want to seek additional, professional help. Call your college, university, or community college and ask for the academic counselor. Tell the counselor that you have a level of test anxiety that sometimes keeps you from being able to take an exam. The counselor may be willing to help you or may suggest someone else you should talk to.

Step 3: Make a Plan

Time to complete: 50 minutes
Activity: Construct a study plan

Maybe the most important thing you can do to get control of yourself and your exam is to make a study plan. Too many people fail to prepare simply because they fail to plan. Spending hours on the day before the exam poring over sample test questions not only raises your level of test anxiety, it is also no substitute for careful preparation and practice.

Don't fall into the cram trap. Take control of your preparation time by mapping out a study schedule. If you're the kind of person who needs deadlines and assignments to motivate you for a project, here they are. If you're the kind of person who doesn't like to follow other people's plans, you can use the suggested schedules here to construct your own.

Even more important than making a plan is making a commitment. You can't develop the skills you need to do well on the LSAT in one night. You have to set aside some time every day for study and practice. Try for at least 20 minutes a day. Twenty minutes daily will do you much more good than two hours the day before the exam. Start now. Even ten minutes a day (just one practice game), with half an hour or more on weekends, can make a big difference in your score—and in your chances of obtaining the score you want!

Schedule A: The 30-Day Plan

If you have at least one month before you take your test, you have plenty of time to prepare—as long as you don't procrastinate! If you have less than a month, turn to Schedule B. Of course, keep in mind that this book will get you ready for the logic games section of the LSAT, not the entire test. You might consider creating similar, concurrent schedules to prepare for the exam as a whole.

Day 1

Skim over any written materials you may have about the LSAT. Learn the specific content and skills that you need to brush up on to prepare for the test. Read the introduction of this book. Look over relevant information on the LSAC website and review actual LSAT example questions there.

Day 2

Read Chapter 1, LSAT Logic, Game Types, and General Strategies. Learn the five-step technique for approaching the whole logic games section, and general strategies for solving logic games. Consider writing down the five steps, along with key elements from each step, and reviewing them before each logic game or logic game section you practice. Take the time to make sure you understand the formal logical rules that are essential to cracking the games.

Days 3–5

Read Chapter 3, "Sequencing Games Review." Experiment and practice with the diagramming and problem-solving techniques presented for sequencing games. Make sure to apply these techniques as you work through the practice games! After each game, compare your approach to the suggested approach and see if you can improve your accuracy or efficiency in the next game.

Day 6

Review any Chapter 3 concepts or techniques that you feel are necessary for you to brush up on.

Days 7–9

Read Chapter 4, "Selection Games Review." Experiment and practice with the diagramming and problem-solving techniques presented for selection games. Make sure to apply these techniques as you work through the practice games! After each game, compare your approach to the suggested approach, and see if you can improve your accuracy or efficiency in the next game.

Day 10

Review any Chapter 4 concepts or techniques that you feel are necessary for you to brush up on.

Days 11–13

Read Chapter 5, "Distribution Games Review." Experiment and practice with the diagramming and problem-solving techniques presented for distribution games. Make sure to apply these techniques as you work through the practice games! After each game, compare your approach to the suggested approach, and see if you can improve your accuracy or efficiency in the next game.

Day 14

Review any Chapter 5 concepts or techniques you feel are necessary for you to brush up on.

Days 15–17

Read Chapter 6, "Matching Games Review." Experiment and practice with the diagramming and problem-solving techniques presented for matching games. Make sure to apply these techniques as you work through the practice games! After each game, compare your approach to the suggested approach, and see if you can improve your accuracy or efficiency in the next game.

Day 18

Review any Chapter 6 concepts or techniques you feel are necessary for you to brush up on.

Days 19–21

Read Chapter 7, "Hybrid Games Review." Experiment and practice with the diagramming and problem-solving techniques presented for hybrid games. Make sure to apply these techniques as you work through the practice games! After each game, compare your approach to the suggested approach, and see if you can improve your accuracy or efficiency in the next game.

Day 22

Review any Chapter 7 concepts or techniques you feel are necessary for you to brush up on.

Days 23–25

Take the two practice logic games sections in Chapter 8 under timed conditions—allow yourself 35 minutes, as you would on the actual exam. Apply the five-step technique to the section, and apply the game-type specific strategies you have learned. After each game, review the answer explanations to see how you can improve your game-solving technique for the next practice section. If you had difficulty with a game, review the techniques and tips in the chapter specific to that game type.

Days 26–28

Take the two practice logic games sections in Chapter 9 under timed conditions—allow 35 minutes, as you would on the actual exam. Apply the five-step technique to the section, and apply the game-type specific strategies you have learned. After each game, review the answer explanations to see how you can improve your game-solving technique for the next practice section. If you had difficulty with a game, review the techniques and tips in the chapter specific to that game type.

Day 29

Quickly refresh yourself on all the suggested game-solving techniques presented in the book. Do one final review of the concepts and techniques related to any game-types you discovered you were weak on while taking the practice logic sections the day before the exam

Relax

Do something unrelated to the exam and go to bed at a reasonable hour.

Schedule B: The 14-Day Plan

If you have two weeks or less before the exam, you may have your work cut out for you. Use this 14-day schedule to help you make the most of your time.

Day 1

Read the introduction and strategies in Chapter 1.

Day 2

Take the practice section in Chapter 8 to identify game types you need help with. Rank order the five game types based on your ability to solve them quickly.

Days 3–5

Read the chapter on the game type you need the most help with. Complete the practice games, and review the explanations.

Days 6–8

Read the chapter on the second game type on your list. Complete the practice games, and review the explanations.

Days 9–10

Read the chapter on the third game type on your list. Complete the practice games, and review the explanations.

Day 11

Read the chapter on the fourth game type on your list. Complete the practice games, and review the explanations.

Day 12

Read the chapter on the fifth game type on your list. Complete the practice games, and review the explanations.

Day 13

Take the practice section in Chapter 9, review the answer explanations, and review concepts and techniques with which you were weakest.

Day before the exam

Relax. Do something unrelated to the exam and go to bed at a reasonable hour.

Step 4: Learn to Manage Your Time

Time to complete: 10 minutes to read, many hours of practice!
Activities: Use these strategies as you take the practice games and sections in this book
Steps 4, 5, and 6 of the LearningExpress Test Preparation System put you in charge of your exam by showing you some test-taking strategies that work. Practice these strategies as you take the sample test in this book, and then you'll be ready to use them on test day.

First, take control of your time on the exam. The LSAT Analytical Reasoning (Logic Games) section has a time limit of 35 minutes, which may give you more than enough time to complete all the questions—or not enough time. It's a terrible feeling to hear the examiner say, "five minutes left," when you're only three-quarters of the way through the test. Here are some tips to keep that from happening to you.

- Follow directions. Carefully read the LSAT Analytical Reasoning directions ahead of time and know them well, so you don't have to re-read them after the exam begins. Ask questions before the exam begins if there is anything you don't understand. Write down the beginning time and ending time of the exam in your booklet.
- Pace yourself. Glance at your watch every few minutes, and compare the time to how far you've gotten in the test. Each game should take you about 8 minutes. If you're falling behind, pick up the pace a bit.
- Keep moving. Don't waste time on one question. If you don't know the answer, skip the question and move on. Circle the number of the question in your test booklet in case you have time to come back to it later. Do not let one question on one game bog you down!
- Keep track of your place on the answer sheet. If you skip a question, make sure you skip it on the answer sheet too. Check yourself every few questions to make sure the question number and the answer sheet number are still the same.
- Don't rush. Although you should keep moving, rushing won't help. Try to keep calm and work methodically and quickly.

Step 5: Learn to Use the Process of Elimination

Time to complete: 20 minutes
After time management, your most important tool for taking control of your exam is using the process of elimination wisely. As discussed in Chapter 1, the proper Process of Elimination will be a bit different for LSAT Analytical Reasoning than it is for other sections of the LSAT. It's standard test-taking wisdom that you should always read all the answer choices before choosing your answer, since this will ensure that you are choosing the best answer. That standard wisdom does NOT apply to logic games. For every question, there is one objectively and provably correct answer choice, and four incorrect choices.

The LSAT, and especially the Analytical Reasoning section, is a test of efficiency as much as it is a test of problem-solving or logical abilities, so you need to shave off unnecssary time expenditures as much as possible. Reviewing other answer choices is simply a waste of time once you have found the correct answer choice. The key, of course, is knowing that your answer choice is correct. As long as you diagram correctly and make no logical mistakes in your deductions, you will be in a position to mark the correct answer choice with confidence and move on to the next question. By working through this book, you will practice these techniques and gain the analytical strength to get the right answer and fearlessly circle it.

So what use does the Process of Elimination (POE) have on the LSAT? Plenty. First, some questions, such as "Test-the-Rules" questions (which appear in almost every logic game), are better approached by elimating all the incorrect answer choices rather than finding the correct answer choice.

Second, you may not always know how to apply your diagramming techniques and deductions to find the correct answer right away. In these cases, the POE will work at least as well here as on any other test—in fact, sometimes it works better, because you might know that an answer choice is incorrect.

Let's review how to find the right answer by POE, when you can't easily find it directly.

Understand the Question

As you read a question, you may find it helpful to underline important information or make some notes about what you're reading. When you get to the heart of the question, circle it and make sure you understand what it is asking. Keep an eye out for the words 'NOT' and 'EXCEPT'—they make a big difference to the question. If you miss these words when reading a question, wrong answer choices will seem right, and right answer choices will seem wrong. If you're not sure of what's being asked, you'll never know whether you've chosen the right answer. If after reading the question, you really have no idea what it is asking, it sometimes helps to take a quick look at the answer choices for some clues.

For example, if the question asks "which one of the following could be a partial, accurate list of the people who are on the flight," you might not know what is being asked right away. But if you look at the answer choices, you may have a better idea of what the question is asking:

    a. Paul, Theresa
    b. Paul, Ryan
    c. Paul, Sam, Theresa
    d. Ryan, Sam, Theresa
    e. Paul, Ryan, Sam, Theresa

The answer choices might help you realize that the question is looking for a subset of a larger list, where that subset only includes people on the flight and where that subset could be any size.

What you do next depends on the type of question you're answering.

Eliminating Wrong Answers in Logic Games

When using POE on a typical test, you might start by marking the answers that seem unreasonable. POE for logic games will be a bit different. There are certainly reasons to think that an answer will probably be incorrect, and we will discuss these reasons in the next section. Moreover, it will be helpful to use these reasons as a guide when figuring out which answers to try to eliminate first. But when it comes to actually eliminating answers, the best thing you can do is test the answer and make logical inferences to see that the answer is wrong. There are a number of ways in which you can know an answer is wrong. Here are a few important ones.

Rule Violations

The most straightforward way to eliminate an answer choice is to see that it violates one of the restricions in the game setup. For example, in a game that asks you to place seven flights in the order of their departure from an airport, one of the restrictions may be that flight A departs after flight D. Then if you have a question that asks for an acceptable departure order, you can eliminate any answer choice in which flight A does not depart after flight D. For example, the question might be "if flight C departs before flight F, which one of the following must be the order of departures, from first to last?" Whatever the right answer is, you can surely eliminate the answer choice 'C, B, A, E, D, F, G,' since it violates the restriction that flight A departs after flight D.

Use Prior Work

Each logic game will have five to seven questions accompanying it. Sometimes, diagrams you created, deductions you made, and answers you found for a previous question will help eliminate answer choices on a later question. When trying to use POE, remember to look at previous work or answers to see if they can help.

For example, suppose a question asks "which one of the following CANNOT be the departures sequence, in order from first to last?" Suppose you find that the correct answer choice is 'C, B, A, E, D, F, G.' Then suppose another question asks "if E departs fourth, which one of the following MUST be the departure sequence, in order from first to last?" If' 'C, B, A, E, D, F, G' appears as one of your answer choices, you can immediately eliminate it, because you know from the earlier question that it can't be the departure sequence.

Interchangeables

Sometimes two entities will be indistinguishable with respect to their role in the game. These entities are 'interchangeables.' If a set of answer choices includes an answer choice for both members of an interchangeable duo, then both of those answer choices must be wrong. This is because each question demands one and only one answer—and if two essentially indistinguishable answers appear, then neither one of them can be the one and only answer.

Let's look at an example. Suppose in the game setup, there are no restrictions that mention the entities B and G. And suppose the question reads "if E departs fourth, which one of the following MUST depart sixth?" And suppose the you have the following answer choices:

- **a.** A
- **b.** B
- **c.** D
- **d.** F
- **e.** G

Since B and G are indistinguishable with respect to the roles they play in the game, and are not mentioned in the question, neither of them can be the one that must depart sixth; if B departs sixth, and it's pretty much the same as G, then G must depart sixth as well. So you can immediately eliminate both of these choices.

Be careful with this technique. Sometimes B and G will appear indistinguishable, but might actually be indirectly distinguishable. For example, B might be included on a list of flights to Chicago given in the setup, and G might be included on a list of flights to Detroit given in the setup. If a restriction involves all flights to Chicago (e.g., "the last three flights are flights to Chicago"), then the two flights might play different roles in the game, and you cannot apply this technique.

There are other ways to eliminate wrong answers in logic games without knowing what the right answer is, and these will become apparent as you work through the practice games and answer explanations in this book. The basic idea, though, is that when you don't know what the right answer is, do what you can to eliminate answer choices you can fully determine are incorrect. Whatever you do, don't waste too much time with any one answer choice. If it's the right answer, you may be able to eliminate all the others, and if it's a wrong answer, working with the other answer choices may help you make inferences that allow you to eliminate that answer as well. By quickly eliminating at least some wrong answer choices, you put yourself in a position to move to the guessing phase and increase your probability of getting the right answer without losing overall efficiency.

If you haven't eliminated any answers at all, skip the question temporarily, but don't forget to mark the question so you can come back to it later if you have time. If you're certain that you could never answer this question in a million years, pick an answer and move on. The test has no penalty for wrong answers.

Guess on Every Question

You will not be penalized for wrong answers on the LSAT. This is very good news. It means you should absolutely answer every single question on the test. If you're hopelessly lost and can't even cross off one answer choice, make sure that you don't leave it blank. Even if you only have 30 seconds left and 10 questions to answer, you should just guess on all of those last questions.

Of course, if you can eliminate even one of the choices, you improve your odds of guessing correctly. If you can identify three of the choices as definitely wrong, you have a 50% chance of answering the question correctly.

If You Finish Early

Use any time you have left to do the following:

- Go back to questions you marked to return to later, and try them again.
- Check your work on all the other questions. If you have a good reason for thinking your reasoning was incorrect and your response is wrong, change it.
- Review your answer sheet. Most tests are scored in such a way that questions with more than one answer are marked wrong.
- Make sure you've put the answers in the right places and you've marked only one answer for each question.
- If you've erased an answer, make sure you've done a good job of it.
- Check for stray marks on your answer sheet that could distort your score.

Whatever you do, don't waste time when you've finished a test section. Make every second count by checking your work over and over again until time is up.

Step 6: Know When to Guess

Time to complete: 20 minutes
Activity: Take the Guessing Quiz
On the LSAT, the number of questions you answer correctly yields your raw score. So you have nothing to lose and everything to gain by guessing. Frankly, even if you're a play-it-safe kind of person with terrible intuition, you're still safe in guessing every time because the exam has no guessing penalty. The best thing would be if you could overcome your anxieties and go ahead and mark an answer. Second, if you apply Step 5 and learned how to eliminate wrong answers even when you don't know the right answer, your chances of guessing correctly are significantly improved. Third, even if you have a bad LSAT guessing intuition, there are a few ways you can improve that intuition, which you will see after the guessing quiz.

So if you don't know the answer, go ahead and guess!

Your Guessing Ability

The following are a few logic game questions, some without any game setup. You're not supposed to know the answers (they are modified from actual logic games). Rather, this is an assessment of your ability to guess when you don't have a clue. Read each question carefully, just as if you did expect to answer it. If the question has a game setup and you think that you might be able to deduce the right answer by playing the game, don't! This is meant to test your guessing intuition for situations in which you don't know how to play the game.

1. Which one of the following statements cannot be true?
   a. Exactly two nurses are chosen.
   b. Exactly two foreign professionals are chosen.
   c. Exactly three foreign professionals are chosen.
   d. Exactly two local professionals are chosen.
   e. Exactly three local professionals are chosen.

   Five books are to be chosen from seven—A, B, C, D, E, F and G—according to the following restrictions:
   If either A is not chosen or B is not chosen, C is chosen.
   If C is chosen, D is not chosen.

2. If D is chosen, which one of the following must be chosen?
   a. A
   b. C
   c. E
   d. F
   e. G

   Five books are to be chosen from seven—A, B, C, D, E, F and G—according to the following restrictions:

   If either A is not chosen or B is not chosen, C is chosen.
   If C is chosen, D is not chosen.
   If F or E are chosen, D is chosen
   If F is not chosen, B is not chosen.

3. If A is not chosen, which one of the following could be chosen?
   a. B
   b. D
   c. E
   d. F
   e. G

Answers

1. C
2. A
3. E

How Did You Do?

You may have not been able to avoid reasoning through the last two questions in your head, and getting the answers. But if you managed to refrain from reasoning through the deductions, then you will have a better sense of how you guess. If you got even one answer correct, then you're doing pretty well. If you got two or three, then you're a terrific LSAT logic games guesser. Regardless, you can learn how to guess when you absolutely have to on these kinds of questions.

Guessing on Logic Games

The three questions on the guessing quiz reperesent three sorts of questions for which educated guessing might work:

Numerical Restrictions

The answer to the first question is that 'exactly three foreign professionals are chosen.' When you encounter 'cannot-be-true' questions for logic games that involve numerical restrictions, the answer choices with the highest numbers involved are often correct. This is because a larger block of entities (three entities vs. two) will have less freedom in the mechanics of a numbers-driven game. For example, if the game specifies that only five professionals can be chosen, and three of them must be domestic rather than foreign, then although zero, one, or two foreign professionals could be chosen, three could not.

Must-Be Questions

The correct answer for the second question is that entity A must be chosen. You could have guessed A by noting that A is mentioned in the game setup. Most of the other entities presented in the answer choices, except for C, are not involved in any of the restrictions. So there is no reason that they must be chosen. Something that must be chosen is probably involved in some restrictions.

Could-Be Questions

The opposite logic applies for "could-be" questions. The correct answer for the third question is that entity G could be chosen. G is the only entity of those presented in the answer choices that is not involved in any of the restrictions. So there probably can't be anything preventing it from being chosen.

These are just some of the question types for which noticing patterns in the answer choices can help you guess. As you work through the sample questions in this book, you will see more instances where you might have guessed an answer. Take note of them for those moments on the LSAT when you need to guess.

Step 7: Reach Your Peak Performance Zone

Time to complete: 10 minutes to read; weeks to complete!
Activity: Complete the Physical Preparation Checklist

To get ready for a challenge like a big exam, you have to take control of your physical, as well as your mental state. Exercise, proper diet, and rest will ensure that your body works with, rather than against, your mind on test day, as well as during your preparation.

Exercise

If you don't already have a regular exercise program going, this is actually an excellent time to start one. If you're already keeping fit—or trying to get that way—don't let the pressure of preparing for an exam fool you into quitting now. Exercise helps reduce stress by pumping wonderful feel-good hormones called endorphins into your system. It also increases the oxygen supply throughout your body and your brain, so you'll be at peak performance on test day.

A half hour of vigorous activity—enough to break a sweat—every day should be your aim. If you're really pressed for time, every other day is OK. Choose an activity you like and get out there and do it. Jogging with a friend always makes the time go faster as does listening to music.

But don't overdo it. You don't want to exhaust yourself. Moderation is the key.

Diet

First of all, cut out the junk. Go easy on caffeine and nicotine, and eliminate alcohol and any other drugs from your system at least two weeks before the exam.

What your body needs for peak performance is a balanced diet. Eat plenty of fruits and vegetables, along with protein and complex carbohydrates. Foods that are high in lecithin (an amino acid), such as fish and beans, are especially good "brain foods."

Rest

You probably know how much sleep you need every night to be at your best, even if you don't always get it. Make sure you do get that much sleep, though, for at least a week before the exam. Moderation is important here, too. Extra sleep will just make you groggy.

If you're not a morning person and your exam will be given in the morning, you should reset your internal clock so that your body doesn't think you're taking an exam at 3 a.m. You have to start this process well before the exam. The way it works is to get up half an hour earlier each morning, and then go to bed half an hour earlier that night. Don't try it the other way around; you'll just toss and turn if you go to bed early without getting up early. The next morning, get up another half an hour earlier, and so on. How long you will have to do this depends on how late you're used to getting up. Use the "Physical Preparation Checklist" on page 37 to make sure you're in tip-top form.

Step 8: Get Your Act Together

Time to complete: 10 minutes to read; time to complete will vary
Activity: Complete Final Preparations worksheet
Once you feel in control of your mind and body, you're in charge of test anxiety, test preparation, and test-taking strategies. Now it's time to make charts and gather the materials you need to take to the exam.

Gather Your Materials

The night before the exam, lay out the clothes you will wear and the materials you need to bring with you to the exam. Plan on dressing in layers because you won't have any control over the temperature of the exam room. Have a sweater or jacket you can take off if it's warm. Use the checklist on the worksheet entitled "Final Preparations" on page 38 to help you pull together what you'll need.

Follow Your Routine

If you usually have coffee and toast every morning, then you should have coffee and toast before the test. If you don't usually eat breakfast, don't start changing your habits on exam morning. Do whatever you normally do so that your body will be used to it. If you're not used to it, a cup of coffee can really disrupt your stomach. Doughnuts or other sweet foods can give you a stomache ache, too. When deciding what to have for breakfast, remember that a sugar high will leave you with a sugar low in the middle of the exam. A mix of protein and carbohydrates is best: Cereal with milk or eggs with toast will do your body a world of good.

Physical Preparation Checklist

For the week before the test, write down what physical exercise you engaged in and for how long and what you ate for each meal. Remember, you're trying for at least half an hour of exercise every other day (preferably every day) and a balanced diet that's light on junk food.

Exam minus 7 days
Exercise: _____ for ____ minutes

Breakfast:

Lunch:

Dinner:

Snacks:

Exam minus 6 days
Exercise: _____ for ____ minutes

Breakfast:

Lunch:

Dinner:

Snacks:

Exam minus 5 days
Exercise: _____ for ____ minutes

Breakfast:

Lunch:

Dinner:

Snacks:

Exam minus 4 days
Exercise: _____ for ____ minutes

Breakfast:

Lunch:

Dinner:

Snacks:

Exam minus 3 days
Exercise: _____ for ____ minutes

Breakfast:

Lunch:

Dinner:

Snacks:

Exam minus 2 days
Exercise: _____ for ____ minutes

Breakfast:

Lunch:

Dinner:

Snacks:

Exam minus 1 day
Exercise: _____ for ____ minutes

Breakfast:

Lunch:

Dinner:

Snacks:

Step 9: Do It!

Time to complete: 10 minutes, plus test-taking time
Activity: Ace Your Test!

Fast-forward to exam day. You're ready. You made a study plan and followed through. You practiced your test-taking strategies while working through this book. You're in control of your physical, mental, and emotional state. You know when and where to show up and what to bring with you.

In other words, you're better prepared than most of the other people taking the test with you. You're psyched!

Just one more thing. When you're done with the exam, you will have earned a reward. Plan a night out. Call your friends and plan a party, or have a nice dinner for two—whatever your heart desires. Give yourself something to look forward to.

And then do it. Go into the exam, full of confidence, armed with the test-taking strategies you've practiced until they're second nature. You're in control of yourself, your environment, and your performance on exam day. You're ready to succeed.

So do it. Go in there and ace the LSAT! And then, look forward to your new career.

Final Preparations

Getting to the Exam Site

Location of exam site: _____

Date: _____

Departure time: _____

Do I know how to get to the exam site? Yes _____ No _____   If no, make a trial run.

Time it will take to get to exam site: _____

Things to Lay Out the Night Before

Clothes I will wear _____

Sweater/jacket _____

Watch _____

Photo ID _____

Admission card _____

4 No. 2 pencils _____

Other: _____

_____   _____

_____   _____

C H A P T E R

3 ▶ Sequencing Games Review

In a sequencing game, you are given a set of entities to put in sequential order. The entities can be persons, places, or things, and the order can be spatial, temporal, or some other metric. For example, it may be a list of cities (the entities) to visit on a trip (temporal order), a set of friends (the entities) to seat around a table (spatial order) or a list of television shows (the entities) to rank according to popularity (a non-spatial/temporal metric).

The key to mastering sequencing games is to understand the types of conditions that govern the sequencing, and to symbolize those conditions. These conditions, either indirectly or directly, result in a set of sequencing "players." The ultimate aim of symbolizing these players is to produce a relative ordering of some of the entities, which can then be mapped onto a diagram of slots representing the number of places in the sequence (e.g., five slots for a sequence from first to fifth).

To make the examples more concrete, let's pretend that we have a sequencing game in which five flights—A, B, C, D, and E—depart from an airport one at a time. To make the sequencing visual, we diagram five slots, labeled 1 through 5 from left to right.

$$
\underline{} \quad \underline{} \quad \underline{} \quad \underline{} \quad \underline{}
$$
$$
1 \quad 2 \quad 3 \quad 4 \quad 5
$$

In general, entities to the left will be "before" or "of a lower number" in the sequence than entities to the right. The general strategy for diagramming sequencing games is straightforward: to put entities into the slots. This process is relatively self-explanatory and will become apparent as we work through practice games.

There are eight common players in sequencing games. In this chapter, we will look at the game conditions that often produce them, and recommended methods for symbolizing them. These common players are:

- Ordered Blocks
- Unordered Blocks
- Restricted Blocks
- Numbered Sequence Blocks
- Sequence Strings
- Partially Unordered Sequence Strings
- Joint Sequence Strings
- Floaters

The Eight Common Sequencing Players

As we will see, symbolizing restrictions will often result in large, consolidated symbolizations (the "Joint Sequence Strings") that are effectively their own diagrams. As the practice games will illustrate, sometimes it will be useful to refer to these symbolizations independently of the slots-diagram when answering a question, and other times it will be useful to refer to those symbolizations in order to help place those entities into the slots-diagram.

Ordered Blocks

We might be given the information that two entities are immediately next to one another in a sequence. For example, we might be told that flight A departs immediately after flight B. This could mean that flight B is first and flight A is second, or that flight B is third and flight A is fourth. We call it an ordered block because we know that A and B will be placed on the diagram next to one another, and know the order in which they will be placed. We symbolize the block by just placing the letters next to each other, in the proper order:

BA

We might also symbolize bigger blocks, if we know that A immediately follows B, which immediately follows D:

DBA

The blocks work visually by immediately telling us where a set of entities might fit in an ordering. For example, if flight C departs second, then we know that the BA block must fit somewhere into slots 3–5, and that therefore neither A nor B can depart first.

Here are some examples of conditions that would give ordered blocks:

Flight A departs immediately after Flight B.
Adam has his interview the day immediately after Raja's interview.
Mona sits just to the left of Lillja.
Wells sits immediately to the left of Anand.

Unordered Blocks

We might be given the information that two entities are immediately next to one another in a sequence without knowing which one comes first. For example, we might be told that Flight A departs either immediately before or after flight B. This could mean that flight A is first and flight B is second, or that flight B is first and flight A is second.

We call this an unordered block because we know that A and B will be placed on the diagram next to one another, but we do not know their relative order. We symbolize the block by just placing the letters next to each other, with a slash in between them to remind ourselves that we do not know the order, and that A could come before B, or B could come before A:

A/B

We might also symbolize bigger blocks. For example, if we know that there are no other flights that separate flights A, B, and D, we could write:

A/B/D

If we know that A immediately follows B, and that D is either immediately before B or after A, we could combine ordered and unordered blocks to write:

(BA)/D

As with ordered blocks, these unordered blocks work visually by immediately telling us where a set of entities might fit in an ordering. For example, if flight C departs second, then we know that neither A nor B can depart first.

Here are some examples of conditions that would give unordered blocks:

> Flight A departs either immediately before or after flight B.
> Adam has his interview either the day immediately before or after Raja's interview.
> Mona sits either just to the left or right of Lillja.
> Wells sits next to Anand.

Restricted Blocks

We might be given the information that certain entities are *not* placed next to one another. For example, we might be told that Flight A does not depart immediately before or after Flight B. Flight A might be first and flight B third, or flight B second and flight A fifth.

We call it a restricted block because it restricts a certain block from existing. We can symbolize it by drawing a non-sequenced block, and crossing it out, as follows:

~~A/B~~

Here are some examples of conditions that would yield restricted blocks:

> Flight A neither departs immediately before nor after flight B.
> Adam does not have his interview on the day immediately before or after Raja's interview.
> Wells does not sit next to Anand.

Numbered Sequence Block

Sometimes we might be given the number of places in the sequence between two entities. For example, we might be told that there are exactly two flights that depart between Flight A and B. So flight A might be first and flight B might be fourth, or flight B third and flight A sixth. We could symbolize this numbered sequence block with two place holders in between A and B, and a slash to indicate that A and B could be reversed in order:

A_/_B

Here are some examples of conditions that would yield numbered sequence blocks (in particular, with exact numbers):

> There are exactly two flights that depart between flight A and flight B.
> There are exactly three interviews in between Adam's interview and Raja's interview.
> There are exactly three seats in between Wells and Anand.

We might also be told that there are at least a certain number of places in the sequence between two entities. For example, we might be told that there are at least two departures in between flight A and flight B. So flight A might be first and flight B is fourth, or flight B first, and flight A fifth; as long as two or more departures separate the flights. We can symbolize this numbered sequence block by adding a '+' sign, to indicate that the exact number of spaces in the symbolization—or more—must exist between the two entities:

A_/_+B

Here are some examples of conditions that would yield these kinds of numbered sequence blocks:

> There are at least two flights that depart between flight A and flight B.

There are at least two interviews either after Adam's interview and before Raja's interview, or after Raja's interview and before Adam's interview.

There is at least one seat between Mona and Lillja.

Sequence Strings

We might be given information that provides a relative ordering for some of the entities. For example, we might be told that flight A departs after flight B. This differs from the Ordered Block, because we are not told that flight A is *immediately* after flight B. Rather, we are just told that flight A departs at some point after flight B. Flight B might be first and flight A third, or flight B second and flight A fifth.

We call it a sequence string because we string the entities together by a line, and can string multiple entities together if we know their relative order. We would symbolize the condition that flight A departs after flight B as:

B——A

We can also get bigger strings. Suppose we are told that flight A departs after flight B, but before flight D. Then we can symbolize this condition:

B——A——D

These sequence strings work visually by telling us where the strings might fit in a sequence. For example, suppose we are told that flight B does not depart first or second. Since there are two flights to the right of B on this string, flight B must depart third. Otherwise, if it departed fourth or fifth, there would not be enough room for the rest of the string to the right of flight B.

Here are some examples of conditions that would give sequence strings:

Flight A departs after flight B, but before flight D.

Adam has his interview before Raja has his interview.

Mona sits to the right of Lillja, but to the left of Justin.

Wells sits to the right of Anand.

Partially Unordered Sequence String

As a variation on the sequence string, we might be given information that places two entities in relative order with respect to a third, but not with respect to each other. For example, we might be told that flights F and G depart after flight D. So we might have D depart first, F second, and G third; or D departs second, G third, and F fifth.

We call it partially unordered because unlike sequence strings, in which all the entities involved are ordered with respect to one another (B before A before D), some of the entities are not ordered with respect to one another (F might be before G or after G, as long as both are after D). We can symbolize the partially unordered sequence string by using two slashes to indicate not only that the order of F relative to G is unknown, but also that they may or may not depart one right after the other (like the slash for the unordered block):

D——F//G

This symbolization means that F departs sometime after D, and G departs sometime after D, but that G might be before F or after F, and either immediately so or not.

Here are some examples of conditions that would give us partially unordered sequence strings:

Flights F and G depart after flight D.

Both Adam's and Raja's interviews take place sometime before Cory's interview.

Mona sits to the left of both Lillja and Justin.

Joint Sequence Strings

Perhaps the most important element of many sequencing games is the joint sequence string. These are not given to you in the restrictions, but are rather produced by you as you piece together the information given in different restrictions. In particular, if you have two separate sequence strings and the two strings have at least one element in common, then you can join them.

For example, suppose you are given the information that flight A departs after flight B, but before flight D:

B———A———D

And suppose you are given the information that flight C departs after flight D:

D———C

Since the two strings have the entity D in common, you can join them at D:

B———A———D———C

This combines two pieces of information into one, and is far more helpful than the two disjointed strings.

This is a relatively simple string joining; there are more complicated connections that might be made as well. For example, suppose we are also told that flight E departs before flight D:

E———D

Then we again have a point of connection D, but that point of connection is embedded in the first string, so we can't simply produce a longer, linear string as we did before. Instead, we can draw a line down from the point of connection, and an arrow with the other entity involved, indicating that E must depart sometime before D:

It is crucial for sequencing games to understand what this symbolization means, or to come up with your own method of symbolizing how to join different relative sequences (B before A before D before C, and E before D). This symbolization indicates that E occurs to the left of D (before D). The arrow helps to remind us that it's not the case that E could only come in between A and D, but rather that E could occur *anywhere* to the left of D. E could occur first (furthest left, indicating that E departs first), or in between B and A, or in between A and D. It just could not occur after D.

Although we use this joint sequence string symbolizing technique throughout the rest of this book, it is only a suggestion. Many find it intuitive to use vertical lines and arrows (as we do here), but some find it more intuitive to use greater than and less than signs, or diagonal lines (see figure 1). If the technique presented here is not intuitive for you, try your own method, but make sure that it doesn't confuse you into thinking that elements are more restricted than they actually are, like thinking that E must occur in between A and D, rather than anywhere to the left of D.

Figure 1

Let's try a more complicated example now, along with a more involved symbolization.

Eight flights—A, B, C, D, E, F, G, and H—
   depart one at a time, according to the following restrictions:
Flight A departs after flight B, but before flight D.
Flight C departs after flight D.
Flight E departs before flight D.
Flights F and G depart after flight D.
Flight H departs after flight E.

The symbolizations for the restrictions taken in isolation are:

Flight A departs after flight B, but before flight D.

B————A————D

Flight C departs after flight D.

D————C

Flight E departs before flight D.

E————D

Flights F and G depart after flight D.

D————F//G

Flight H departs after flight E.

E————H

Now, how do we join these sequence strings? We already joined the first two:

B————A————D————C

We can also join the third and the fourth restrictions (the fourth being a partially unordered sequence string, discussed above):

E————D————F//G

Now, we can join these two sequence strings at the point of connection—that is, by D, the entity that both have in common. To do this, we use one string as a primary string, and draw a line under the point of connection D, from which we draw the remaining elements of the secondary string.

B————A————D————C
←——E——+—F//G→

What about the fifth restriction, that H is after E? We can again join this to the symbolization we have by drawing a line under E, with H in an arrow pointing to the right, as follows:

B————A————D————C
←——E——+—F//G→
├—H————————→

This simply means that H occurs somewhere to the right of E.

To get a sense of how these symbolizations help with sequencing games, let's take the following question:

If flight H departs before flight B, then which one of the following must be true?
a. E departs first
b. E departs second
c. F departs sixth
d. G departs sixth
e. C departs eighth

The symbolization shows us that E must be to the left of H. If H is to the left of B, then E must be to the left of B, because H departs after E. That is, we can imagine shifting H to the left of B, forcing E to move left of B as well, and E stays to the left of H).

B————A————D————C
E———————————+—F//G→
├—H→

So now we can symbolize the ordering as:

E————H————B————A————D————C
                              ├—F//G→

Since the only 'unsettled' elements are F and G, which are somewhere to the right of D, everything to the left of D is settled—, and in particular, E must depart first. The correct answer, then, is A—, that E departs first.

We might have also arrived at this answer without having first produced the master joint sequence string by joining sequence strings given by the restrictions as needed. That is, we could note that H departing before B joins the string given by the first and fifth restrictions, and then join the other strings. The point of the initial, master joint sequence symbolization, however, is to compile all the information we can into one diagram, so that we can just refer to that one diagram as we work through all the questions, rather than construct a new diagram from scratch for every question and have to check each restriction individually.

Two more points should be made about sequence strings in general. First, ordered blocks can be elements on a joint sequence string. For example, suppose we are told that:

> Flight A departs immediately after Flight B
> Flight A departs after flight D.

Then we have an ordered block (BA) and a sequence string (D———A) which can be integrated into a joint sequence string:

> D———BA

Second, unordered blocks can be elements on a joint sequence string. Suppose we are told that:

> Flight A either departs immediately before flight B or immediately after flight B.
> Flight A departs after flight D.

Then we have an unordered block (A/B) and a sequence string (D———A) which can be integrated into a joint sequence string:

> D———A/B

The important point to keep in mind is that these various players can all be integrated together. Very rarely, the symbolizations will not easily allow for integration; in these instances, you must adapt your symbolization to the circumstance to make sure you capture the information in one place, or be content to leave the information visually separated and try to mentally integrate it or reason with it as needed.

Finally, a note about answering sequencing questions: some questions will introduce new sequencing information. Often, you will want to modify your sequencing diagram—or create a new diagram using the original one as a reference—to incorporate new information. This will usually mean creating a new primary string. You will gain practice with this technique by working through the practice logic games.

Floaters

The final major common player to pay attention to in sequence games is the floater. Floaters are entities that have absolutely no restrictions on them. That is, they do not appear in any of the restrictions, and also do not have restrictions placed on them indirectly. Always keep in mind which entities can float into any position when attempting to sequence.

A Final Note about Sequencing Games

It is important to realize that sequencing games will not always allow for the creation of the players we just described, or master joint sequence strings, or any sequence strings at all up front. Some sequencing games—especially ones that are heavy on conditional statements (e.g., 'If Wells goes first, then Anand is third')—will not lend themselves to such techniques. We have discussed these techniques because they are unique to sequencing games.

Practice Game 1

Seven jobs—painting, window washing, caulking, landscaping, insulating, roofing, and brick-work—are to be performed to improve a house, one at a time, according to the following conditions:

The window washing happens before the painting.
The caulking happens after the insulating, but before the window washing.
Both the roofing and landscaping happen after the caulking.
The brickwork happens before the roofing.

1. Which one of the following could be the order of the jobs, from first to last?
   a. Landscaping, insulating, caulking, brick-work, window washing, painting, roofing
   b. Brickwork, insulating, painting, caulking, landscaping, window washing, roofing
   c. Insulating, brickwork, caulking, roofing, window washing, landscaping, painting
   d. Brickwork, caulking, landscaping, roofing, window washing, insulating, painting
   e. Insulating, caulking, landscaping, roofing, window washing, brickwork, painting

2. Which one of the following is a complete and accurate list of the last jobs performed?
   a. Painting
   b. Painting, roofing
   c. Roofing, landscaping
   d. Roofing, landscaping, window washing
   e. Painting, roofing, landscaping

3. If the brickwork happens after the window washing, then which one of the following is the earliest that the roofing could occur?
   a. Second
   b. Third
   c. Fourth
   d. Fifth
   e. Sixth

4. If the roofing happens fourth, then which one of the following is the least number of tasks separating the brickwork from the painting?
   a. One
   b. Two
   c. Three
   d. Four
   e. Five

5. Which one of the following is a complete and accurate list of the jobs any one of which could be the second task performed?
   a. Caulking
   b. Brickwork, caulking
   c. Insulating, brickwork, caulking
   d. Insulating, brickwork, roofing
   e. Insulating, caulking, brickwork, landscaping

Practice Game 2

A job applicant has to interview with a company's top six executives—Emmett, Fernandez, Garg, Hinton, Isaac, and Jimenez—one at a time, according to the following conditions:

Emmett is either the first or second person to interview the applicant.
If Garg is the second to interview the applicant, then Jimenez is the fourth to interview the applicant.
If Hinton is the sixth to interview the applicant, then Garg is either the second or third person to interview the applicant.
Fernandez interviews the applicant immediately after Garg interviews the applicant.

1. Which one of the following could be the sequence in which the executives interview the applicant, from first to last?
   a. Emmett, Hinton, Garg, Fernandez, Jimenez, Isaac
   b. Garg, Fernandez, Hinton, Emmett, Isaac, Jimenez
   c. Emmett, Jimenez, Isaac, Garg, Fernandez, Hinton
   d. Emmett, Fernandez, Jimenez, Garg, Hinton, Isaac
   e. Emmett, Garg, Fernandez, Isaac, Jimenez, Hinton

2. Which one of the following statements CANNOT be true?
   a. Isaac interviews the applicant first.
   b. Hinton interviews the applicant second.
   c. Fernandez interviews the applicant second.
   d. Jimenez interviews the applicant fifth.
   e. Hinton interviews the applicant sixth.

3. If Isaac interviews the applicant after Fernandez interviews the applicant, and exactly two executives interview the applicant in between Isaac and Fernandez, then which one of the following statements CANNOT be true?
   a. Emmett interviews the applicant first.
   b. Garg interviews the applicant second.
   c. Jimenez interviews the applicant third.
   d. Hinton interviews the applicant fifth.
   e. Isaac interviews the applicant sixth.

4. If Emmett interviews the applicant either immediately before or immediately after Garg interviews the applicant, then which one of the following is a complete and accurate list of the executives any one of which could be the fourth executive to interview the applicant?
   a. Isaac
   b. Jimenez
   c. Fernandez, Hinton
   d. Fernandez, Jimenez
   e. Fernandez, Hinton, Isaac, Jimenez

5. If Hinton is the last executive to interview the applicant, then which one of the following is a complete and accurate list of the spots in which Isaac could interview the applicant?
   a. Fifth
   b. First, second
   c. First, second, fifth
   d. First, third, fifth
   e. First, second, fourth, fifth

Practice Game 3

Six friends—Alan, David, Marcello, Pedro, Rahul, and Sanjay—attend a baseball game. They sit in Section 5, Row H, seats 1 to 6. Seat 1 is on the left, and the seats increase in number as they go to the right. The friends sit according to the following restrictions:

> Pedro does not sit immediately next to Sanjay.
> Rahul sits either immediately to the left or immediately to the right of Sanjay.
> Marcello sits to the left of David.
> Both Alan and Pedro sit to the left of Marcello.
> Rahul sits to the right of Pedro.

1. Which one of the following could be the order in which the friends sit, from left to right?
   a. Alan, Marcello, Pedro, Rahul, Sanjay, David
   b. Alan, Rahul, Pedro, Marcello, Sanjay, David
   c. Alan, David, Pedro, Marcello, Sanjay, Rahul
   d. Alan, Pedro, Rahul, Sanjay, Marcello, David
   e. Alan, Sanjay, Rahul, Pedro, Marcello, David

2. Which one of the following is a complete and accurate list of the friends any one of which could sit in seat 1?
   a. Alan
   b. Marcello
   c. Alan, Pedro
   d. Sanjay, Pedro
   e. Alan, Pedro, Sanjay

3. Which one of the following is a complete and accurate list of the seats any one of which could be the seat in which Sanjay sits?
   a. Seat 3, seat 5
   b. Seat 4, seat 5, seat 6
   c. Seat 2, seat 4, seat 5, seat 6
   d. Seat 3, seat 4, seat 5, seat 6
   e. Seat 2, seat 3, seat 4, seat 5, seat 6

4. If Rahul sits in seat 2, then for how many of the six seats is the occupant determined?
   a. Two
   b. Three
   c. Four
   d. Five
   e. Six

5. If Sanjay sits to the left of Marcello, then which one of the following is a complete and accurate list of the friends any one of which could be the friend sitting in seat 4?
   a. Alan
   b. Alan, Sanjay
   c. Rahul, Sanjay
   d. Rahul, Sanjay, Marcello
   e. Sanjay, Rahul, Alan

Practice Game 4

An admissions committee ranks six students—A, B, C, D, E, and F—for further consideration. The highest-ranked student ranks first. The ranking is consistent with the following conditions:

Student A is ranked the second highest.
Both student C and student E are ranked higher than B.
Student D and student F have consecutive ranks, not necessarily in that order.

1. Which one of the following could be the ranking of students, from lowest to highest?
   a. B, A, E, D, F, C
   b. B, C, F, D, A, E
   c. B, D, E, C, A, F
   d. C, D, F, B, A, E
   e. E, F, D, C, A, B

2. What which one of the following is a complete and accurate list of the ranks any one of which could be student B's rank?
   a. Sixth
   b. Third, fifth
   c. Fourth, sixth
   d. Second, fifth, sixth
   e. Fourth, fifth, sixth

3. If student D is ranked higher than student C, then which one of the following statements could be true and which one could be false?
   a. Student B is ranked first.
   b. Student C is ranked second.
   c. Student D is ranked third.
   d. Student A is ranked fourth.
   e. Student E is ranked fifth.

4. Which one of the following is a complete and accurate list of all the students any one of which could be ranked fourth?
   a. Student D, student F
   b. Student C, student E
   c. Student C, student D, student F
   d. Student B, student D, student F
   e. Student B, student C, student D, student F

5. If student E is ranked third, then which one of the following statements CANNOT be true?
   a. Student D is ranked sixth.
   b. Student C is ranked fifth.
   c. Student F is ranked fifth.
   d. Student F is ranked fourth.
   e. Student B is ranked fourth.

Practice Game 5

Seven songs—H,I, J, K, L, M and N—are selected on a jukebox. They are played one at a time, according to the following conditions:

> H is played second.
> J is either played third or played fifth.
> K is played before J.
> N is either played immediate after M or immediately before L.
> At least one song is played in between song J and song K.

1. Which one of the following could be a list of the songs played in order from first to last?
   a. K, L, H, I, J, M, N
   b. M, H, N, K, J, L, I
   c. L, H, J, M, N, K, I
   d. K, H, I, J, N, L, M
   e. K, H, M, N, J, I, L

2. Song K could be played:
   a. Third
   b. Fourth
   c. Fifth
   d. Sixth
   e. Seventh

3. If song K is played after song H is played, then which one of the following songs must be played after J is played?
   a. Song I
   b. Song K
   c. Song L
   d. Song M
   e. Song N

4. If song N is played third, then the sixth song to be played must be:
   a. Either song L or song M.
   b. Either song M or song I.
   c. Either song L or song I.
   d. Either song M or song K.
   e. Either song L or song K.

5. If exactly three songs are played in between song L and song J, then which one of the following is a complete and accurate list of all the songs that could be played fifth?
   a. Song N
   b. Song M, song J
   c. Song M, song N, song J
   d. Song M, song N, song I
   e. Song M, song N, song J, song I

Practice Game 6

An outdoors club picks seven checkpoints for an orienteering course. The checkpoints—L, M, N, O, P, Q, R—are to be arranged in order according to the following conditions:

Checkpoints M and P both occur before checkpoint R.
Checkpoint P occurs before checkpoint Q.
Checkpoint O occurs before checkpoint M.
Either checkpoint R occurs immediately after checkpoint L, or checkpoint L occurs immediately after checkpoint R.
Checkpoint P is not the first checkpoint.

1. Which one of the following could be a list of the checkpoints, in order from first to last?
   a. M, N, O, P, L, R, Q
   b. N, O, P, M, Q, R, L
   c. N, Q, O, P, M, L, R
   d. O, N, M, R, L, Q, P
   e. O, P, M, Q, R, N, L

2. Which one of the following checkpoints CANNOT be the third checkpoint?
   a. Checkpoint M
   b. Checkpoint N
   c. Checkpoint P
   d. Checkpoint Q
   e. Checkpoint R

3. Which one of the following statements CANNOT be true?
   a. Checkpoint Q is second.
   b. Checkpoint O is second.
   c. Checkpoint M is second.
   d. Checkpoint N is third.
   e. Checkpoint M is third.

4. If checkpoint O is the fourth checkpoint, then each of the following statements must be true EXCEPT:
   a. Checkpoint N is first.
   b. Checkpoint P is second
   c. Checkpoint Q is third.
   d. Checkpoint M is fifth.
   e. Checkpoint L is sixth.

5. If checkpoint M occurs before checkpoint P, then what is the earliest checkpoint Q could appear in the course?
   a. First
   b. Second
   c. Third
   d. Fourth
   e. Fifth

Practice Game 7

Seven parts—Q, R, S, T, U, V, and X—are added to a car chassis on a Mustang assembly line, one at a time. The order in which they are added is consistent with the following conditions:

> The sixth part to be added is either part Q or part S.
> If part T is added before part S, then part U is added second.
> Part U is added immediately after part V.
> Part V is added before both part T and part X.
> Part R must be added either immediately before or immediately after part S.

1. Which one of the following could be a list of the parts in the order in which they are added?
   a. V, U, T, X, Q, R, S
   b. V, U, S, T, R, Q, X
   c. U, V, S, R, X, Q, T
   d. Q, V, U, T, R, S, X
   e. V, U, X, S, R, Q, T

2. If part Q is added last, then each of the following statements must be true EXCEPT:
   a. V is added first.
   b. U is added second.
   c. T is added third.
   d. R is added fifth.
   e. S is added sixth.

3. Each of the following parts could be added last EXCEPT:
   a. Part Q
   b. Part R
   c. Part S
   d. Part T
   e. Part X

4. If part R is added last, then which one of the following statements must be true?
   a. Part V is added first.
   b. Part Q is added third.
   c. Part T is added fourth.
   d. Part X is added fifth.
   e. Part T is added fifth.

5. If part T is added after part X but before part S, then which one of the following is a complete and accurate list of all the parts any one of which could be added fifth in the assembly line?
   a. part Q
   b. part R, part Q
   c. part S, part T
   d. part Q, part R, part X
   e. part Q, part R, part T

Practice Game 8

Six speakers—A, B, C, D, E, and F—are to speak at a rally, one at a time. Their line-up is determined by the following conditions:

D speaks either second or third.
A speaks before C.
C either speaks immediately before or immediately after E.
F speaks after E.
B does not speak immediately before or immediately after F.

1. Which one of the following could be the speaker list, in order from first to last?
   a. B, D, A,C, E, F
   b. D, B, A, C, E, F
   c. C, D, E, F, A, B
   d. A, F, D, E, C, B
   e. E, C, D, F, A, B

2. Which one of the following is a complete and accurate list of the spot speaker E could have in the line-up?
   a. Third spot, fourth spot
   b. Fourth spot, fifth spot
   c. Fifth spot, sixth spot
   d. Fourth spot, fifth spot, sixth spot
   e. Third spot, fourth spot, fifth spot

3. If there is exactly one speaker in between speaker A and speaker D, then all of the following statements must be true EXCEPT:
   a. A speaks first.
   b. B speaks second.
   c. D speaks third.
   d. C speaks fourth.
   e. F speaks sixth.

4. If speaker B immediately precedes speaker C in the line-up, then how many people speak in between speaker A and speaker F?
   a. Zero
   b. One
   c. Two
   d. Three
   e. Four

5. Which one of the following is a complete and accurate list of the speakers any one of which could speak second?
   a. B
   b. A, B
   c. A, B, D
   d. B, D, C
   e. A, D, E

Setup, Answers, and Explanations

Practice Game 1

All the restrictions in this game provide some sort of sequence string.

> The first restriction: W———P
> The second restriction: I———C———W
> The third restriction: C———R//L (Note that this is a partially unordered sequence string, so the unknown order of R relative to L is symbolized with a double-dash.)
> The fourth restriction: B———R

Now try to combine these sequence strings into a joint sequence string. The first and second strings can be straightforwardly combined into:

> I———C———W———P

Combine the third string with this string by joining them at the common entity C:

> I—C—W—P
> ├—R//L→

Now combine the fourth string with this string by joining the two at the common entity R:

> I—C—W—P
> ├—R//L→
> ←B—┤

This will be the larger joint sequence string that will provide a jumping-off point for answering the questions.

Question 1

The correct answer is choice **c**. This question is a "Test-the-Rules" question. The first restriction rules out choice **b**, since the window washing occurs after the painting. The second restriction rules out choice **d**, since both the caulking and the window washing occur before the insulating. The third restriction rules out choice **a**, since the landscaping occurs before the caulking. The fourth restriction rules out choice **e**, since the roofing occurs before the brickwork.

Question 2

The correct answer is choice **e**. Consult the sequence diagram to see which entities could be the right-most on the diagram. P does not need to have anything to its right. R and L are on an arrow pointing to the right, and are not ordered with respect to one another, so either of those could be the right-most entity as well. So each of P, R, and L could be the last job performed—this is choice **e**.

Question 3

The correct answer is choice **d**. Construct a new sequence diagram with the new information that W—B. You will want to create a new string with W and B integrated, so the primary string will now be:

> I—C—W—B—P

The rules tell us that roofing must occur after the caulking and brickwork. The L and R will have to be separated and added as secondary strings:

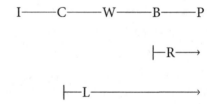

Although L must occur after C, there is no restriction that keeps R from occurring before L. So now we can see that the left-most spot for R could be fifth—choice **d**.

Question 4

The correct answer is choice **b**. Construct a new sequencing diagram that is based off the initial diagram and the information that the roofing occurs fourth. The roofing can happen fourth if exactly three jobs happen before it (three entities are to the left of R on the diagram). By consulting the initial sequencing diagram, we see that those three jobs must be I, C, and B. L, W, and P must then be pushed to the right of R. We can then create a new primary string relating I, C, R, W, and P, leaving B and L as secondary strings:

$$I—C—R—W—P$$
$$←B—|—L→$$

We might just as easily have created a primary string relating I, C, R, and L, leaving W—P and B as secondary strings:

$$I—C—R—L$$
$$←B—|—W—P→$$

B must be to the left of R, so the closest we can get it to the right side is just to the left of R. To ensure that P is as far left as possible, we push L as far right as possible, past P. We then have two entities in between B and P, namely, R and W. (The sequence looks like: I-C-B-R-W-P-L.) So the correct answer is **b**.

Question 5

The correct answer is choice **c**. Consult the sequencing diagram to see which could be the second task performed. Consider each entity in turn. I could be second if B was pushed to its left. C could be second if B was to the right of C. B could be second if it fell between I and C. Neither W nor P could be second, as they are preceded by two and three entities, respectively. Neither R nor L could be second, since R is preceded by at least three entities (I, C, and B), and L is preceded by at least two entities (I and C). So I, C, and B could be second, and no others could be second—this is answer choice **c**.

Practice Game 2

The first thing to do is to symbolize the restrictions, and see if any deductions or joint sequence strings can be made from them. It will turn out that there won't be any master sequence string, and this is largely because the restrictions of this sequencing game are largely conditional statements.

The first restriction can be symbolized with a diagram of six slots:

$$←E→$$

$$\underline{} \quad \underline{} \quad \underline{} \quad \underline{} \quad \underline{} \quad \underline{}$$
$$1 \quad 2 \quad 3 \quad 4 \quad 5 \quad 6$$

The second restriction can be symbolized:

$G = 2 \rightarrow J = 4$ [and the contrapositive, $J \neq 4 \rightarrow G \neq 2$]

The third restriction can be symbolized:

$H = 6 \rightarrow G = 2$ or 3 [and the contrapositive, $(G \neq 2$ and $G \neq 3) \rightarrow H \neq 6$]

The fourth restriction gives us an ordered block:

GF

Although we don't have a sequence string to work with, a couple of observations can be made. One, the GF block entails that F cannot be first. Two, if F were second, then the GF block would take up spots 1 and 2, leaving no room for E; so F cannot be second. Three, the GF block means that G cannot be last (sixth). Four, I has no restrictions on it, and so is a floater.

We can capture most of this information in the diagram:

$$←E→$$

$$\underline{} \quad \underline{} \quad \underline{} \quad \underline{} \quad \underline{} \quad \underline{}$$
$$1 \quad 2 \quad 3 \quad 4 \quad 5 \quad 6$$
$$\cancel{F} \quad \cancel{F} \quad \quad \quad \quad \cancel{G}$$

Question 1

The correct answer is choice **a**. This question is a "Test-the-Rules" question. The first restriction rules out **b**, since Emmett is neither first nor second. The second restriction rules out **e**, since Garg is second but Jimenez is not fourth. The third restriction rules out **c**, since Hinton is sixth, but Garg is not second or third. The fourth restriction rules out **d**, since Fernandez does not go directly after Garg.

Question 2

The correct answer is choice **c**. Check to see if any of our up-front observations are being stated. Choice **c** states that F cannot be second, which we noted in the up-front observations, and so this is the correct answer. Notice that choices **b** and **d** represent situations that were already determined to be possible in the answer to question 1 (in choice **a** of question 1, Hinton is second and Jimenez is fifth).

Question 3

The correct answer is choice **c**. If I goes three spots after F, then the fact that there are only six spots limits the position of F to either the first, second, or third spot. But we know from the up-front observations that F cannot be in the first or second spot. So F must be in the third spot, and I in the sixth spot:

```
        ←E→
 _  _  F  _  _  I
 1  2  3  4  5  6
 F̶  F̶        G̶
```

But our ordered block 'GF' indicates that G must be in spot 2. And that forces E into spot 1. By the second restriction, since G is in spot 2, J must in be in spot 4, leaving H for spot 5:

```
 E  G  F  J  H  I
 1  2  3  4  5  6
```

Now check each answer choice against this diagram. The diagram makes choices **a**, **b**, **d**, and **e** all true. Choice **c** is the correct answer because according to the diagram, Jimenez does not interview the applicant third, but fourth.

Question 4

The correct answer is choice **d**. First, assess what the new information means. The new restriction that Emmett interviews the applicant either immediately before or immediately after Garg amounts to an unordered block, E/G. We can combine this block with the ordered block GF to create the ordered block EGF. Since E must either be in the first spot or second spot, we get two possible scenarios:

```
S1
 E  G  F  _  _  _
 1  2  3  4  5  6
```

```
S2
 _  E  G  F  _  _   (I, H, J)
 1  2  3  4  5  6
```

We write (I, H, J) in the second scenario to remind ourselves that these three entities are to be distributed into the remaining slots (and don't write this in the first scenario because we are about to distribute them). In the first scenario, G is second, so J must be fourth, leaving I and H to be distributed into slots 5 and 6:

```
S1
 E  G  F  J  I/H
 1  2  3  4  5 6
```

Now we consult these two diagrams to see which entities could be in the fourth spot. In S1, J is in the fourth spot. In S2, F is in the fourth spot. So the list of entities that could be in the fourth spot includes Jimenez and Fernandez, and no other entities—that is, choice **d**.

Question 5

The correct answer is choice **c**. If H is sixth, then G must be in spot 2 or spot 3. Consider each option as a separate scenario.

Scenario 1: If G is in spot 2, then J is in spot 4. And since G is in spot 2, E is forced into spot 1. And since G is in spot 2, F must be in spot 3. This leaves I for spot 5. So we have:

$$\underline{E}\ \underline{G}\ \underline{F}\ \underline{J}\ \underline{I}\ \underline{H}$$
$$1\ \ 2\ \ 3\ \ 4\ \ 5\ \ 6$$

Scenario 2: If G is in spot 3, then F must be in spot 4. So we have:

$$\overset{\leftarrow E\rightarrow}{}$$
$$\_\ \_\ \underline{G}\ \underline{F}\ \_\ \underline{H}$$
$$1\ \ 2\ \ 3\ \ 4\ \ 5\ \ 6$$

So where can Isaac go? In Scenario 1, Isaac is in spot 5. In Scenario 2, Isaac can go into spots 1, 2 and 5. So Isaac could go first, second or fifth, and couldn't go in any other spots—choice **c**.

Practice Game 3

The first restriction gives us a restricted block:

~~P/S~~

The second restriction gives us an unordered block:

S/R

The third restriction gives us a sequence string:

M—D

The fourth restriction gives us a partially ordered sequence string:

A//P—M

The fifth restriction gives us a sequence string:

P—R

We can combine the sequence strings making up the third and fourth restrictions:

A//P—M—D

We can add in the fifth restriction as a secondary string:

A//P—M—D

├—R→

Finally, we can add the replace R with the unordered block from the second restriction:

A//P—M—D

├—S/R→

This sequence diagram captures all the information in the second through fifth restrictions. The only other piece of information to keep in mind is the first restriction, the restricted block.

Question 1

The correct answer is choice **d**. This question is a "Test-the-Rules" question. The second restriction rules out choice **b**, since Sanjay is not sitting immediately next to Rahul. The third restriction rules out choice **c**, since Marcello is not to the left of David. The fourth restriction rules out choice **a**, since Pedro is not to the left of Marcello. The fifth restriction rules out choice **e**, since Rahul is not to the right of Pedro.

Question 2

The correct answer is choice **c**. Consult the sequence diagram to see who could sit in seat 1—that is, who could be the left-most in the diagram. Only A and

P, since they are unordered relative to one another, could be first. S and R must be to the right of P, and so must M and D. So the correct answer includes Alan and Pedro and no others, choice **c**. Double-check that the first restriction, which is not captured in the diagram, doesn't rule out either of these options—it doesn't since it only says that P and S cannot be adjacent, which could be the case whether A is first or whether P is first (just place S to the right of, say, M).

Question 3

The correct answer is choice **d**. We want all the seats that Sanjay could be in. Consult the diagram and see where S can go, considering each seat in turn. S can't be in 1, because at the very least P will be to his left. Can S be in 2? If S is in 2, then P must be in 1, since P must be to S's left. But then we will violate the restrictive block, prohibiting P from being immediately next to S. So S can't be in seat 2. So we have eliminated choices **c** and **e**. What about seat 3? S could be 3rd, with P-A to his left. What about seat 4? S could be 4th, with A-P-R to his left. S could be 5th, with A-P-M-R to his left. S could be sixth, with A-P-M-D-R to his left. So S could be in seats 3, 4, 5 and 6—choice **d**.

Question 4

The correct answer is choice **e**. Consult the diagram to see what happens when Rahul is in seat 2. If R is in 2, then P must be in 1 (since P must be to the left of R). S must then be in 3, to maintain the S/R unordered block. This leaves A, M, and D, for seats 4 through 6—which must be in that order, according to the diagram. So we have:

$$\underline{P}\ \underline{R}\ \underline{S}\ \underline{A}\ \underline{M}\ \underline{D}$$
$$1\ 2\ 3\ 4\ 5\ 6$$

So every one of the six seats has a determinate occupant, and the answer is choice **e**.

Question 5

The correct answer is choice **e**. Consult the diagram to see what happens with the new information that

S—M. Since S/R is a block, this simply cuts off the arrow allowing S/R to be moved to the right:

$$A//P\text{——}M\text{——}D$$
$$\vdash S/R\dashv$$

To see more concretely what this means, divide up this sequencing diagram into two scenarios, based on the unordered sequence pair A//P. In one scenario, A will be the left of P, and in another scenario, A will be to the right of P.

$$S1:\ A\text{——}P\text{——}M\text{——}D$$
$$\vdash S/R\dashv$$

$$S2:\ P\text{——}A\text{——}M\text{——}D$$
$$\vdash\text{——}S/R\text{——}\dashv$$

Note that S1 really allows for only one possibility, since P and S cannot be next to one another:

$$S1:\ A\text{-}P\text{-}R\text{-}S\text{-}M\text{-}D$$

S2 can be subdivided yet again, with the S/R block in between P and A, or in between A and M:

$$S2.1:\ P\text{——}S/R\text{——}A\text{-}M\text{-}D$$

$$S2.2:\ P\text{-}A\text{——}S/R\text{——}M\text{-}D$$

Note again that S2.1 is restricted by the restricted block preventing P and S from immediately adjacent, and so just becomes: P-R-S-A-M-D.

To summarize, our three scenarios are:

$$S1:\ A\text{-}P\text{-}R\text{-}S\text{-}M\text{-}D$$

$$S2.1:\ P\text{-}R\text{-}S\text{-}A\text{-}M\text{-}D$$

$$S2.2:\ P\text{-}A\text{——}S/R\text{——}M\text{-}D$$

Now look at seat 4 for each. In S1, S sits in seat 4. In S2.1, A sits in seat 4. In S2.2, S or R could sit in seat 4. So seat 4 could be occupied by S, R, or A, and by no other entity. This is choice **e**.

This is admittedly a fairly complicated way to answer this question. Another approach would be to use the information you have gained from previous questions. You can see from the answer to Question 1 that S has to be on the list, which rules out choice **a**. You can see from the diagram produced to answer Question 4 that A has to be on the list, which rules out choice **c**. You can rule out any answer choice which includes M since at least four letters have to come before M (we know A//P must precede M from the initial joint sequence string, and given the question stem, S/R must also precede M)—that is, we can rule out choice **d**. This leaves only choices **b** and **e**, so you just have to check whether R could be fourth without violating any of the restrictions.

Practice Game 4

This game asks for a ranking of six students—and the first question asks for the ranking from lowest to highest—so draw six slots, labeled 1 to 6, with 6 on the left and 1 on the right. (If you started by drawing the slots in reverse order, you would simply have to flip your diagram once you got to the first question and realized it would be easier to draw it in the opposite order for the sake of that question).

$$\underline{\quad}\ \underline{\quad}\ \underline{\quad}\ \underline{\quad}\ \underline{\quad}\ \underline{\quad}$$
$$6\quad 5\quad 4\quad 3\quad 2\quad 1$$

The first restriction can be directly entered into the diagram:

$$\underline{\quad}\ \underline{\quad}\ \underline{\quad}\ \underline{\quad}\ \underline{A}\ \underline{\quad}$$
$$6\quad 5\quad 4\quad 3\quad 2\quad 1$$

The second restriction gives us a partially unordered sequence string:

B—C//E

The third restriction gives us an unordered sequence block:

D/F

Since there are no entities in common, the strings cannot be joined. We can make a couple immediate observations, however. B cannot be first or third (because they would be no room for C and E to its right), and neither C nor E can be sixth. We could proceed to the questions, or we could quickly see if breaking down B's position into three scenarios (sixth, fifth, and fourth) will be useful. Again, be cautious about sinking too much time into creating scenarios, especially if you're looking to produce three (rather than two) scenarios. In general, if you find that scenarios are getting too confusing, or eating too much of your time, just proceed to the questions and figure out scenarios as needed. In this set of answer explanations, we make use of the three scenarios that depend on B's placement:

S1
$$\underline{B}\ \underline{\quad}\ \underline{\quad}\ \underline{\quad}\ \underline{A}\ \underline{\quad}$$
$$6\quad 5\quad 4\quad 3\quad 2\quad 1$$

S2
$$\underline{\quad}\ \underline{\quad}\ \underline{B}\ \underline{\quad}\ \underline{A}\ \underline{\quad}$$
$$6\quad 5\quad 4\quad 3\quad 2\quad 1$$

S3
$$\underline{\quad}\ \underline{\quad}\ \underline{B}\ \underline{\quad}\ \underline{A}\ \underline{\quad}$$
$$6\quad 5\quad 4\quad 3\quad 2\quad 1$$

In S3, C and E must fill spots 3 and 1, leaving D and F to fill spots 6 and 5:

S3
$$\underline{D/F}\ \underline{B}\ \underline{C/E}\ \underline{A}\ \underline{E/C}$$
$$6\quad 5\quad 4\quad 3\quad 2\quad 1$$

(Keep in mind that the slash between E and C in spots 3 and 1 do not indicate an unordered block, as it does for D/F, but rather the two possibilities for spot 3 and the two possibilities for spot 1.)

For S2, the unordered block D/F can only fit in the two-spot block consisting of spots 4 and 3; leaving E and C to be distributed between spots 6 and 1. But this would violate our sequence string B—C//E. So S2 is not a possibility, and B cannot be fifth

For S1, this is not an issue, since B is in spot 6. There are two possibilities for placing the D/F block, each way leaving C and E for the remaining spots:

S1.1

$$\underline{B}\ \ \underline{D/F}\ \ \underline{C/E}\ \ \underline{A}\ \ \underline{C/E}$$
$$6\ \ \ 5\ 4\ \ \ \ 3\ \ \ \ \ 2\ \ \ \ \ 1$$

S1.2

$$\underline{B}\ \ \underline{C/E}\ \ \underline{D/F}\ \ \underline{A}\ \ \underline{C/E}$$
$$6\ \ \ 5\ \ \ \ 4\ \ \ \ \ 3\ \ \ 2\ \ \ \ 1$$

So our three scenarios are:

S1.1
$$\underline{B}\ \ \underline{D/F}\ \ \underline{C/E}\ \ \underline{A}\ \ \underline{C/E}$$
$$6\ \ \ 5\ \ 4\ \ \ \ 3\ \ \ \ 2\ \ \ \ 1$$

S1.2
$$\underline{B}\ \ \underline{C/E}\ \ \underline{D/F}\ \ \underline{A}\ \ \underline{C/E}$$
$$6\ \ \ 5\ \ \ \ 4\ \ \ \ 3\ \ \ 2\ \ \ \ 1$$

S3
$$\underline{D/F}\ \ \underline{B}\ \ \underline{C/E}\ \ \underline{A}\ \ \underline{E/C}$$
$$6\ \ \ \ 5\ \ \ \ 4\ \ \ \ \ 3\ \ \ 2\ \ \ \ 1$$

Question 1

The correct answer is choice **b**. This question is a "Test-the-Rules" question. The first restriction rules out choice **a**, since A is not ranked second highest. The second restriction rules out choices **d** and **e**, since in **d**, C is ranked lower than B, and in choice **e**, both C and

E are ranked lower than B. The third restriction rules out choice **c**, since D is not adjacent to F.

Question 2

The correct answer is choice **c**. Consult the three sequence diagrams to see where B could go. In S1.1 and S1.2, B is sixth. In S3, B is fourth. Since these exhaust our scenarios, B could be fourth or sixth, and no other rank—choice **c**.

Question 3

The correct answer is choice **c**. Start with the new information that C—D. The only scenario in which C can appear before D is S1.2.

S1.2
$$\underline{B}\ \ \underline{C/E}\ \ \underline{D/F}\ \ \underline{A}\ \ \underline{C/E}$$
$$6\ \ \ 5\ \ \ \ 4\ 3\ \ \ 2\ \ \ \ 1$$

So C must appear in spot 5, forcing E into spot 1:

$$\underline{B}\ \ \underline{C}\ \ \underline{D/F}\ \ \underline{A}\ \ \underline{E}$$
$$6\ \ \ 5\ \ \ 4\ 3\ \ \ 2\ \ \ \ 1$$

Now we consider each answer choice, and see whether the statement could be both true and false. Choice **a** is incorrect because B is in fact ranked sixth—it can't be true that B is ranked first. Choice **b** is incorrect because C is in fact ranked fifth—it can't be true that C is ranked second. Choice **c** is correct because D could be ranked third; but it could also be ranked first, such that it would be false that D is ranked third. Choice **d** is incorrect because A is in fact ranked second, so it couldn't be the case that it's ranked fourth. Choice **e** is incorrect because E is in fact ranked first, so it couldn't be the case that it's ranked fifth.

Question 4

The correct answer is choice **d**. Consult the diagram to see which students could be in spot 4. In S1.1 and S1.2, students D and F could be in spot 4. In S3, B is in spot 4. So B, D, and F are the students that could be in spot 4, and no other students could be—choice **d**. Also, you know from question 1 that the list has to include F, and you know from question 2 that the list has to include B, so this narrows the options down to choices **d** and **e**. The only difference between the choices is C, and if you try to put C fourth you will see that it doesn't work.

Question 5

The correct answer is choice **b**. If E is ranked third, then we must be in scenario S1.1 or S3. In either case, C is forced into spot 1:

S1.1

B	D/F	E	A	C
6	5 4	3	2	1

S3

D/F	B	E	A	C
6 5	4	3	2	1

Now check each answer choice against these two diagrams, looking for a statement that is not accommodated by one or both of these diagrams. Choice **a** is incorrect because D is ranked sixth in S3. Choice **b** is correct because C is not ranked fifth in either scenario. Choices **c** and **d** are incorrect because F could be ranked fifth or fourth in S1.1. Choice **e** is incorrect because B is ranked fourth in S3.

Practice Game 5

Start with a seven slots, with the first song at the left and seventh song at the right:

_	_	_	_	_	_	_
1	2	3	4	5	6	7

Now incorporate and symbolize the restrictions. Put H in slot 2. Since H must either be third or fifth, see if creating two scenarios will be useful, one with J third, and one with J fifth:

S1

_	H	J	_	_	_	_
1	2	3	4	5	6	7

S2

_	H	_	_	J	_	_
1	2	3	4	5	6	7

The third restriction places K before J. For now, symbolize it as:

K—J

The fourth restriction says that there must be one of two ordered blocks:

MN or NL

The fifth restriction gives a numbered sequence block:

J/_+K

Remember that the slash indicates the positions of J and K can be reversed, and the one space and plus sign that at least one spot must be in between. Since we already have a restriction ordering J and K, we can combine the two to produce:

K_+J

This indicates that there must be at least one space in the sequence string K—J.

Now see how the third through fifth restrictions might play into the two scenarios. In S1, since K must precede J, we have:

S1

K	H	J	_	_	_	_
1	2	3	4	5	6	7

In S2, K must precede J, but must have at least one space separating K from J; so K must either be first or third. So subdivide S2:

S2.1

<u>K</u> <u>H</u> _ _ <u>J</u> _ _
1   2   3   4   5   6   7

S2.2

_ <u>H</u> <u>K</u> _ <u>J</u> _ _
1   2   3   4   5   6   7

These three scenarios, S1, S2.1, and S2.2, now incorporate all the information given in the first, second, third, and fifth restrictions. So we can ignore those restrictions going forward, and only keep in mind one restriction, that MN or NL. By considering the diagrams spatially, we can observe that for S2.2, the slot block 6–7 must contain either MN or NL:

S2.2

                     (MN
_ <u>H</u> <u>K</u> _ <u>J</u> or NL
1   2   3   4   5   6 7

So in summary, our three scenarios are:

S1

<u>K</u> <u>H</u> <u>J</u> _ _ _ _
1   2   3   4   5   6   7

S2.1

<u>K</u> <u>H</u> _ _ <u>J</u> _ _
1   2   3   4   5   6   7

S2.2

                     (MN
_ <u>H</u> <u>K</u> _ <u>J</u> or NL
1   2   3   4   5   6 7

Question 1

The correct answer is choice **e**. This question is a "Test-the-Rules" question. The first restriction rules out choice **a**, since H is not second. The second restriction rules out choice **d**, since J is neither third nor fifth. The third restriction rules out choice **c**, since K is not before J. The fourth restriction rules out choice **b**, since N does not immediately follow M, nor does L immediately follow N.

Question 2

The correct answer is choice **a**. Consult the diagrams to see when K could be played. K is played first in S1 and S2.1, and third in S2.2. So the correct answer is **a**, third. It could be helpful to note for future questions that K can't be fourth, fifth, sixth, or seventh.

Question 3

The correct answer is choice **e**. If K follows H, then we must be in S2.2. According to the diagram for scenario 2.2, the space after J—namely, spots 6 and 7—must be filled either by MN or NL. Either way, N appears in that space. So choice **e** is correct.

Question 4

The correct answer is choice **b**. If N is third, then we must be in S2.1 (since S1 has J in spot 3, and S2.2 has K in spot 3). So we have:

S2.1

<u>K</u> <u>H</u> <u>N</u> _ <u>J</u> _ _
1   2   3   4   5   6   7

Now, we consider our restriction that MN or NL. Since MN can clearly not occur, we must have NL. That means that L is in spot 4, leaving M and I for spots 6 and 7:

<u>K</u> <u>H</u> <u>N</u> <u>L</u> <u>J</u> M/I
1   2   3   4   5   6 7

Now look at the sixth spot. It could be filled by M or I, and not by anything else. So **b** is the correct answer.

Question 5

The correct answer is choice **e**. If there are exactly three songs in between L and J, we have a numbered sequence block:

L_/_ _J

Consider the diagrams to see in scenarios this block could fit, and in how many ways. In S1, since J is third, we would have to fit the block J _ _ _ L into the scenario, and we would have:

S1

<u>K</u> <u>H</u> <u>J</u> _ _ _ <u>L</u>
1 2 3 4 5 6 7

We now have to accommodate MN or NL. If we have MN, there are two ways to accommodate it, either in the 4–5 space, or 5–6 space, leaving I for the remaining space:

S1.1

<u>K</u> <u>H</u> <u>J</u> <u>M</u> <u>N</u> <u>I</u> <u>L</u>
1   2   3   4   5   6   7

S1.2

<u>K</u> <u>H</u> <u>J</u> <u>I</u> <u>M</u> <u>N</u> <u>L</u>
1   2   3   4   5   6   7

If we use NL, we must have N in spot 6, leaving I and M to be distributed into spots 4 and 5, either with I in 4 and M in 5, or vice versa:

S1.3

<u>K</u> <u>H</u> <u>J</u> <u>I</u> <u>M</u> <u>N</u> <u>L</u>
1   2   3   4   5   6   7

S1.4

<u>K</u> <u>H</u> <u>J</u> <u>M</u> <u>I</u> <u>N</u> <u>L</u>
1   2   3   4   5   6   7

So much for scenario 1. What about fitting the block L_/_ _J into scenarios 2.1 and 2.2? A brief glance at the diagram for 2.1 shows us that this block cannot fit into that scenario.

For 2.2, L would have to be spot 1. That would force MN into spots 6 and 7, leaving I for spot 4:

<u>L</u> <u>H</u> <u>K</u> <u>I</u> <u>J</u> <u>M</u> <u>N</u>
1   2   3   4   5   6   7

Now, look to see which songs appear in spot 5. In S1.1, it's N, in S1.2 it's M, in S1.3 it's M, and in S1.5 it's I. In S2.2, it's J. So M, N, J and I, and nothing else, can appear in spot 5. That's choice **e**.

This is admittedly a complicated way to answer this question. You could also approach this question by first noting that J must either be third or fifth, and that each of these options will determine where L has to be. If J is third, then L must be seventh, and if J is fifth, then L must be second. So J can be fifth, and we can rule out any answer choice that does not include J—namely, choices **a** and **d**. Now look at the remaining answer choices: **b**, **c**, and **e** each include M, so we don't have to worry about M. We only need to decide if N can be fifth and if I can be fifth to determine which of the three remaining answer choices is correct. You need to place N fifth, and see if you can construct an acceptable scenario, in which three spaces separate L and J. You can:

<u>K</u> <u>H</u> <u>J</u> <u>M</u> <u>N</u> <u>I</u> <u>L</u>
1   2   3   4   5   6   7

Same with I:

<u>K</u> <u>H</u> <u>J</u> <u>M</u> <u>I</u> <u>N</u> <u>L</u>
1   2   3   4   5   6   7

So the correct answer choice is **e**. The trick to this approach is to use commonalities among the answer choices (that M appears in **b**, **c**, and **e**) to focus your efforts. You will still have to construct scenarios (in which N is fifth and in which I is fifth), but if you see that J's presence on the list rules out two answer choices, and that the remaining three have an element in common, then you might save some time over using the initial scenarios.

Practice Game 6

First, symbolize the restrictions, and then see how to put them together.

The first restriction is a partially unordered sequence string:

M//P—R

The second restriction:

P—Q

The third restriction:

O—M

The fourth restriction is an unordered block:

R/L

The fifth restriction:

P ≠ 1

First, consolidate the fourth and first restrictions:

M//P—R/L

Next, add the second restriction (P—Q) as a secondary string:

M//P—R/L

⊢Q→

Finally, add the third restriction (O—M). This is a bit tricky. If you add it directly to the primary string, you get:

O—M//P—R/L

⊢Q→

As long as you are clear on what this symbolization means, go ahead and use it. In particular, keep in mind that you could have the following order: P—O—M--etc.

If, however, this symbolization is confusing, modify the primary string by making O—M part of the primary string (connected directly in relative order with R), and add P on a secondary string. We can do this because M//P—R simply tells us that both M and P are to the left of R, but not about the order of M and P:

O—M—R/L

←P⊣

Of course, we need to keep Q attached to P, as yet another secondary string:

O—M—R/L

←P⊣

⊢Q→

This symbolization captures all the information in the first through fourth restriction, so just keep in mind the fifth restriction (that P ≠ 1) when consulting the diagram. Also keep in mind that N is a floater, since there are no restrictions on it.

Question 1

The correct answer is choice **b**. This question is a "Test-the-Rules" question. The first restriction rules out choice **d**, since P is not before R. The second restriction rules out choice **c**, since P is not before Q. The third restriction rules out choice **a**, since O is not before M. The fourth restriction rules out choice **e**, since R and L are not adjacent to one another.

Question 2

The correct answer is choice **e**. Consult the diagram:

$$O—M—R/L$$

$$←P—|$$

$$|—Q→$$

Your ideal approach to this question should be to look at the diagram and try to see which letters could not be third—R and L, because they are preceded by three letters—and then check the answer choices for one of these letters, without testing each choice. R appears in choice **e**.

If you don't do this, you could check each answer choice against the diagram, keeping in mind that N can be used as a floater. Try to see if the letter in each answer choice could be third (if letters can be moved in a way consistent with the diagram so that the letter in that answer choice is third). M could be third, if O and P preceded it, so choice **a** is incorrect. N could be third, if O and N preceded it, so **b** is incorrect. P could be third, if O and M preceded it, so **c** is incorrect. Q could be third if preceded by O and P, so **d** is incorrect. R cannot be third, because it has at least three checkpoints preceding it (O, M, and R), so **e** is the correct choice.

Question 3

The correct answer is choice **a**. Consult the diagram to see which letter cannot appear second. R and L could not appear second, since there are two letters before them—but neither R nor L appear in the answer choices.

So take each answer choice in turn. Could Q appear second? If Q were second, then according to the diagram, P would have to be first. But, keeping in mind the fifth restriction, P cannot be first. So Q cannot be second—choice **a**.

Question 4

The correct answer is choice **e**. If O is the fourth checkpoint, then we have:

$$\frac{\quad\ \ \quad\ \ \quad\ \ \ O\ \quad\ \ \quad\ \ \quad}{1\ \ \ 2\ \ \ 3\ \ \ 4\ \ \ 5\ \ \ 6\ \ \ 7}$$

Consulting our diagram, we see that the string M—R/L must fill the spaces to the right, as there are only three slots:

$$\frac{\quad\ \ \quad\ \ \quad\ \ \ O\ \ \ M\ \ R/L}{1\ \ \ 2\ \ \ 3\ \ \ 4\ \ \ 5\ \ \ 67}$$

This forces P—Q to the left of O. Keeping in mind that P cannot be first, we see that P—Q must take up spots 2 and 3, leaving N for spot 1:

$$\frac{N\ \ \ P\ \ \ Q\ \ \ O\ \ \ M\ \ R/L}{1\ \ \ 2\ \ \ 3\ \ \ 4\ \ \ 5\ \ \ 67}$$

Consulting this diagram, we see that N is in fact first, so **a** is incorrect; P is in fact second, so **b** is incorrect; Q is in fact third, so **c** is incorrect; M is in fact fifth, so **d** is incorrect; but L is not necessarily sixth (it could be seventh), so **e** is the correct answer.

Question 5

The correct answer is choice **d**. If M occurs before P, then by consulting the diagram we see that P must be in between M and R/L. So we can modify the diagram to:

O—M—P—Q—R/L

We can see now that the farthest left we can push Q (the earliest it can occur) is the fourth spot, after O, M and P. This is choice **d**.

Practice Game 7

First, draw out seven spots for the seven parts:

$$\underline{\hspace{1em}}\ \underline{\hspace{1em}}\ \underline{\hspace{1em}}\ \underline{\hspace{1em}}\ \underline{\hspace{1em}}\ \underline{\hspace{1em}}\ \underline{\hspace{1em}}$$
$$1\ \ 2\ \ 3\ \ 4\ \ 5\ \ 6\ \ 7$$

Then, symbolize the restrictions.

The first restriction:

6 = Q or S

The second restriction:

T—S →U = 2

U ≠ 2 →S—T [contrapositive]

The third restriction:

VU

The fourth restriction:

V—T//X

The fifth restriction:

R/S

Now see if any of the sequence strings can be joined. Combining the third and fourth restrictions, we have:

VU—T//X

We can also add the information from the third and fifth restrictions into the second restriction:

T—S/R →V = 1 and U = 2

Note, however, that since this is a conditional statement, the information that R/S and VU have not been captured by this modified restriction, and the fifth restriction must still be considered.

All in all, we have:

6 = Q or S

T—S/R →V = 1 and U = 2

VU—T//X
R/S

Now we can turn to the questions.

Question 1

The correct answer is choice **e**. This question is a "Test-the-Rules" question. The first restriction rules out choice **a**, since neither Q nor S are in spot 6. The second restriction rules out choice **d**, since T precedes S, but U is not second. The third restriction rules out choice **c**, since V does not precede U. The fifth restriction rules out choice **b**, since R and S are not adjacent to one another.

Question 2

The correct answer is choice **c**. Write out the 7 spots, and start filling them in. It will be obvious how to apply the rules as you proceed. If Q is in the spot 7, then by the first restriction, S must be in spot 6. If S is in spot 6, R can only be in spot 5. Since S and Q take up the last two spots, T must occur before S, and U must be in spot 2. If U is in spot 2, then V must be in spot 1. This leaves T and X for spots 3 and 4:

$$\underline{V} \quad \underline{U} \quad \underline{T/X} \quad \underline{R} \quad \underline{S} \quad \underline{Q}$$
$$1 \quad 2 \quad 3 \ 4 \quad 5 \quad 6 \quad 7$$

Given this diagram, the only statement that doesn't have to be true is that T is added third, since T could also be in the fourth spot. So **c** is the correct answer.

Question 3

The correct answer is choice **c**. First, consult the diagram to see which parts can obviously not be added last. Since V and U have parts to their right, neither can be added last. But V and U do not appear in the answer choices. This is a difficult question, and one approach is to take each part in turn and seeing if it could be added last. We are looking for definitive proof that a part cannot be added last. We saw in the last question that Q could be added last, so **a** is incorrect. If R is added last, then S would have to be in spot 6. Since T would be before S, U would have to be in spot 2, and V in spot 1. Q, T, and X could then fill spots 3, 4, and 5. So it seems R could be last, and we can move on to the next choice. If S were in spot 7, then Q would have to be in spot 6 to satisfy the first condition. But then we would break the R/S block from the fifth condition. So S definitely cannot be in spot 7, and **c** is the correct answer choice.

Since taking each choice in turn can often turn out to be time-consuming, you might instead save this question for last and use whatever information you can from other questions to rule out answer choices—that is, to see which parts are added last in the acceptable scenarios you come across or produce for the other questions. Part T is last in the correct answer to Question 1, so choice **d** is ruled out, and part Q is last in the acceptable scenario produced for Question 2, so choice **a** can be ruled out. Part R is last in the acceptable scenario produced for Question 4, so choice **b** is incorrect. That leaves just two choices to test, and if we test choice **c** as above, we see that S cannot be last.

Waiting to draw on work you have done for other questions to answer questions like this can save time.

Question 4

The correct answer is choice **a**. Write out the 7 spots, and start filling them in by applying the restrictions. If R is in spot 7, then S must be in spot 6. Since there is no room to the right of S, T must be to the left of S, and therefore U must be in spot 2, carrying V with it into spot 1. This leaves Q, T, and X to fill spots 3, 4, and 5:

$$\underline{V} \quad \underline{U} \quad \underline{Q/T/X} \quad \underline{S} \quad \underline{R}$$
$$1 \quad 2 \quad 3 \quad 4 \quad 5 \quad 6 \quad 7$$

Take each answer choice in turn. Since V is indeed added first, choice **a** is correct.

Question 5

The correct answer is choice **e**. We have the new information that X—T—S. We can incorporate this with our existing sequence strings to produce:

$$VU—X—T—S/R$$

This gives a relative order to six of the seven parts, so try to map the string onto the seven slots. The first restriction says that Q or S must be in spot 6. See what would happen if Q were in spot 6:

$$\underline{\quad} \ \underline{\quad} \ \underline{\quad} \ \underline{\quad} \ \underline{\quad} \ \underline{Q} \ \underline{\quad}$$
$$1 \quad 2 \quad 3 \quad 4 \quad 5 \quad 6 \quad 7$$

$$VU—X—T—S/R$$

Since the S/R block cannot be broken up, the entire string of 6 letters VU—X—T—S/R would have to be to the left of Q—but there are only 5 spots to the left of Q. So Q cannot be in spot 6, and S must instead by spot 6. Since T cannot be to the right of S (given the string VU—X—T—S/R), it must be to the left of S, which implies (via the second restriction, T—S/R -> V = 1 and U = 2) that V and U take up spots 1 and 2 respectively:

V U _ _ _ S _
1 2 3 4 5 6 7

Now, R must be either to the immediate right of S or immediate left of S, so we can produce two scenarios. In scenario 1, with R to the left of S, X and T must be forced into spots 3 and 4, leaving Q for spot 7:

S1

V U X T R S Q
1 2 3 4 5 6 7

In scenario 2, R is to the right of S, leaving X—T and Q to fill spots 3, 4, and 5. X—T and Q can be ordered in three ways (Q before X—T, in between X—T, or after X—T): QXT, XQT, or XTQ.

So the second scenario looks like:

S2
Q X T
X Q T
X T Q
V U _ _ _ S R
1 2 3 4 5 6 7

Now see which parts could appear in spot 5. In S1, R appears in spot 5. In S2, T or Q appear in spot 5.

Since Q, R, and T, and no other parts can appear in spot 5, the correct answer is **e**.

Practice Game 8

Six speakers have to be assigned to six spots:

_ _ _ _ _ _
1 2 3 4 5 6

The first restriction:

D = 2 or 3

The second restriction:

A—C

The third restriction:

E/C

The fourth restriction:

E—F

The fifth restriction:

F/B

The second, third, and fourth restrictions produce sequence strings that can be joined together into:

A—E/C—F

We have four of the six speakers in a sequence string, so the sequence possibilities will probably be fairly limited. From the first restriction, we know that D must be either second or third, so let's graph our string A—E/C—F onto two scenarios, one scenario in which D is second and one scenario is which D is third:

S1

_ D _ _ _ _
1 2 3 4 5 6

S2

_ _ D _ _ _
1 2 3 4 5 6

Keep in mind that B cannot be next to F, as per the fifth restriction. In S1, E/C—F will have to take spots 4–6, since E/C cannot fit into spot 1, and since if E/C took spots 3 and 4, that would leave B and F next to one another in spots 5 and 6 (A must be in spot 1, so B cannot be there). So if E/C—F takes spots 4–6, A and B are distributed into spots 1 and 3:

S1

A/B D B/A E/C F
 1   2   3   45   6

What about S2? Given our string A—E/C—F, we can see that E/C cannot fit into spots 1 and 2, because that would leave no room for A. So E/C—F must again squeeze into spots 4–6, leaving A and B to be distributed into spots 1 and 2:

S2

A/B B/A D E/C F
 1   2   3 45   6

Question 1

The correct answer is choice **a**. This question is a "Test-the-Rules" question. The first restriction rules out choice **b**, since D is neither second nor third. The second restriction rules out choices **c** and **e**, since A does not precede C. (The third restriction also rules out choice **c**, since C and E are not adjacent to one another). The fourth restriction rules out choice **d**, since E does not precede F.

Question 2

The correct answer is choice **b**. Consult the scenario diagrams to see where speaker E could be. In both S1 and S2, speaker E could be in either spot 4 or spot 5, and no other spot. This is choice **b**.

Question 3

The correct answer is choice **d**. If there is one space in between A and D, we cannot be in S1 (since A must either be to D's immediate right or left there). So we must be in S2, and A must be in spot 1, meaning that B is in spot 2:

A B D E/C F
1 2 3 45   6

Since A is first, B is second, D is third, and F is sixth, choices **a**, **b**, **c**, and **e** all must be true. Since C could speak fifth, it isn't the case that C must speak fourth; and so **d** is the correct answer.

Question 4

The correct answer is choice **e**. If B is just before C, then we cannot be in S2 (since E/C is immediately preceded by D), and so we must be in S1, with B in spot 3 and A in spot 1:

A D B E/C F
1 2 3 45   6

We can now see that since A speaks first and F sixth, four people must speak in between them—answer choice **e**.

Question 5

The correct answer is choice **c**. Consult the scenario diagrams to see which speakers could be in spot 2. In S1, spot 2 is taken by D. In S2, spot 2 is taken by A or B. So A, B, and D, and no other speakers, could speak second. This is choice **c**. You could also use the answer from question 1 to eliminate choices **a** and **b** and then go from there. It's easy to show that neither E nor C can be second.

Selection Games Review

In a selection game, you are given a group of entities from which some are to be selected. The entities can be people, places, or things. The selection is always done according to a certain set of rules (for example, that if entity A is selected, entity B is not selected), and these rules are sometimes based on certain characteristics of those entities (for example, that if one of the green-colored entities is selected, one of the red-colored entities must be selected). Some selection games specify how many entities are to be selected (information which is often crucial to understanding the game-play and answering the questions), while some leave that open-ended.

There are two things you should understand before approaching selection games: the different types of domains (i.e., the groups of entities from which you are selecting), and the different types of typical rules.

We consider both here, as well as methods for diagramming the actual selection of entities.

Know the Domain Types

The group of entities from which you are selecting (let's call this the domain) can take on different levels of complexity, which will dictate the difficulty of the game and the types of conditions given and questions asked.

Simple Domain

The simplest domain is a plain list of some number of entities, with no further distinction between them. For example, you may be asked to select five students for a class section from a group of seven students labeled A, B, C, D, E, F, and G. The list of seven students is your simple domain.

Subgroups Domain

Some domains consist of subgroups. For example, you may be asked to select five students from a group of seven students, some of whom are female (A, B, and C) and some of whom are male (D, E, F, and G). The two subgroups are the females and males.

Cross-Group Domain

Finally, there is the "cross-group" domain, in which the domain is broken down along two or more dimensions. For example, you may be asked to select five students from a group of seven students, some of whom are female and domestic A, some of whom are female and international (B and C), some of whom are male and domestic (D, E, and F), and some of whom are male and international (G). In this case, there are two ways to divide the domain into two groups, resulting in four groups.

You may also be given subgroups and cross-groups for which specific members are not specified. For example, you may be asked to select from a group of seven students, three of whom are female and four of whom are male; or to select from a group of seven students, one of whom is female and domestic, two of whom are female and international, three of whom are male and domestic, and one of whom is male and international. Usually, LSAT does not give you a cross-group without a breakdown, such as three female, four male, three domestic, four international.

Diagramming the Domain

The kind of domain you are given (simple, subgroup, or cross-group) should dictate what your diagram of the entity group will look like. This diagram may be all there is to diagramming a selection game. If you have a simple domain, just list the entities in that domain:

A B C D E F

If you have a group consisting of subgroups, use capitalization to distinguish them, and perhaps label them as well (e.g., we label the Female group "F" and the male group "M" below). If the entities are named A, B, C, etc., you might write:

F: A B C
M: d e f g

If the entities are not named or otherwise specified, you might write:

F F F M M M M

If you are given cross-groups, there are a few options, and you should see what works best for you as you go through the practice games. The most visual way to capture cross-group information is with a grid. The advantage of the grid is that you can visualize how to apply conditions involving two different characteristics of a domain (in the example we have been using, male/female and domestic/international).

If the entities are specified or named:

	d	i
f	A	B C
m	D E F	G

If the entities are not specified, you can represent them by dots:

	d	i
f	•	• •
m	• • •	•

This allows you to visually grasp the effects of the rules. For example, if a condition tells you that at least two females are chosen, a quick glance at the upper row of the grid (representing all females) tells you that you can circle a dot in the upper-right box, since at least one in that box will have to be selected. If another condition tells you that at least three domestic are chosen, a quick glance at the left column of the grid (representing all domestic students) tells you that you can circle two in the lower left-hand box (since there is only one female domestic student, at least two male domestic students must be chosen). These kinds of inferences are often easier with the aid of a grid such as this, since it allows you to be flexible in how you visualize the relevant groups (for the female students, look at the top row; for the domestic students, look at the left column; for the male international students, look at the bottom-right box; etc).

Another method for symbolizing the cross-group entities is to use capitalization to capture one of the dimensions. For example, domestic could be represented by lowercase letters and international by upper-case letters:

f F F m m m M

The advantage of this sort of representation is that it takes less time to write out. The disadvantages are that one of the dimensions is only represented by capitalization (lower-case for domestic vs. upper-case for international), while the other is represented by particular letters ("f" for female and "m" for male), which might lead to confusion (e.g., forgetting which case represents domestic and which international).

Also, the inferences may not be as visually apparent (e.g., the condition that three domestic are chosen requires you to look at the "f" and three "m" across two "F", rather than down the "d" column in the grid, perhaps making the implication of the condition—that two "m" must be chosen—less obvious).

You might try to avoid the first problem by using two different sets of two letters for each dimension—i.e., d and i for domestic and international and m and f for male and female:

df if if dm dm dm im

But this notation still doesn't allow for an easy visual grasp of the rules.

You should experiment with different approaches to see which is more efficient for you—if you are good at grasping deductions without visual aids, you might save time forgoing the grids.

Diagramming the Selection

If a simple domain or subgroup game does not specify how many entities are to be selected, it is usually most efficient to just circle and cross out symbols directly on your entity list as you learn information (for entities you know are definitely selected or definitely not selected). For example:

(A) B Ϲ D E

Another example:

Group 1: A (B) C
Group 2: Ð E F
Group 3: (G) H I

You may also wish to keep a separate space for the entities definitely *not* selected (the "out" group). You can do this by writing:

OUT: D, F, H

This information was captured by crossing entities off the entity list, but some students find it helpful to specifically create an "out" group as well.

Even if you use the entity grid for cross-group domains as discussed above, then whether or not the game specifies how many entities are to be selected, it usually helps to circle and cross out symbols on the grid itself as you learn new information.

If a simple or subgroup domain specifies how many entities are to be selected, then consider using slots to keep track of what's been selected, and what entities are still available to select from. For example:

A _ C _ _   A̶ B C̶ D E

This is particularly useful for subgroup domains, since the restrictions and questions can use a mix of information about specific entities and their subgroup types. For this reason, keep information about specific entities above the spaces, and information about subgroup types below the spaces. For example, if we know that five entities are to be selected, two from group 1, two from group 2, and one from group 3, we might write:

B _ _ _ G
1 1 2 2 3

Group 1: A (b) C
Group 2: D̶ E F̶
Group 3: (G) H̶ I

Finally, a note about replicating your diagrams: For cross-group domain entity grids, it is often helpful to leave space underneath your letters or slots so that you can put a check or x-mark or dot (or some other mark) to indicate selection or exclusion (rather than crossing out or circling). This allows you to use the same diagram or entity-list multiple times (by making it easy to erase your marks), rather than have to redraw the grid. If you want to keep the information from each question, you should also draw an entity list next to each question. Or, you could just have an "in" and "out" column next to each question into which you place entities as you select or exclude them. The upside is that you retain information as you move from question to question that could be time-saving

(e.g., a diagram showing that a certain selection list is acceptable). The downside is that you will spend a little extra time drawing diagrams (both the entity grid and entity list/columns). You will have to experiment with diagramming to see what works best for you.

Know the Rule Types

A typical selection game will present a set of rules that will determine how the selection must, can, or can't occur. One thing nearly all selection games have in common is that they tend to be logic-heavy: the rules are often conditional statements, sometimes involving disjunctions ("or" clauses) and conjunctions ("and" clauses). Understanding, manipulating, and connecting these statements will require a basic command of symbolic logic, which will allow you to draw inferences.

There are six basic types of rules that are typical in selection games.

Concrete Rules

Concrete rules tell you which entities are definitely selected.

> B is selected.
> C and D are in the section.

Positive Conditionals

Simple positive conditionals tell you that if one entity is selected, another entity will be selected.

> If A is selected, B is selected.
> If C is in the section, D is in the section.

More complicated positive conditionals involve disjunction and conjunction clauses.

> If either A or B are selected, D will be selected.
> If C is in the section, both F and G will be in the section.

Negative Conditionals

A simple negative conditional tells you that if one entity is selected, another entity will not be selected; or that if one entity is not selected, another entity will be selected.

> If A is selected, B will not be selected.
> If C is not in the section, D must be in the section.

More complicated negative conditionals involved disjunction and conjunction clauses.

> If either A or B is selected, D will not be selected.
> If C is not selected, E and F will both be selected.

Positive vs. Negative Conditionals

We have separated positive and negative conditionals because they usually operate differently in logic games—especially when the conditionals are simple rather than complex.

Positive conditionals tell you how selecting one entity will pull in another entity—if you choose A, you must also choose B. And their contrapositives tell you that if one entity isn't chosen, another cannot be—if you don't choose B, you can't choose A.

By contrast, negative conditionals tell you how selecting one entity will preclude the selection of another. If you select A, you cannot select B. Notice that the contrapositive says that if you select B, you cannot select A. This means that such negative conditionals really amount to statements that two entities cannot be selected together, symbolized by our box with a line through it (a selection anti-block):

$$\boxed{\text{A̶B̶}}$$

Further, a negative conditional tells you that at least one of the two entities involved must not be selected; that is, one of the two entities will be in the

"out" group. If you prefer pure symbolic logic, a negative conditional such as A → ≠ B (that one entity precludes another) is equivalent to:

1. B → ≠ A (the contrapositive, that the selection of the latter entity precludes the former)
2. ≠ B or ≠ A (one of the two entities involved must not be selected)
3. ≠ (B and A) (the two entities cannot be selected together)

This information can also be symbolized by writing that either A or B must be in the "out" group, rather than using pure symbolic logic:

> OUT: A or B

Biconditional Rules

Biconditional rules are positive conditionals that also work in reverse. For example, suppose we have a positive conditional saying that if A is selected, B must be selected. As we know, this does not mean that if B is selected, A must be selected. Biconditionals, however, add this extra bit of information in. So they will say: If A is selected, B is selected, and if B is selected, A is selected. This essentially means that either A and B must be chosen together, or neither can be chosen. In more formal terms, the statement that "if A, then B, and if B, then A" is equivalent to the statement "if not B, then not A, and if not A, then not B." The latter is what gives us the idea that if any one of them isn't chosen, then neither can be chosen. These rules are equivalent to this selection block:

$$\boxed{\text{AB}}$$

Remember that biconditionals are often stated using the phrase "if and only if." For example, the rule discussed here might have been stated: "A is selected if and only if B is selected."

Disjunction Rules

Disjunction rules are like diluted concrete rules. They tell us that one or both of two entities must be selected (but don't tell us which one).

Examples:

Either A or B must be selected.
Either A is in the section or B is in the section.

Remember that "or" statements are not exclusive by default—that is, if we say that "either A or B must be selected," we are not ruling out the possibility that both A and B are selected.

Also note a strange fact about disjunction rules: they can be disguised as conditional statements. Take the rule "if A is not selected, then B is selected." This seems like a negative conditional. But what it really says is that either A must be selected or B must be selected. If we don't select A, we must select B; and if we don't select B, then must select A, as the contrapositive says; so we must select one or the other, or both.

Disjunction rules are sometimes useful for breaking up a diagram of possible selections into two scenarios. This creation of two scenarios should usually come after *all* other bits of the diagram have been filled out and other deductions have been made.

Number Rules

Perhaps the most difficult rules are number rules. They are also often the most important rules, playing a large role in driving the mechanics of a game. Number rules always tell us something about the number, or relative number, of entities to be selected.

At least three domestic students are selected.
More males are selected than females.
If exactly two females are chosen, one international student is chosen.
If A is selected, at most two domestic students are selected.

Practice Game 1

A dish contains one or more of six spices—salt, pepper, chili, basil, garlic, and oregano—according to the following conditions:

> If it contains salt, it contains pepper.
> If it contains chili, it does not contain basil.
> If it does not contain salt, it contains garlic.
> If it contains either chili or pepper, it contains garlic.

1. Which one of the following could be a complete and accurate list of the spices in the dish?
   a. Basil, chili, garlic, pepper
   b. Chili, oregano, pepper, salt
   c. Basil, oregano
   d. Garlic, oregano, pepper, salt
   e. Basil, garlic, oregano, salt

2. Which one of the following must be true?
   a. The dish contains salt.
   b. The dish contains garlic.
   c. The dish contains either chili or basil.
   d. The dish contains pepper.
   e. The dish contains either chili or pepper.

3. If the dish contains exactly five spices, all of the following must be true EXCEPT:
   a. The dish contains chili.
   b. The dish contains salt.
   c. The dish contains pepper.
   d. The dish contains garlic.
   e. The dish contains oregano.

4. If the dish does not contain pepper, what is the largest number of total spices the dish could contain?
   a. One
   b. Two
   c. Three
   d. Four
   e. Five

5. If the dish contains salt, what is the least number of total spices the dish could contain?
   a. One
   b. Two
   c. Three
   d. Four
   e. Five

Practice Game 2

Five books are selected for a syllabus from three history books (A, B, and C), four philosophy books (D, E, F, and G), and two literature books (H and I). At least one of each kind is selected, according to the following conditions:

If more than one philosophy book is chosen, both literature books are chosen.
If D is chosen, I is not chosen.
Either C or B must be chosen.
If B is chosen, then either D or F (or both) must be chosen.

1. Which one of the following could be a complete and accurate list of the books chosen for the syllabus?
a. A, B, E, F, I
b. A, E, F, H, I
c. A, B, C, D, I
d. C, F, G, H, I
e. A, B, D, F, G

2. If book E is selected, then which one of the following cannot be true?
a. H and I are both selected.
b. B and G are both selected.
c. B and H are both selected.
d. A and C are both selected.
e. C and G are both selected.

3. If book A is selected, then which one of the following must be true?
a. Exactly one philosophy book is selected.
b. Exactly one history book is selected.
c. Exactly two history books are selected.
d. Exactly two philosophy books are selected.
e. Exactly two literature books are selected.

4. If book I is the only literature book selected, then the syllabus must include which one of the following pair of books?
a. F and D
b. B and H
c. A and F
d. C and G
e. A and E

5. Suppose we replace the first restriction (if more than one philosophy book is chosen, at least two literature books are chosen) with the restriction that if more than one philosophy book is chosen, at most one literature book is chosen. Now, if E and G are the only philosophy books selected, which one of the following could be true?
a. C and I are both selected.
b. A and B are both selected.
c. D and I are both selected.
d. H and I are both selected.
e. B and G are both selected.

Practice Game 3

A section is comprised of at least four students chosen from among three male students (A, B, and C), and four female students (D, E, F, G). The students are chosen according to the following restrictions:

> At least two female students are chosen.
>
> D cannot be in the section without E.
>
> If either student A or E is in the section, G cannot be.
>
> The section must have either student B or student D (or both).

1. Which one of the following could be a complete and accurate list of the students in the section?
   a. A, B, C, F
   b. B, C, E, F
   c. A, C, F, G
   d. A, C, E, F
   e. A, B, D, F, G

2. If student G is in the section, which two students must also be in the section?
   a. A and B
   b. B and C
   c. E and C
   d. D and G
   e. E and B

3. If student A is in the section, which one of the following cannot be true?
   a. B is not in the section.
   b. E is not in the section.
   c. D is in the section.
   d. C is not in the section.
   e. F is in the section.

4. Which one of the following statements cannot be true?
   a. Exactly four females are in the section.
   b. Exactly three females are in the section.
   c. Exactly three males are in the section.
   d. Exactly two males are in the section.
   e. Exactly two females are in the section.

5. If student B is not in the section, which one of the following could be true?
   a. Neither A nor D is in the section.
   b. Neither C nor E is in the section.
   c. Neither C nor F is in the section.
   d. Neither C nor G is in the section.
   e. Neither E nor F is in the section

Practice Game 4

Four species of trees are selected to populate a new park from among four deciduous species (A, B, D, and G) and five evergreen species (C, E, F, H, I). Each species is available for planting in exactly one of two possible ways, either as a sapling or fully-grown tree. The species available as saplings are A, F, H, and I, and the species available fully-grown are B, C, D, E, and G. The trees are selected according to the following conditions:

Exactly two deciduous trees and exactly two evergreen trees are selected.
Exactly two saplings and exactly two fully-grown trees are selected.
The park must include either species I or species C or both.

1. Which one of the following could be a complete and accurate list of the trees selected for the park?
a. A, D, E, H
b. D, F, G, I
c. A, C, E, I
d. F, G, H, I
e. B, C, D, E

2. Which two species cannot be both selected?
a. B and D
b. F and H
c. C and A
d. H and I
e. G and A

3. If species A and E are selected, which other species must be selected?
a. C
b. B
c. F
d. G
e. I

4. If species E is selected, which one of the following cannot be selected?
a. A
b. B
c. D
d. G
e. H

5. If species C is selected, which one of the following must also be selected?
a. A
b. B
c. D
d. E
e. I

Practice Game 5

At least four and at most five bands are selected from eight entrants for a music competition. The entrants include two folk bands from Chicago, two jazz bands from Chicago, three folk bands from Milwaukee, and one jazz band from Milwaukee. The bands are chosen according to the following restrictions:

At least two jazz bands are selected.
At least one band from Milwaukee is selected.
At least one band from Chicago is selected.
If the Milwaukee jazz band is selected, at least two Milwaukee folk bands must be selected.

1. Which one of the following could be a complete and accurate list of the bands selected for the competition?
   a. One Milwaukee jazz band, one Milwaukee folk band, two Chicago folk bands, two Chicago jazz bands
   b. Two Chicago folk bands, two Chicago jazz bands
   c. One Chicago jazz band, two Chicago folk bands, two Milwaukee folk bands
   d. One Chicago jazz band, one Milwaukee jazz band, two Milwaukee folk bands
   e. Three Milwaukee folk bands, one Milwaukee jazz band.

2. If both Chicago folk banks are selected, which one of the following must be true?
   a. Exactly one Milwaukee jazz band is selected.
   b. Exactly one Chicago jazz band is selected.
   c. No Milwaukee folk band is selected.
   d. Exactly one Milwaukee folk band is selected.
   e. Exactly two Milwaukee folk bands are selected.

3. Which one of the following cannot be true?
   a. No Milwaukee folk band is selected.
   b. Exactly one Milwaukee folk band is selected.
   c. Exactly one Chicago folk band is selected.
   d. Exactly two Chicago folk bands are selected.
   e. Exactly one Chicago jazz band is selected.

4. If exactly one Chicago jazz band is selected, which one of the following must be true?
   a. At least two Chicago bands are selected
   b. At least three Chicago bands are selected
   c. At least three folk bands are selected
   d. At least three Milwaukee bands are selected.
   e. At most three Milwaukee bands are selected.

5. If exactly two Milwaukee bands are selected, which one of the following statements must be true?
   a. Exactly one Chicago folk band is selected.
   b. Exactly two Chicago folk bands are selected.
   c. Exactly two Chicago jazz bands are selected.
   d. Exactly one Milwaukee jazz band is selected.
   e. Exactly one Milwaukee folk band is selected.

Practice Game 6

Four members are selected for a medical expedition from a group of nine medical professionals, including six nurses (A, B, D, F, G, and H) and three doctors (C, E, and I), six of whom are local (A, E, F, G, H, and I) and three of whom are foreign (B, C, and D), according to the following conditions:

At least two nurses are chosen.

At least one doctor is chosen.

If C is chosen, then at least two local nurses must be chosen.

If either E or I are chosen, then B must be chosen.

1. Which one of the following could be a complete and accurate list of the expedition members?
   a. A, B, C, D
   b. A, D, F, G
   c. A, B, C, F
   d. A, C, E, I
   e. A, E, F, G

2. If exactly one local nurse joins the expedition, then which one of the following statements must be true?
   a. A is selected.
   b. B is selected.
   c. D is selected.
   d. E is selected.
   e. F is selected.

3. Which two professionals cannot both be chosen for the expedition?
   a. A and C
   b. E and I
   c. B and C
   d. C and E
   e. B and F

4. If C is not selected, which one of the following could NOT be an accurate, partial list of the professionals chosen for the expedition?
   a. A, F, G
   b. A, B, E
   c. G, H, I
   d. A, B, H
   e. D, E, F

5. Which one of the following statements cannot be true?
   a. Exactly three nurses are chosen.
   b. Exactly two foreign professionals are chosen.
   c. Exactly three foreign professionals are chosen.
   d. Exactly two local professionals are chosen.
   e. Exactly three local professionals are chosen.

Practice Game 7

A student applies to at most five of eight colleges—A, B, C, D, E, F, G, and H—according to the following restrictions:

> She applies to at most three among A, B, C, and D.
> She applies to at least two among E, F, and G.
> If she applies to C, then she does not apply to D.
> If she applies to A, then she applies to both B and C.
> If she does not apply to A, then she applies to H.

1. Which one of the following could be a complete and accurate list of the colleges to which she applies?
   a. A, B, E, F   No C
   b. B, C, F, G   No A, No H
   c. A, B, C, E
   d. C, D, E, F, H   only 1
   e. A, B, C, F, G

2. If the student applies to college H, then which one of the following statements must be true?
   a. She does not apply to A.
   b. She does not apply to B.
   c. She does not apply to C.
   d. She does not apply to E.
   e. She does not apply to F.

3. The student cannot apply to both of which two schools?
   a. Both H and B
   b. Both D and A
   c. Both A and C
   d. Both F and B
   e. Both D and E

4. If the student applies to college D, then which one of the following must be true?
   a. She applies to A.
   b. She applies to B.
   c. She applies to E.
   d. She applies to G.
   e. She applies to H.

5. If the student applies to college A, then which one of the following could NOT be a partial, accurate list of the colleges to which she applies?
   a. E, C
   b. C, G
   c. E, F, G
   d. B, E, F
   e. B, F, G

Practice Game 8

A textbook is to be translated into at least one of seven languages—Arabic, Chinese, French, German, Hindi, Russian, and Spanish—according to the following conditions:

If it is translated into French, it is translated into German.
If it translated into Arabic or Chinese or both, it will not be translated into Russian.
If it is not translated into Arabic, it is translated into Hindi.
If it is translated into Spanish, it will not be translated into German.

1. Which one of the following could be a complete and accurate list of the languages into which the book is translated?
   a. Chinese, German
   b. Arabic, French, Spanish
   c. French, German, Hindi, Chinese
   d. Arabic, French, German, Spanish
   e. Arabic, Chinese, Russian, Spanish

2. If the book is translated into Russian, then what is the maximum number of languages into which the book could be translated?
   a. One
   b. Two
   c. Three
   d. Four
   e. Five

3. Which two languages CANNOT be a pair into which the book is translated?
   a. Spanish and French
   b. Russian and French
   c. German and Hindi
   d. Spanish and Hindi
   e. Arabic and Chinese

4. If the book is not translated into Hindi, which one of the following must be true?
   a. It is translated into Spanish.
   b. It is translated into German.
   c. It is not translated into French.
   d. It is not translated into German.
   e. It is not translated into Russian.

5. If the book is neither translated into Hindi nor German, then which one of the following could be an accurate, partial list of the languages into which it is translated?
   a. Chinese, French
   b. Spanish, Chinese
   c. Russian, Arabic
   d. Spanish, Chinese, Russian
   e. Spanish, Arabic, French

Setup, Answers, and Explanations

Practice Game 1

This selection game uses a simple domain and doesn't have number restrictions, so a simple list of the entities will suffice for the diagram:

s p c b g o

The first restriction can be symbolized:

$s \rightarrow p$ ($\neq p \rightarrow \neq s$)

The second restriction:

$c \rightarrow \neq b$ ($b \rightarrow \neq c$; either $\neq b$ or $\neq c$)

This can also be symbolized:

b̶c̶

Note that this puts either b or c in the out group, so you could also write:

OUT: b or c

The third restriction:

$\neq s \rightarrow g$ ($\neq g \rightarrow s$; g or s)

Note that this is a disguised disjunction. This restriction says that either g or s must be selected.

The fourth restriction:

(c and p) $\rightarrow$ g

The contrapositive is:

$\neq g \rightarrow$ ($\neq c$ and $\neq p$)

Now look for connections among the restrictions. The third restriction and the contrapositive of the first restriction link up:

$\neq p \rightarrow \neq s \rightarrow g$

The contrapositives:

$\neq g \rightarrow s \rightarrow p$

Looking at the restrictions, the salt seems to play an important role (at least it appears in two rules—although the chili and garlic do so as well). It's also the case that both the salt being in the dish has implications (that the pepper is selected) and the salt not being in the dish has implications (that the garlic is selected). So to try to get a handle on the action of the game, experiment with dividing it up into two scenarios—one in which salt is chosen, and one in which it is not.

If the salt is chosen, then according to the first restriction, pepper is also chosen. If pepper is chosen, then according to the fourth restriction, garlic is also chosen. So we have:

S1
Ⓢ Ⓟ c b Ⓖ o

If the salt is not chosen, we know that garlic is chosen. So we have:

S2
s̶ p c b Ⓖ o

Notice what we have done with the restrictions. The first restriction, third restriction, and fourth restriction are all satisfied in these two scenarios (the fourth restriction is satisfied because in both scenarios, garlic is chosen, and so the conditional representing the fourth restriction is true).

We have effectively made it such that only the second restriction is relevant to further game play (i.e., we only need to consider the second restriction now), given the two scenarios. As we proceed, we only need to worry about the fact that c and b cannot both be chosen.

TIP

Folding up rules into your diagrams is an essential strategy. Try to diagram scenarios (without dividing up into too many scenarios) such that as many restrictions as possible are satisfied. Then you can focus on the remaining restrictions while resting assured that your diagrams are taking care of the rest.

Now we can turn to our questions.

Question 1

The correct answer is choice **d**. This is a "Test-the-Rules" question. The first restriction rules out **e**, since salt is chosen but pepper is not. The second restriction rules out **a**, since both chili and basil are chosen. The third restriction rules out **c**, since neither salt nor garlic is chosen. The fourth restriction rules out **b**, since pepper is chosen but garlic is not.

Question 2

The correct answer is choice **b**. This is where diagramming ahead of time really pays off. In both possible scenarios, we see that g is selected. Circle this answer choice, and move on.

If you had not diagrammed, you could also get the answer by noting that the answer to question 1 rules out **c**, and that **d** can't be the answer because if it were true, **e** would be true as well. You are left with **a**, **b**, and **e**, which could be tested one at a time by seeing if the statement could be made false without violating any of the restrictions. When you get to **b**, you will see that you can't put garlic in the out group without violating a restriction: if g is out, then by the contrapositive of the fourth restriction, c and p are out as well; but if p is out, then by the contrapositive of the first restriction, s is out; but then the third restriction (saying that either s or g must be in) must be violated.

Question 3

The correct answer is choice **a**. Since we can't have both b and c, at least one of these two must not be selected. But if we are choosing five of six spices, then there can only be one spice that is not selected, and so that spice must be either b or c, and the rest must be in the dish.

If you are using the scenario diagrams, you should note that if the dish contains exactly five spices, we must be in scenario 1 since scenario 2 contains at most four spices. Since there are five spices, and we can select at most one of c or b, we must have the oregano. So our diagram is:

$$\text{(s)} \ \text{(p)} \ c \ b \ \text{(g)} \ o$$

Now check each answer choice against the diagram. Salt, pepper, garlic, and oregano must all be selected. But basil could be selected, and chili not. So the correct answer is **a**.

Question 4

The correct answer is choice **c**. If the dish does not contain pepper, we must be in scenario S2, since in S1, the dish contains pepper. Our diagram is now:

$$\textbf{s} \ \textbf{p} \ c \ b \ g \ o$$

Now we see what the greatest number of ingredients we could select is (we circle as many as we can). In addition to g (already selected), we can select one of c and b, and we can select o. That leaves us with a maximum of three spices, answer choice **c**.

Question 5

The correct answer is choice **c**. If the dish contains salt, we must be in scenario 1, since scenario 2 has the dish lacking salt. In scenario 1, salt, pepper, and garlic must be selected. As our diagram indicates, beyond that, nothing must be selected. Therefore, the least number of spices the dish could contain is three, answer choice **c**.

You could also answer this question by just applying the rules one at a time, and keeping track of what must be selected. By the first restriction, since salt is selected, pepper must be selected. The second restriction doesn't force us to select anything. The third is already satisfied since we have selected salt. The fourth forces us to also choose garlic. So we have:

$$\text{(s)} \ \text{(p)} \ c \ b \ \text{(g)} \ o$$

Now, cycle back through the rules to make sure that we don't have to select anything else (can cross out c, b, and o).

Practice Game 2

Since we are choosing five books from three sub-groups, we want to diagram five spaces, and characterize those spaces as either philosophy (p), history (h), or literature (l).

We can also keep track of what's selected and definitely not selected with a list of each group:

> h: A B C
> p: D E F G
> l: H I

The first rule is a number rule, so see if the rule allows you to create different scenarios. Since there are five spots, and there is at least one of each genre in the syllabus, there can be one, two, or three philosophy books chosen. If there is one philosophy book chosen, the first restriction does not apply (and we would be left with one required spot for literature, one required spot for history, and two spots that could go either way ("l/h")). If there are two chosen, the first restriction applies, and the specific number of each type of book is fixed: two philosophy, two literature, and one history. If three philosophy books were to be chosen, then there would be two literature books, and no more room for a history book—so there can't be three philosophy books chosen. We are left with two scenarios, one with one philosophy book chosen, and one with two philosophy books chosen:

S1: _ _ _ _ _
    p l/h l/h l   h

S2: _ _ _ _ _
    p p l l h

Now consider the other rules, and start making deductions that can be applied to these diagrams. We could go one of two routes—either noting a couple of bits of information about these diagrams and moving the questions, or going into a bit more depth with the initial deductions. Which you ought to do depends on how quickly you are able to make initial deductions. If you can make them quickly, it might pay off to do them up front; but if they generally take a bit longer for you, cut off the initial deduction process earlier and just make deductions as the questions require.

The less involved route:

The third restriction tells us that one of the history books must be C or B. so we can write "C/B" into the required history slot for both S1 and S2. We also note that since there are only two literature books, there must be at least two history books in S1. Then, just keep the other rules handy:

S1: _ _ _ _ <u>C/B</u>
    p h l/h l   h

S2: _ _ _ _ <u>C/B</u>
    p p l l h

B → (D or F)
(not D and not F) → not B

The more involved route:

We start with the deductions just made. Then, we look at S2 more carefully. In S2, there are two literature books required, and only two to choose from, so those spots can be filled in with H and I. According to the second restriction, D and I cannot be chosen together. Since we have I, we know that D cannot be one of the philosophy books. So we can write E/F/G into the two philosophy spots. So we have:

S2: <u>E/F/G</u> <u>E/F/G</u> <u>H</u> <u>I</u> <u>C/B</u>
         p   p   l   l   h

The fourth restriction can't be easily incorporated into the diagram, so we just note that:

B → (D or F)
(~not D and ~not F) → ~not B

There is not much else to add to S1, so we leave that as it is:

S1: __ __ __ __ <u>C/B</u>
      p h l/h l h

With some visual sense of how the game works, we can now turn to the questions.

Question 1

The correct answer is choice **d**. This is a "Test-the-Rules" question. The first restriction rules out **a**, since there are two philosophy books, but only one literature book. The second restriction rules out **c**, both D and I have been selected. The third rule rules out **b** since neither book C nor book B have been selected. Choice **e** violates the restriction in the setup—there is no literature book.

Question 2

The correct answer is choice **b**. We start by supposing that E is selected. There is nothing that can be

immediately deduced from the rules given this new information. So we turn to the answer choices and test each one to see if the two books in the choice could also be selected; if so, that's not the correct answer. Can E, H, and I be selected? S2 seems to allow this, so **a** seems incorrect, and we move on. Can E, G, and B be selected? Since E and G are selected, there are two philosophy books chosen, and we must be in S2. Realizing this fixes the entire selection: E, G, H, I, B. Is that a possible selection? No, the fourth restriction is violated, because B is selected, but neither D nor F is selected.

So G and B cannot be selected, and choice **b** is correct. Circle this answer and move on to the next question.

Question 3

The correct answer is choice **a**. If book A is selected, we must be in scenario 1, as a brief glance at scenario 2 tells us that there is no room for A there. S1 shows us that there is only one philosophy spot, so **a** must be the correct answer.

Question 4

The correct answer is choice **c**. If book I is the only literature book selected, then we must be in scenario 1, since scenario 2 has two literature books. (You could also see this by applying the contrapositive of the first restriction—since only one literature book is selected, only one philosophy book can be selected, requiring all three history books). Now see if you can fill out the diagram for scenario 1:

__ <u>I</u> __ __ __
 p l h h h

h: A B C
p: D E F G
l: H Ⓘ

Since there are three history slots, we know that A, B, and C are chosen. Since B is chosen, by the fourth restriction, either D or F must be chosen (for the philosophy slot). But since I is chosen, D cannot be chosen by the second restriction. So F must be the philosophy book. We now have a full syllabus:

> $\underline{F}$ $\underline{I}$ $\underline{A}$ $\underline{B}$ $\underline{C}$
> p   l   h   h   h
>
> h: (A)(B)(C)
> p: Đ E (F) G
> l: H (I)

We can now scan our answer choices for a pair on this syllabus. F and A are on the list, so choice **c** is the correct answer.

Question 5
The correct answer is choice **a.** Our strategy will be to start with the new information, that the only philosophy books chosen are E and G, and then apply the new first restriction along with the other restrictions. Since E and G are the only philosophy books chosen, D and F are out.

> $\underline{E}$ $\underline{G}$ _ _ _
> p p
>
> h: A B C
> p: Đ E F̶ G
> l: H I

Since there are two philosophy books chosen, the new first restriction kicks in so that we know only one literature book is chosen, and therefore, those two history books must be chosen:

> $\underline{E}$ $\underline{G}$ _ _ _
> p p l h h
>
> h: A B C
> p: Đ (E) F̶ (C)
> l: H I

Since D and F are out, we can apply the contrapositive of the fourth restriction to rule out B, leaving A and C as the two history books:

> $\underline{E}$ $\underline{G}$ _ $\underline{A}$ $\underline{C}$
> p p l h h
>
> h: (A) B̶ (C)
> p: Đ (E) F̶ (G)
> l: H I

The only remaining spot is a literature book, and we could either have H fill the spot or I fill the spot without violating the remaining restrictions; the second restriction is not violated because D is not selected, and the third restriction is not violated because C has been selected. So we have:

> $\underline{E}$ $\underline{G}$ $\underline{H/I}$ $\underline{A}$ $\underline{C}$
> p p l h h
>
> h: (A) B̶ (C)
> p: Đ (E) F̶ (G)
> l: H I

Now scan the answer choices for a set of two selections compatible with this diagram. I and C are possible given this diagram, so **a** is the correct answer. Since B is not chosen, choices **b** and **e** are ruled out. Since D is not chosen, **c** is ruled out. Since there is no room for both H and I, **d** is ruled out.

Practice Game 3
This game has a subgroup domain, but does not specify the number to be selected (beyond saying that there must be at least four students). So our diagram is just a list of the entities in the domain:

> M: A, B, C
> F: d, e, f, g

We now turn to the restrictions. The first restriction says that there must be at least two females, so we can write "at least 2" next to the female group:

M: A, B, C
F: d, e, f, g (at least 2)

The second restriction, which says that if d is in the section, e must be in the section, can be written:

d → e (and not e → not d)

The third restriction can be written:

(A or e) → not g and "g → (not A and not E)"

The fourth restriction can be written:

B or d

This can also be written as "not d → B" and "not B → d" (disguised disjunctions).

Now look for connections between the restrictions. The third restriction can be connected with the contrapositive of the second restriction, which can be connected with the disguised disjunction version of the fourth restriction:

g → not A and not e → not d → B

Question 1

The correct answer is choice **b**. This is a standard "Test-the-Rules" question. The first restriction rules out **a**, since only one female is selected. The second restriction rules out **e**, since D is in the section, but e is not. The third restriction rules out **c**, since A is in the section and g is in the section as well. The fourth restriction rules out **d**, since neither B nor d are in the section.

Question 2

The correct answer is choice **b**. Start by seeing what deductions can be made from the information that G is selected. We have already done the work before getting to the question (with the long conditional chain we constructed). g is in, A is out, e is out, d is out, and B is in:

M: A̶, Ⓑ, C
F: d̶, e̶, f, Ⓖ (at least 2)

Since we must have at least 2 females, f must be in as well, and since we must have at least four students, C must be in the section. Now check each answer choice against your diagram.

M: A̶, Ⓑ, Ⓒ
F: d̶, e̶, f, Ⓖ (at least 2)

Choice **a** is incorrect because A is out. Choice **b** is correct because both B and C are in the section. Circle this answer choice and move on to the next question.

Question 3

The correct answer is choice **b**. If A is in the section, then according to the contrapositive of the third restriction, g is not selected.

M: Ⓐ, B, C
F: d, e, f, g̶ (at least 2)

Since we need at least two of d, e, and f, and since d cannot be selected without e, we are going to need e in the section (the way we might think e is not selected is if d and f are selected—but selecting d requires selecting e). So choice **b** is the correct answer.

If you did not see this deduction right away, then you might have considered each answer choice in turn. Is it possible for B to not be in the section? It seems so, since the only restriction on B is the fourth, which can be satisfied by making sure d is in the section:

M: (A), B̶, C
F: (d), e, f, g̶ (at least 2)

Circle e, and you have an acceptable roster. So **a** is incorrect.

Now try choice **b**. If e is not selected, then d is not selected. So g, d, and e are not selected. These three are females, and so restriction 1 will be violated, and choice **b** is the correct answer.

Question 4

The correct answer is choice **a**. You need to try each answer choice in turn, to see if it could be true. For questions like this, the answer choices that put the most numerical strain on the situation should be the first suspects. Can all four females be in the section? Test each rule with d, e, f, and g in the section. According to the third restriction, if e is in the section, g cannot be—so **a** violates the third restriction, and is the correct answer.

Question 5

The correct answer is choice **d**. If B is not selected, then d must be selected (by the fourth restriction). If d is selected, then e must be selected (by the second restriction). If e is selected, g cannot be selected (by the third restriction). So we have:

M: A, B̶, C
F: (d), (e), f, g̶ (at least 2)

Take each answer choice in turn, and test it against this diagram. The diagram says that D must be in the section, so choice **a** is incorrect. The diagram says that e is in the section, so **b** and **e** are incorrect. That leaves **c** and **d**. Note at this point that the diagram says that at least two of the remaining letters, A, C and f, must be selected to get the required four students. That rules out choice **c**, so choice **d** is the correct answer.

Practice Game 4

This game uses a cross-group domain, so drawing a grid will clarify the characteristic of each entity and the mechanics of the game by providing a visual framework. In this diagram, "d" is for "deciduous," "S" for "sapling," etc. Write the short form of the restrictions next to the grid. We write "2 of each category" to remind ourselves that each row (the s row and f row) and each column (the d column and e column) will have to have exactly two species underlined (selected for the park).

	d	e
S	A	H I F
F	B D G	C E

2 of each category
I or C

Remember to leave enough space under the letters representing the species for you to underline and erase as you go through questions and consider the relevant scenarios (this will save you the trouble of recreating the grid again and again). You can also write an "in" and "out" column next to each question to keep information concerning previous selection scenarios you found acceptable.

It might pay off to do a bit of thinking about how the selection could occur up front.

This grid should help. You want two of each column, and two of each row, so consider the various ways that could happen. You could have one tree selected from each of the four boxes. Or you could have two selected from one box, and two selected from the box diagonal to that box (this could only occur for the lower left and upper right boxes, as there is only one tree in the upper left box). Could you have two in one box, and one in a box above it or next to it? No, because then you would have three in a column or row, and that violates our restriction that there are exactly two in each column and row. For the same reason, you could not have three selected from a single box.

So we are really left with two possibilities: 1) one from each box, or 2) two from the lower left and two from the upper right. In either scenario, we must make sure that the restriction that either I or C is selected is satisfied.

Question 1

The correct answer is choice **b**. A scan of the distribution of letters from each answer choice on your grid should immediately tell you which work and which don't. Choice **a** gives you one in each box, but neither I nor C are selected, so choice **a** is incorrect. Choice **b** gives you two in the lower left box and two in the upper right box, and I is selected, so choice **b** is correct. Choice **c** does gives you three in the right column (meaning three evergreens are selected), and so is incorrect. The same goes for choice **d**. Choice **e** gives you four in the lower row (four fully-grown trees), and so is incorrect.

Question 2

The correct answer is choice **b**. Take each answer choice and check it against diagram to see if it is possible to select those two. That is, mark the two given in your answer choice (either in your head or with your pencil on the diagram), and then see if you can select two others in keeping with the restriction. Since B and D are in the lower-left box, if they are selected, we must also select two from the upper-right box. We could choose I, to satisfy the requirement that I or C be selected, and one other species. So it is possible to choose both B and D and choice **a** is incorrect. Since H and F are in the upper-right box, if they are selected, then we must also select two from the lower left box. Notice, however, that we need to select I or C—and neither I nor C are in the lower-left box.

So H and F cannot both be selected, and **b** is the correct answer. Circle this answer choice and move on to the next question.

Question 3

The correct answer is choice **e**. If both A and E are selected, then we have one species selected from the upper-left box, and one from the lower-right box. So we must select one from each of the two remaining boxes (lower-left, and upper-right), otherwise we cannot get a distribution that leads to two from each row and two from each column (we already figured this out before we attacked the questions). Remember that I or C must be selected—but C is not available, because it's in the lower-right box.

We must select I, so choice **e** is correct.

Question 4

The correct answer is choice **e**. If E is selected, then we must select one from each box (as we discovered in the set-up, we must either select two each from the lower-left and upper-right boxes, or select one from each of the boxes). Since E is already selected from the lower-right box, C cannot be. So I must be selected, to satisfy the condition that either I or C is selected. If I is selected from the upper-right box, then nothing else from that box can be selected—in particular, neither H nor F can be selected. We now have a couple of trees we know cannot be selected, so scan the answer choices to see if they show up.

H appears in choice **e**, so **e** is correct.

Another way to look at this is to see that since E is selected, and either I or C must be selected, we already have two evergreens. So we cannot have another evergreen, and therefore neither H nor F can be chosen.

Question 5

If C is selected, then again, we must select one from each of the four boxes. Since A is the only choice available in the upper-left box, A must be selected. So **a** is the correct answer. Note that we don't need to necessarily select I, since the condition that I or C must be selected is already satisfied.

Practice Game 5

This game has a cross-group domain, so start by sorting the entities into a grid. Since the entities aren't named, just use dots. Write the short form of the rules next to the grid, or in the grid. The restrictions that at least two jazz bands must be selected, at least one Chicago band must be selected, and at least one Milwaukee band must be selected, can be written directly into the grid.

	C (at least 1)	M (at least 1)
f	• •	• • •
j (at least 2)	• •	•

Select 4–5

Mj →2 + Mf [0 -1 Mf → no Mj]

Now consider each rule, and see if any up-front deductions can be made. The first restriction says that at least 2 jazz bands must be selected. This means that at least one Chicago jazz band must be selected, since there is only one Milwaukee jazz band. So you can go ahead and underline a Chicago jazz band (and get rid of the restriction that at least one Chicago band must be selected, since that is satisfied, and change the note that at least two jazz bands must be selected to a note that at least one more jazz band must be selected).

	C	M (at least 1)
f	• •	• • •
j (at least 1 more)	• ⊙	•

Mj → 2+ Mf [0–1 Mf → no Mj]

The rest of the restrictions don't seem to immediately yield deductions or concrete information that can be incorporated into the diagram, so move on to the questions. Consider keeping a list of what's selected next to each question, for reference in subsequent questions.

Question 1

The correct answer is choice **d**. This is a standard "Test-the-Rules" question. The first restriction rules out choices **c** and **e**, since only one jazz band is selected. The second restriction rules out choice **b**, since no Milwaukee band is selected. The third restriction rules out choice **e**, since no Chicago band is selected (but that was already ruled out). The fourth restriction rules out choice **a**, since the Milwaukee jazz band is selected, but only one Milwaukee folk band is selected.

Question 2

The correct answer is choice **a**. If both Chicago folk bands are selected, then we select both bands in the upper left box.

	C	M (at least 1)
f	⊙ ⊙	• • •
j (at least 1 more)	• ⊙	•

Select 4–5

Mj → 2+ Mf [0–1 Mf → no Mj]

We now consider what other selections we might make. We need at least one more jazz band (one more entity from the lower row), so we could select either the other band in the lower-left box, or the band in the lower-right (or both). But if we select a band on the lower right—that is, an Mj—then we'll need to select at least 2 Mf's (the fourth restriction). So we would end up with six bands selected, and that would violate the rule that we can select only 4–5 bands. So we can't select the Mj (and we can cross that out). So we need to select the other Cj (and can underline that).

	C	M (at least 1)
f	⊙ ⊙	• • •
j (at least 1 more)	⊙ ⊙	✗

Select 4–5

Mj → 2+ Mf [0–1 Mf → no Mj]

Now, we still need to select at least one band from Milwaukee (at least one from the right column). But we just crossed out Mj, so we need one Mf (and no more, otherwise we would have more than five bands).

So we have:

	C	M (at least 1)
f	⊙ ⊙	⊙ ✗ ✗
j (at least 1 more)	⊙ ⊙	✗

Select 4–5
Mj → 2+ Mf [0–1 Mf → no Mj]
In: Cf Cf Cj Cj Mf

Now we can test each answer choice against this diagram. Choice **a** is incorrect because the Milwaukee jazz band is not selected. Choice **b** is incorrect because two Chicago jazz bands are selected. Choice **c** is incorrect because one Milwaukee folk band is selected, which is choice **d**—circle your answer choice and move on to the next question.

Question 3

The correct answer is choice **a**. First, see if any choices can be eliminated based on other questions. The acceptable selection list for Question 2 rules out choices **b** and **d**. The answer to Question 1 rules out **e**. You are left with **a** and **c**—take each answer choice and try to determine whether it could be accommodated on the diagram. If no Milwaukee folk band is selected, then it can't be the case that the Milwaukee jazz band was selected. This is apparent by considering the contrapositive of the fourth restriction [or the fourth rule diagrammed into the grid]. So no Milwaukee band is selected at all. But this would violate the second restriction, that at least one Milwaukee band is selected.

So it can't be the case that no Milwaukee folk band is selected, and **a** is the correct choice. Circle this answer and move on to the next question.

If you did not have the information from the other questions, you would start by looking for the most numerically implausible answer choice (the one that says no member of some group is selected), and testing it for compatibility with the diagram. And if you don't have a sense of which is the most

numerically implausible, you would just test each answer choice in turn for compatibility with the diagram; the further the correct answer appears down the list, the longer it will take you to do the problem. So try to see if information from other questions can save you some time.

Question 4

The correct answer is choice **d**. If exactly one Chicago jazz band is selected, then the other jazz band we need (as per the first restriction) must be the Milwaukee jazz band (glancing at the grid makes this immediately obvious). By the fourth restriction, we know that two Milwaukee folk bands must be selected. So our diagram looks like:

	C	M (at least 1)
f	• •	⊙ ⊙ •
j (at least 1 more)	✗ ⊙	⊙

Select 4–5
Mj → 2+ Mf [0–1 Mf → no Mj]

We can select one more from the remaining bands, if we like, without violating any restrictions. Scan the answer choices to see if any concrete information shows up. Choice **d** is correct because the diagram shows that at least three Milwaukee bands must be chosen. Circle this answer choice and move on to the next question.

Choice **a** is incorrect because according to the diagram, we could select just one Chicago band. This makes choice **b** incorrect as well. Choice **c** is incorrect because according to the diagram, we could select just two folk bands. Choice **e** is incorrect because according to the diagram, we could choose four Milwaukee bands.

Question 5

The correct answer is choice **c**. We must figure out how exactly two Milwaukee bands could be selected.

They could either both be Milwaukee folk bands, or a combination of one Milwaukee folk band and one Milwaukee jazz band. But if we had the Milwaukee jazz band, we would need two Milwaukee folk bands to satisfy the fourth restriction, and we would end up with three Milwaukee bands. So we can't choose the Milwaukee jazz band (cross it out), and we need to choose two Milwaukee folk bands (circle them). Since we need one more jazz band (besides the one already selected Chicago jazz band), and the Milwaukee jazz band is crossed out, we must select the other Chicago jazz band. So our diagram looks like:

	C	M (at least 1)
f	• •	⊙ ⊙ ✗
j (at least 1 more)	⊙ ⊙	✗

We can select an additional band from the upper-left box if we want. Now scan the answer choices to see if any of the concrete information we have in this diagram is mentioned. Choice **c** says that exactly two Chicago jazz bands are selected, so that is the correct answer.

Choices **a** and **b** are incorrect because according to the diagram, we could either select no Chicago folk bands or one Chicago folk band. Choice **d** is incorrect because no Milwaukee jazz bands are selected. And choice **e** is incorrect because exactly two Milwaukee folk bands are selected.

Practice Game 6

Since this game involves a cross-group domain, set up a grid in which you place all the nine candidates. Symbolize the restrictions, and either incorporate them into the diagram or write them next to the diagram.

	N (at least 2)	D (at least 1)
l	A, F, G, H	E, I
f	B, D	C

$C \rightarrow$ at least 2 lN [if 0–1 lN $\rightarrow$ not C]

(E or I) $\rightarrow$ B [not B $\rightarrow$ (not E and not I)]

The restrictions do not produce any immediate deductions, so proceed to the questions.

Question 1

The correct answer is choice **c**. This is a standard "Test-the-Rules" question. Refer to the grid as you check each restriction. The first restriction rules out choice **d**, as only one nurse is chosen (only one letter from the left column). The second restriction rules out choice **b**, since no doctor is chosen (no entity from the right column). The third restriction rules out choice **a**, since C is chosen, but two are not chosen from the upper-left box (the local nurses). The fourth restriction rules out choice **e**, since E is chosen, but B is not.

It might be helpful to note that the correct answer choice, in which A, B, C and F are selected, means that one possible complete selection list includes 2 lN, 1fN, and 1fD.

Question 2

The correct answer is choice **b**. If exactly one local nurse is selected, then C cannot be selected (this is apparent by considering the contrapositive of the third restriction), so cross C out. If C is not selected, then either E or I must be selected, since at least one doctor must be selected. If E or I is selected, then by the fourth restriction, B must be selected, so circle B. Scan the answer choices—choice **b** says that B must be selected, and so is the correct answer.

	N (at least 2)	D (at least 1)
l	A, F, G, H (exactly 1)	E, I
f	Ⓑ, D	∈

$C \rightarrow$ at least 2 lN [if 0–1 lN $\rightarrow$ not C]

(E or I) $\rightarrow$ B [not B $\rightarrow$ (not E and not I)]

Question 3

The correct answer is choice **d**. We want to rule out the answer choices consistent with a full selection that does not violate any of the restrictions. We saw in Question 1, choice **c**, that A, B, C, and F is an acceptable selection, so that rules out **a**, **c**, and **e**. E and I can be selected, as long as B is selected and another entity (not C), so **b** is incorrect. That leaves choice **d**.

If you had not answered Question 1, then you would have to check each answer choice in turn to see if you could make a full selection consistent with that choice which does not violate any restrictions. Choices **a** through **c** would give no inconsistencies. When you reach choice **d**, you would reason as follows. If C and E are both selected, then B must be selected (by the fourth restriction, because E is selected), and two local nurses (A, F, G, and H) must be selected (by the third restriction, because C is selected).

But that would mean that five professionals are selected (C, E, B, and two of A, F, G, and H)—so it can't be that C and E are both selected. So **d** is the correct answer.

Question 4

The correct answer is choice **a**. If C is not selected, then since at least one doctor must be selected, E or I must be selected. If E or I is selected, then B must be selected, so circle B.

	N (at least 2)	D (at least 1)
l	A, F, G, H	E, I
f	Ⓑ, D	∈

C → at least 2 lN [if 0–1 lN → not C]
(E or I) → B [not B → (not E and not I)]

So the selection will have to be: E or I, B, and 2 more.

Now consider each answer choice, and see whether it is ruled out by this diagram. Can A, F, G be a partial list? No, because there is only one spot left,

and we need to have at least two other entities: B, and either E or I. So **a** is the correct answer.

Question 5

The correct answer is choice **c**. Test the most numerically restrictive answer choices first. (If you had answered Question 1, where the acceptable list was 2 lN, 1fN, and1fD, you could rule out choices **b** and **d** before testing the most numerically restrictive answer choice). Can exactly three nurses be chosen? It seems we can—for example, a selection of A, F, G, C does not violate any restrictions. So choice **a** is incorrect. Now move to choice **c**. Can exactly three foreign professionals be chosen? If three foreign professionals are chosen, then we choose all three on the bottom row, including C. And if C is chosen, we must choose two from the upper left box. But that would leave us with a total of five selected. So all three foreign professionals can't be chosen, and **c** is the correct answer.

You might have also realized that since there are only three foreign professionals available (vs. six nurses available), the most numerically restrictive choice is really **c**, and not **a**—and you would have saved a bit of time.

Practice Game 7

This game has a simple domain type, so list the entities:

A B C D E F G H

Symbolize the restrictions:

At most 3 of A, B, C, D
At least 2 of E, F, G
C → not D [D → not C]
A → (B and C) [(not B or not C) → not A]
not A → H [not H → A] [A or H]

Now see if any deductions can be made from the rules. Not C seems to be a linking element—combining the third restriction, contrapositive of the fourth restriction and gives us:

$$D \rightarrow \text{not } C \rightarrow \text{not } A \rightarrow H$$

Next, look for positive information about what must be selected. We know that two of E, F, and G must be selected. So we can start a selection list.

E/F/G E/F/G (__ __ __)

Notice that the fourth restriction is numerically restrictive—if A is chosen, then we have a full selection list:

E/F/G E/F/G A B C

This seems a fairly concrete scenario, so let's see if we can set up two scenarios, one in which A is chosen, and one in which A is not. If A is not chosen, then by the fifth restriction, H must be. So we have:

E/F/G E/F/G H (__ __)   A̶

We can now choose 0–2 of B, C/D, or E/F/G. We cannot choose both C and D (by the third restriction). We can write "E/F/G" again because two of those three will have been selected, and one will be left to choose from.

These two scenarios are not as concrete as we might like them, but they are enough to start attacking the questions. We have:

S1
E/F/G E/F/G A B C

S2
E/F/G E/F/G H (__ __) A̶
     0–2 of B, C/D, or E/F/G.

Since the scenarios are not very concrete, we will also show how to answer the questions without the scenarios.

Question 1

The correct answer is choice **e**. The first restriction does not rule anything out. The second restriction rules out choice **c**, since it includes only one of E, F and G. The third restriction rules out choice **d**, since she applies to both C and D. The fourth restriction rules out choice **a**, since A is chosen but C is not. The fifth restriction rules out choice **b**, since she applies to neither A nor H.

Question 2

The correct answer is choice **a**. If the student applies to college H, then we must be in scenario 2. We know right away that she does apply to college A in that scenario, so choice **a** is correct.

Without the scenarios, we could observe that H and at least 2 of E, F, and G take up 3 spots, leaving at most two spots left. Since A has two followers (B and C), there's no room for A.

Question 3

The correct answer is choice **b**. Compare each answer choice to the scenarios to see if either can accommodate that set of two schools. Choice **a** is incorrect because Scenario 2 allows an application to both H and B. Choice **b** is correct because A is only chosen in Scenario 1; according the scenario 1 diagram, it is not possible to select D.

Without the aid of the scenarios, you could also see that **b** is correct by looking at the deduction chain we made up front:

$$D \rightarrow \text{not } C \rightarrow \text{not } A \rightarrow H$$

Question 4

The correct answer is choice **e**. A quick glance at our scenarios shows us that if the student applies to college D, we must be in scenario 2. And in scenario 2, the only sure piece of information is that she applies to H. This is choice **e**.

Without the scenarios, you would reason as follows. Since we have D, we cannot have C (third restriction). Since we do not have C, we cannot have A (fourth restriction). Since we do not have A, we must have H (fifth restriction). Since the student applying to H is an answer choice, we stop here.

Question 5

The correct answer is choice **c**. If the student applies to A, we know we are in scenario 1.

S1
E/F/G E/F/G A B C

Check each answer choice to see whether it is compatible with this diagram. E and C could be selected, so **a** is incorrect. C and G could be selected, so **b** is incorrect. E, F, and G could not be selected— there is room for only two of the three—and so **c** is the correct answer.

Without the scenarios, you would reason as follows. If we have A, we must have B and C (fourth restriction). By the first restriction, D must be excluded. But more relevantly, this also only leaves two extra spots, so any answer choice with three letters none of which are A, B, and C will have to be incorrect. This is choice **c**.

Practice Game 8

This game has a simple domain, so merely list the symbols for the entities:

F S R H A G C

Now, symbolize the rules:

F →G [not G → not F]
(A or C) → not R [R → (not A and not C)]
not A → H [not H → A] [A or H]
S → not G [G →not S] [~~GS~~]

The last restriction can also be written as disjunction in an "out" column next to your entity list. If we do this, we can also write in the third restriction as a disjunction in an "in" column:

F S R H A G C
IN: A or H
OUT: G or S

Now look for connections among rules. The first and fourth restrictions connect up through G:

S → not G → not F [and F → G → not S]

The second and third rules connect up through A:

not H → A → not R [and R → (not A and not C) → H]

The other thing to keep in mind is that there is a disguised disjunction: any selection of languages must have either A or H or both.

We now turn to the questions.

Question 1

The correct answer is choice **c**. This is a standard "Test-the-Rules" question. The first restriction rules out **b**, since French is chosen but German is not. The second restriction rules out choice **e**, since both Arabic and Russian are chosen. The third restriction rules out choice **a**, since neither Arabic nor Hindi are present. The fourth restriction rules out **d**, since both Spanish and German are chosen.

Question 2

The correct answer is choice **d**. If the book is translated into Russian, then we know from our deduction chain, R → (not A and not C) → H, that A and C are not selected, and H is selected. So we have:

F S (R) (H) A̶ G C̶
OUT: G or S

There are now two selected (R, H), and three left (F, S, G) to select from. Can we select all three? We know from the fourth restriction that G and S cannot be selected together. So the most we can select is one of those two (G or S) and F, in addition to R and H. Let's pick one to see if it works: G, F, R, H. This selection does not violate any of the restrictions, so it works. And so the maximum number we can select is four, choice **d**.

Note that if picking one of the two, G or S, had not worked, we would have had to try the other before concluding that we can't have four entities selected.

Question 3

The correct answer is choice **a**. Test each answer choice in turn to see if a selection including the two languages is consistent with all the restrictions. Suppose Spanish and French are both selected. Go through each restriction to see what happens. By the first restriction, since French is selected, German must be selected. The second restriction does not impact these selections, since we haven't selected Arabic, Chinese, or Russian yet. The third restriction simply says that we must add Arabic or Hindi to this selection. The fourth restriction says that since Spanish is selected, German cannot be selected. Here is our contradiction; if both Spanish and French are selected, we would have to both select and rule out German, so it can't be that both Spanish and French are selected. The correct answer is **a**.

We could also very easily arrive at this conclusion by glancing at our deduction chain, S → not G → not F, which immediately tells us that if Spanish is selected, French cannot be. Your first instinct for a question like this is to glance at deductions you have already made to see if the answer is obvious.

Question 4

The correct answer is choice **e**. Look again at your deduction chains to see what follows from the book not being translated into Hindi. According to the chain not H → A → not R, the book must be translated into Arabic and not translated into Russian. Scan the answer choices—choice **e** is that the book is not translated into Russian.

Question 5

The correct answer is choice **b**. If the book is not translated into Hindi, then according to the deduction chain not H → A → not R, it is translated into Arabic and not translated into Russian. If the book is not translated into German, then according to the deduction chain S → not G → not F, it is also not translated into French. So we have:

$$\cancel{F} \; S \; \cancel{R} \; \cancel{H} \; \textcircled{A} \; G \; C$$

Now check each answer choice against this selection diagram. Choices **a** and **e** are incorrect because they include French, which is crossed out. Choices **c** and **d** are ruled out because they include Russian, which is crossed out. Choice **b** includes Spanish and Chinese—two languages that could be selected according to the selection diagram—and nothing else.

So **b** is the correct answer.

CHAPTER 5 ▶ Distribution Games Review

In a distribution game, you are given a set of entities that are to be distributed into two or more groups. The entities can be persons, places, or things—for example, it may be a set of eight movies which are to be classified into drama, comedy, and thriller genres, or it may be a set of college students who are to be divided into three sections. The distribution into groups takes place according to certain rules given to you (for example, that if student X is in Section 1, student Y must be in Section 2, or that there must be at least two students in each section).

In some ways, distribution games are similar to selection games—indeed, one can think of a selection game as a distribution game with just two groups into which to distribute the entities—namely the "in" group and the "out" group—such that each entity is distributed into exactly one group. For this reason, many of the game rules in distribution games will be similar to those we have seen in selection games. But there will be some rule types that are somewhat different.

What's Being Distributed: Domain Types and Symbolizing the Domain

We saw that in selection games there are three types of domains (or master group of entities that are to be distributed)—the simple domain, the subgroup domain, and cross-group domain. Fortunately, distribution games virtually never feature the cross-groups, which are much more complex than simple groups and subgroups.

Nevertheless, recognizing simple domains and sub-group domains when you see them in distribution games will help you anticipate and understand the kinds of rules and diagramming that will be at work in the game.

Simple Domain

The simplest domain is a plain list of some number of entities, with no further distinction between them. For example, you may be asked to distribute seven students—A, B, C, D, E, F, and G—into two sections, Section 1 and Section 2. The list of seven students is your simple domain.

Your diagram for the simple domain will simply be a list of the entities:

A B C D E F

Subgroup Domain

Some domains consist of subgroups—that is, a further distinction is made between entities in the domain. For example, you may be asked to distribute seven students, some of whom are female (A, B, and C) and some of whom are male (D, E, F, and G), into two sections. The two subgroups are the females and males.

The presence of subgroups in the domain allows for a greater variety of game rules. The rules governing the distribution of students into the two sections will not only make reference to the entities (e.g., "if student A is in Section 1, student B is in Section 2"), but also make reference to the subgroups (e.g., "if there is a male in Section 1, at least two females must also be in Section 1").

One way to think about distribution games with subgroup domains is that you are "re-grouping" the entities: for example, a master list of students is grouped into male and female, and you want to re-group those students in Section 1 and Section 2.

When symbolizing a domain consisting of subgroups, use capitalization to distinguish them, and

perhaps label them as well (e.g., we label the female group 'F' and the male group 'M' below).

For example, you might write:

F: A B C
M: d e f g

Understanding Types of Distribution

The matching of entities in the domain to the groups usually occurs in one of four ways, depending on whether or not every entity in the domain is distributed into a group, as well as on whether or not the entities can appear in more than one group. Again, being aware of these nuances will help you anticipate and understand the unique mechanics of different distribution games—in particular, it will draw your attention to whether every entity must find its way into a group and whether you can use entities more than once.

You can visualize these four different kinds of distribution in the following table. For illustration, we suppose here that five entities—A, B, C, D, and E—are to be distributed into two groups, Group 1 and Group 2.

The simplest kind of distribution game is represented in the upper left box—for these games, once you put an entity into a group, you can cross it off your master list. You are told that an entity can't be in a particular group, so you know that it must be in some other group. The other boxes represent slightly more complex distribution games. When you first assess a distribution game, pay attention to what distribution type is at work.

Also note that a two-group game from the upper left box is really a selection game with two groups, the "in" group and the "out" group. This does not apply to any two-group game represented by the other three boxes, nor to any three-or-more group game.

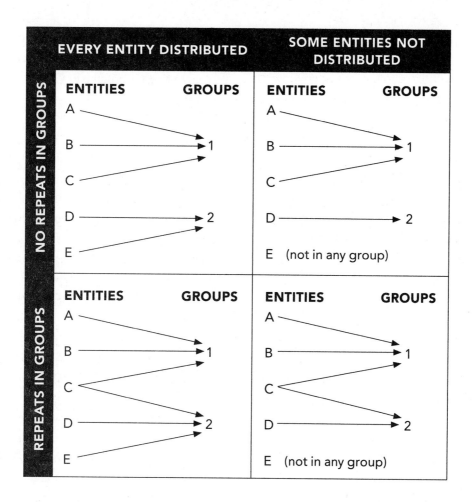

Diagramming the Distribution

How you diagram the action of the game will depend on a number of factors. How you set up the initial diagram will depend on the numerical restrictions on the groups into which the entities are to be distributed.

No Restrictions

If there are no numerical restriction—i.e., if there is no minimum or maximum number of entities in each subgroup—then simply make two columns, labeled with the names of the groups:

Maximums and Minimums

If there is some numerical restriction—that is, if a maximum and minimum are given—draw a series of slots for each group. First, draw the minimum number of slots, and then draw extra slots in parentheses up to the maximum.

For example, if you are told that Group 1 has a minimum of three and maximum of four members, and Group 2 has a minimum of four and maximum of six members, you would draw:

Exact Numbers

If you are given the exact numbers for each group, simply draw the corresponding number of slots. For example, if you are told that Group 1 has four members and Group 2 has five members, you would draw:

```
        1              2
     _ _ _ _        _ _ _ _ _
```

Hybrids

Of course, you can mix and match, depending on the game. For example, if you are told that Group 1 has exactly four members, and Group 2 has a minimum of three and maximum of four, you might draw:

```
        1              2
     _ _ _ _        _ _ _ (_)
```

Subgroup Domains

If you have a subgroup domain, you will want to leave room under your slots so that you can label that spot with a particular subgroup. For example, if you are told that each of two sections (Section 1 and Section 2) must have at least one female student, and that Adam (a male student) is in Section 2, you might draw:

```
        1                2
     _ _ _ _        _  A  _ (_)
     f               f  m
```

The "f" reminds you that at least one student in each group must be female, and the "m" reminds you that A is male—information that might prove useful as you work through a game.

Keeping Track of the Distribution

You will want to keep track of which entities are definitely in a group, which are definitely not in a group, and which could be in a group. Place letters for entities in a group in the slots. If an entity is definitely not in a group, write the letter for that entity next to or under that group and cross it out. If an entity could be in a group, write the letter for that entity next to or under the group and put it in a parentheses. For example, if

we know that D and E are definitely in Group 1, that B is definitely not in Group 2, and we want to remind ourselves that C could be in Group 1, we might draw:

```
        1                2
     _  D  E  _      _  A  _ (_)
        f               f  m
        c                   B
```

You should come up with a tracking system that works for you, as you come across different rules. For example, if an entity must be in one of two groups but cannot be in a third, consider putting a letter for the entity down and drawing two arrows from the entity, one to each of the two groups.

How Things are Distributed: the Rule Types and Major Players

A typical distribution game will present a set of rules which will determine how the selection must, can, or can't occur. There are four basic types of rules typical to a distribution game.

Blocks

A block is a group of entities that must be placed together. If one member of the block is in the group, then the other must be, and vice-versa. Rules that produce blocks tell you that two entities must be in the same group. For example, you may be told that "student A is in the same section as student C." Blocks are symbolized by placing the symbols for two entities next to one another:

AC

Anti-Blocks

An anti-block is a pair of entities that cannot be in the same group. For example, you may be told that "student A is not in the same section as student C," or "if student A is in a Section 1, student C is not in that section."

Note that this negative conditional works the same way as it did in the selection games—the contrapositive is that if student C is in a section, student A is not in that section. Anti-blocks are rarely presented as conditionals in distribution games; usually, the wording is fairly straightforward ("X and Y are not in the same group"). Anti-blocks are symbolized by placing the symbols for the entities next to one another and crossing them out:

~~AC~~

Anti-blocks sometimes make reference to domain subgroups, if those are present. For example, you may be told that "the two males are not in the same section," or that "student A is not in the same section as either of the female students."

Conditionals

We saw in selection games that conditional rules were rampant and took on many different forms. In contrast, distribution games usually have fairly straightforward positive conditionals, such as "if student A is in Section 1, then student C is in Section 2."

Some conditionals will be about the same group (as in selection games)—e.g., "if student A is in Section 1, then student B will also be in Section 1." Occasionally, the conditional will be slightly more complex—e.g., "if student A is in Section 1, then student D is also in Section 1 and student C is in Section 2."

We can symbolize these conditional rules as follows:

$$A1 \rightarrow C2$$
$$A1 \rightarrow (C2 \text{ and } D1)$$
$$A1 \rightarrow B1$$

If you are symbolizing both the entities and groups with letters, it sometimes helps to use parentheses. For example, we might be given the restriction that "if student X is in the morning section, then student Y is in the afternoon section." We might symbolize the sections with a lower-case "m" and "a", so we can write:

$$X(m) \rightarrow Y(a)$$

If the distribution game you are dealing with is really a selection game (that is, if it is a two-group game from the upper-left box, as discussed above), then you can change your symbolizations to make them much simpler. For example, suppose that the condition just given—"if student X is in the morning section, then student Y is in the afternoon section"—applies to a game in which there are just two sections, and every student must be in exactly one section. Then we consider this a selection game, in which the morning section is the "in" group and the afternoon section is the "out" group. Then if a student is in the morning section, we can consider her selected, and if a student is in the afternoon section, we can consider her not selected. So we can rewrite our symbolization:

$$X(m) \rightarrow Y(a)$$
as
$$X \rightarrow \neq Y$$

This means that if X is selected, Y is not selected. This notation often makes such distribution games much easier to handle for many test-takers. To illustrate how this notation works, some of the answer explanations to the practice games in this chapter will use it. You will have to see which method makes more sense to you for such two-group/upper-left-box games.

Number Rules

As in selection games, number rules are often the most important rules, playing a large role in driving the mechanics of a game. Number rules always tell us something about the number, or relative number, of entities that comprise a group. These rules often inform your initial game set-up and the associated diagram.

Section 2 has at most four students.
There is at least one female in every section.
There is at least one male in the same section as student A.

Practice Game 1

Seven census workers—Patrick, Quincy, Ramesh, Shawn, Terry, Unger, and Victoria—are each assigned to survey either the West side or East side of town, but not both. Their assignment is governed by the following restrictions:

If Patrick surveys the West side, then Shawn also surveys the West side.
If Terry surveys the East side, then Unger surveys the West side.
If Ramesh surveys the East side, then both Shawn and Unger survey the East side.
If Victoria surveys the West side, then Patrick surveys the East side and Quincy surveys the West side.
Unger surveys the East side if Patrick surveys the East side.

1. Which one of the following could be a complete and accurate list of the census workers surveying the East side?
   a. Terry, Victoria
   b. Patrick, Quincy
   c. Patrick, Ramesh, Shawn
   d. Ramesh, Shawn, Unger
   e. Patrick, Ramesh, Shawn, Victoria

2. If Ramesh surveys the East side, then which one of the following statements must be true?
   a. Shawn surveys the West side.
   b. Unger surveys the West side.
   c. Patrick surveys the West side.
   d. Terry surveys the West side.
   e. Quincy surveys the West side.

3. If Unger surveys the West side, then each of the following statements must be true EXCEPT:
   a. Patrick surveys the West side.
   b. Shawn surveys the West side.
   c. Victoria surveys the East side.
   d. Ramesh surveys the West side.
   e. Quincy surveys the East side.

4. If Patrick and Shawn survey different sides of the city, then what is the least number of census workers that could be assigned to survey the East side of the city?
   a. one
   b. two
   c. three
   d. four
   e. five

5. Which one of the following CANNOT be a pair assigned to survey the East side?
   a. Shawn and Terry
   b. Patrick and Shawn
   c. Patrick and Unger
   d. Terry and Victoria
   e. Ramesh and Shawn

Practice Game 2

Six journalists—A, B, C, D, E, and F—are assigned to cover the two major events of the day, a political rally and an air show. Each journalist covers one event or the other, but not both, and the assignment of journalists to events is governed by the following rules:

If B covers the political rally, then E also covers the political rally.
If G covers the air show, then both E and F also cover the air show.
If F covers the air show, then C also covers the air show.
If D covers the air show, then F covers the political rally.

1. Which one of the following could be a complete and accurate list of the journalists covering the air show?
   a. F, E
   b. E, F, G
   c. B, F,G
   d. B, D, C
   e. B, D, F

2. If F and C cover different events, then each of the following could be true EXCEPT:
   a. D covers the air show.
   b. G covers the air show.
   c. E covers the air show.
   d. D covers the political rally.
   e. B covers the political rally.

3. If B covers the political rally, then which one of the following must be true?
   a. G covers the political rally.
   b. E covers the air show.
   c. F covers the political rally.
   d. D covers the political rally.
   e. C covers the air show.

4. What is the minimum number of journalists that could be assigned to cover the political rally?
   a. zero
   b. one
   c. two
   d. three
   e. four

5. If G covers the air show, then what is the minimum number of journalists that must cover the airshow?
   a. one
   b. two
   c. three
   d. four
   e. five

Practice Game 3

Seven students—H, I , J, K, L, M and N—are to design a product. They are divided into three teams—an engineering team consisting of three members, a development team consisting of two members, and a branding team consisting of two members. Each student is on one and only one team. The students are divided according to the following restrictions:

Student H is on the development team.
Student J and student K are on the same team.
Student L and student H are on different teams.
If student L is on the engineering team, then student N is on the branding team.

1. Which one of the following could be an acceptable assignment of students to teams?

	Engineering	Development	Branding
a.	M N I	H L	J K
b.	J K H	N I	L M
c.	J K L	H M	N I
d.	J I L	H K	M N
e.	J K L	H N	I M

2. If student N is on the engineering team, then which one of the following statements must be true?
   a. Student I is on the branding team.
   b. Student I is on the development team.
   c. Student M is on the branding team.
   d. Student L is on the branding team.
   e. Student J is on the branding team.

3. Which one of the following is a complete and accurate list of all the students any one of which could be on the development team?
   a. H, I, M
   b. H, M, N
   c. H, I, K, L
   d. H, I, M, N
   e. H, I, K, M, N

4. If student N and student I are on the same team, then each of the following statements must be true EXCEPT:
   a. Student N is on the branding team.
   b. Student M is on the development team.
   c. Student L is on the engineering team.
   d. Student K is on the engineering team.
   e. Student I is on the engineering team.

5. Which one of the following statements CANNOT be true?
   a. Student I is on the branding team.
   b. Student K is on the branding team.
   c. Student M is on the development team.
   d. Student N is on the engineering team.
   e. Student L is on the engineering team.

Practice Game 4

Three artifacts discovered on an archaeological dig—a pot, a coin, and a mirror—are to be examined by six archaeologists—Q, R, S, T, U, and V. Each artifact is examined by exactly two archaeologists, and each archaeologist examines exactly one artifact, subject to the following constraints:

Q and R do not examine the same artifact.
S and T examine the same artifact.
If S examines the coin, then U examines the mirror.

1. Which one of the following could be an acceptable assignment of archaeologists to artifacts?

Coin	Pot	Mirror
a. QR	ST	UV
b. ST	UQ	RV
c. UV	SQ	TR
d. ST	QR	UR
e. ST	RV	UQ

2. If T examines the coin, then which one of the following statements must be true?
   a. V examines the pot.
   b. Q examines the pot.
   c. R examines the mirror.
   d. R examines the pot.
   e. U examines the pot.

3. Each of the following is a pair of archaeologists that could examine the same artifact EXCEPT:
   a. Q and V
   b. R and V
   c. Q and U
   d. V and U
   e. R and U

4. If V examines the mirror, then each of the following statements could be true EXCEPT:
   a. Q examines the coin.
   b. U examines the pot.
   c. U examines the coin.
   d. R examines the coin.
   e. R examines the mirror.

5. If Q examines the pot, then each of the following archaeologists could examine the mirror EXCEPT:
   a. V
   b. S
   c. T
   d. R
   e. U

Practice Game 5

Seven adventure scouts—I, J, K, L, M, N, and O—take two rafts for a white-water rafting trip. Each raft holds at least three and at most four scouts. Every scout boards exactly one of the two rafts, a front raft and a rear raft, according to the following conditions:

If J boards the front raft, then M boards the rear raft.
M and N do not get on the same raft.
N is on the same raft as O.
K is on the rear raft.
If O is on the rear raft, I is also on the rear raft.

1. Which one of the following is an acceptable roster of scouts on rafts?

	Front	Rear
a.	J, M, N, O	I, K, L
b.	N, O, J, I	L, K, M
c.	J, M, N	O, I, K, L
d.	I, J, O, L	M, N, K
e.	L, M, K	N, O, I, J

2. If J and L take different rafts, then how many different possible assignments of scouts to rafts are there?
   a. one
   b. two
   c. three
   d. four
   e. five

3. Which one of the following could be a partial, accurate list of the scouts on the front raft?
   a. J, L, O
   b. K, L, O
   c. I, J, L, N
   d. I, J, L, O
   e. J, K, N, O

4. Which one of the following CANNOT be a pair of scouts in the rear raft?
   a. J and K
   b. L and I
   c. I and M
   d. L and O
   e. K and L

5. Each of the following could be a true statement EXCEPT:
   a. M takes the front boat.
   b. I takes the front boat.
   c. L takes the rear boat.
   d. J takes the front boat.
   e. K takes the rear boat.

Practice Game 6

Six menu times—burgers, pizza, sandwiches, tacos, nachos, and chili—are to appear on three menus: a lunch menu, a dinner menu, and a night menu. Each menu item appears on at least one menu. Each menu has exactly three items. The menus are constructed according the following restrictions:

> One item appears on all three menus.
> Burgers and sandwiches never appear on the same menu.
> Tacos and nachos never appear on the same menu.
> Chili appears on the dinner menu.

1. Which one of the following is an acceptable set of menus?
   a. Lunch: pizza, tacos, chili
      Dinner: chili, burgers, sandwiches
      Night: chili, nachos, tacos
   b. Lunch: pizza, tacos, sandwiches
      Dinner: chili, burgers, nachos
      Night: chili, pizza, tacos
   c. Lunch: pizza, tacos, nachos
      Dinner: chili, pizza, sandwiches
      Night: pizza, burgers, tacos
   d. Lunch: pizza, burgers, tacos
      Dinner: chili, sandwiches, pizza
      Night: pizza, nachos, chili
   e. Lunch: pizza, chili, tacos
      Dinner: pizza, nachos, burgers
      Night: pizza, sandwiches, tacos

2. If chili appears on at most two menus, then which one of the following statements must be true?
   a. Pizza appears on exactly three menus.
   b. Tacos appear on exactly three menus.
   c. Sandwiches appear on exactly three menus.
   d. Pizza appears on exactly two menus.
   e. Tacos appear on exactly two menus.

3. If burgers appear on the lunch and dinner menus and chili appears on the night menu, then which one of the following statements CANNOT be true?
   a. Chili and nachos appear on the lunch menu.
   b. Pizza and nachos appear on the lunch menu.
   c. Chili and tacos appear on the night menu.
   d. Sandwiches and nachos appear on the night menu.
   e. Burgers and tacos appear on the dinner menu.

4. Which one of the following statements must be true?
   a. Chili and pizza appear on a menu together.
   b. Burgers and tacos appear on a menu together.
   c. Burgers and nachos appear on a menu together.
   d. Sandwiches and tacos appear on menu together.
   e. Sandwiches and nachos appear on a menu together.

5. If chili and nachos always appear on a menu together, then which one of the following statements must be true?
   a. Burgers appear on the lunch menu.
   b. Sandwiches appear on the lunch menu.
   c. Tacos appear on the lunch menu.
   d. Burgers appear on the night menu.
   e. Tacos appear on the dinner menu.

Practice Game 7

NASA is launching two simultaneous shuttle missions, using the shuttles Freedom and Independence. Four astronauts are assigned to each shuttle, chosen from three veteran astronauts —A, B, and C—and five novice astronauts—V, W, X, Y, and Z. The astronauts are assigned according to the following conditions:

Astronauts A and C cannot be on the same shuttle.
Astronaut Y is on the Independence.
If Astronaut B is on the Freedom, then Astronaut X is on the Independence
If Astronaut A is on the Independence, then Astronaut Z is on the Freedom.

1. Which one of the following could be the roster of astronauts on board the Freedom?
   a. A, V, Y, Z
   b. A, B, V, X
   c. A, B, C, V
   d. A, V, W, Z
   e. B, C, V, W

2. If Astronaut B and Astronaut X are aboard the same shuttle, then each of the following could be a pair of astronauts on board the same shuttle EXCEPT:
   a. V and W
   b. A and Z
   c. B and C
   d. C and X
   e. B and Z

3. If Astronaut Z is aboard the Independence, then which one of the following statements must be true?
   a. C is aboard the Independence.
   b. A is aboard the Independence.
   c. B is aboard the Freedom.
   d. X is aboard the Independence.
   e. X is aboard the Freedom.

4. If exactly two veteran astronauts are on board the Freedom, then which one of the following statements must be true?
   a. A is aboard the Freedom.
   b. X is aboard the Independence.
   c. C is aboard the Independence.
   d. Z is aboard the Freedom.
   e. B is aboard the Independence.

5. If Astronaut X is aboard the Freedom, then which one of the following statements must be true?
   a. A is aboard the Freedom.
   b. C is aboard the Freedom.
   c. Z is aboard the Freedom.
   d. Exactly two novices are aboard the Freedom.
   e. Exactly three novices are aboard the Freedom.

Practice Game 8

A joint agency task force is formed to investigate two cases—the Appleby case and the Brentwood case. The task force is made up of seven officers: three FBI agents (X, Y, and Z) and four detectives (H, I, J, K). Each case has at least one agent and at least one detective. All officers are assigned to one and only once case, according to the following conditions:

> H and I are not assigned to the same case.
> I and J are assigned to the same case.
> If K is assigned to the Appleby case, then X is assigned to the Brentwood case.
> If Y is assigned to the Appleby case, then I is also assigned to the Appleby case.
> Each case is assigned at least one agent and one detective.

1. Which one of the following could be a complete and accurate list of the officers assigned to the Appleby case?
   a. I, J, K, Y
   b. H, I , J, K
   c. I, K, Y, Z
   d. H, K, X, Z
   e. K, H, Y, Z

2. If H is assigned to the Appleby case, then each of the following could be a pair of officers assigned to the same case EXCEPT:
   a. H and Z
   b. X and Y
   c. H and I
   d. J and K
   e. H and K

3. If exactly three detectives are assigned to the Brentwood case, then which one of the following must be true?
   a. K is assigned to the Appleby case.
   b. H is assigned to the Appleby case.
   c. H is assigned to the Brentwood case.
   d. X is assigned to the Brentwood case.
   e. X is assigned to the Appleby case.

4. If X and Y are both assigned to the Appleby case, then each of the following must be true EXCEPT:
   a. I is assigned to the Appleby case.
   b. J is assigned to the Appleby case.
   c. H is assigned to the Brentwood case.
   d. Z is assigned to the Brentwood case.
   e. K is assigned to the Appleby case.

5. If the Brentwood case is assigned the fewest number of officers possible, then which one of the following must be assigned to the Brentwood case?
   a. H
   b. I
   c. J
   d. X
   e. Y

Setup, Answers, and Explanations

Practice Game 1

First, symbolize the restrictions, and their contrapositives. When finding the contrapositives, note that if some worker does not survey one side of the city, he or she must survey the other. This is a consequence of the fact that this is a two-group distribution game from the upper-left box (along with the fact that if he or she surveys one side of the city, he or she does not survey the other).

The first restriction:

$$P(w) \rightarrow S(w)$$
$$S(e) \rightarrow P(e)$$

The second restriction:

$$T(e) \rightarrow U(w)$$
$$U(e) \rightarrow T(w)$$

The third restriction:

$$R(e) \rightarrow (S(e) \text{ and } U(e))$$
$$S(w) \text{ or } U(w) \rightarrow R(w)$$

The fourth restriction:

$$V(w) \rightarrow P(e) \text{ and } Q(w)$$
$$P(w) \text{ or } Q(e) \rightarrow V(e)$$

The fifth restriction:

$$P(e) \rightarrow U(e)$$
$$U(w) \rightarrow P(w)$$

Notice that the V, Q, and T only appear in one restriction each, and so will have the greatest likelihood of being unrestricted and without a forced assignment, depending on the situation.

Question 1

The correct answer is choice **a**. This is a "Test-the-Rules" question. For each answer choice, you are given a putative complete and accurate list of the workers on the East side; which means any worker not appearing on the list must be assigned to the West side. Keeping this in mind should help you see how the restrictions rule out answer choices.

The first restriction rules out **d**, since Patrick is on the West side, but Shawn is on the East side. The second restriction doesn't rule out any of the answer choices. The third restriction rules out **e**, since Ramesh is on the East side, but Unger is not on the East side. The fourth restriction rules out **b**, since Victoria is on the West side, but Quincy is not on the West side. The fifth restriction rules out **c**, since Patrick is on the East side, but Unger is not.

Question 2

The correct answer is choice **d**. If Ramesh surveys the East side, then by the third restriction, both Shawn and Unger also survey the East side. If Shawn surveys the East side, then by the contrapositive of the first restriction, Patrick also surveys the East side. And if Unger surveys the East side, then by the second restriction, Terry surveys the West side.

It doesn't seem like we can make any more direct deductions from our conditional statements, so we have:

e	w
R S U P	T

Choice **d** says that Terry surveys the West side, which is necessitated by our reasoning and diagram.

Question 3

The correct answer is choice **e**. If Unger surveys the West side, then by the contrapositive of the third restriction, Ramesh surveys the West side, and by the contrapositive of the fifth restriction, Patrick also surveys the West side. If Patrick surveys the West side, then by the first restriction, Shawn also surveys the West side; and by the contrapositive of the fourth restriction, Victoria surveys the East side. It doesn't seem like we can make any more direct deductions from our conditional statements, so we have:

e	w
V	U R P S

According to the diagram, all four of the statements correspond to choices **a** through **d** must be the case; there is no deduction placing Quincy on the East side, so **e** is the correct answer.

Question 4

The correct answer is choice **b**. First, look for the restriction connecting Patrick and Shawn—this is the first restriction, which says that if Patrick surveys the West side, then so does Shawn. So Patrick cannot survey the West side, lest he and Shawn survey the same side. So Patrick surveys the East side, and Shawn surveys the West side. Since Patrick surveys the East side, by the fifth restriction, Unger also surveys the East side. Since Unger surveys the East side, then by the second restriction, Terry surveys the West side. Since Shawn surveys the West side, by the contrapositive of the third restriction, Ramesh also surveys the West side. Since no more immediate deductions can be made, we have:

e	w
P U	S R T

It looks like we must have at least two workers on the East side. But double-check to make sure that the remaining workers, Q and V, can be on the West side without violating any restrictions. The fourth restriction, the only one involving Q and V, would be satisfied if both were on the West side. So the correct answer remains two, choice **b**.

Question 5

The correct answer is choice **a**. First, see if any of the answer choices appear in distribution scenarios you have already found to be acceptable from other answer choices. Choice **d** is ruled out by the answer to Question 1. Choices **b**, **c**, and **e** are ruled out given the diagram through which we answered question 2. That only leaves choice **a**.

Without the aid of previous work, you must go through each pair, and see if the pair could be assigned to the East side or if it would result in a contradiction. If Shawn is assigned to the East side, then Patrick is also assigned to East side (first restriction). If Terry is assigned to the East side, Unger will be assigned to the West side (second restriction), meaning that Patrick would have to be assigned to the West side (fifth restriction)—but we already assigned Patrick to the East side. Choice **a** results in a contradiction, and is thus the correct answer.

Practice Game 2

First, symbolize the restrictions and their contrapositives. Note that this is a two-group distribution game from the upper-left box, and so can be considered a selection game. For this game, we will symbolize the restrictions as though it were a selection game in which the 'in' group is the group covering the air show, and the 'out' group is the group covering the political rally. Every journalist must either be selected (covering the air show) or not selected (covering the political rally). With this in mind, we can symbolize the restrictions like this:

First restriction:

$$\neq B \rightarrow \neq E$$
$$E \rightarrow B$$

Second restriction:

$$G \rightarrow (E \text{ and } F)$$
$$(\neq E \text{ or } \neq F) \rightarrow \neq G$$

Third restriction:

$$F \rightarrow C$$
$$\neq C \rightarrow \neq F$$

Fourth restriction:

$$D \rightarrow \neq F$$
$$F \rightarrow \neq D$$

Notice that A does not appear in any restriction, and so will be a complete floater. Any deductions made will likely be based on a chain of inferences using these conditional statements and additional information, so go to the questions.

Question 1

The correct answer is choice **d**. This is a "Test-the-Rules" question. For each answer choice, you are given a putative complete and accurate list of the journalists assigned to the air show; which means any journalist not appearing on the list must be assigned to the political rally. But since we are considering this a selection game, each answer choice gives a putative complete and accurate list of the journalists selected; which means that any journalist not appearing on the list must not be selected. Keeping this in mind should help you see how the restrictions rule out answer choices. The first restriction rules out **b**, since B is out but E is in. The second restriction rules out **c**, since G is in but E is not. The third restriction rules out **a** since F is in but C is not. The fourth restriction rules out **e**, since D is in, but so is F.

Question 2

The correct answer is choice **b**. First, look for the restriction involving F and C—the third restriction says that if F is selected, C is selected. So let F and C be at the same event (i.e., either both in or both out), F must be out (at the political rally), and C in (at the air show). If F is out, then G must also be out (contrapositive of the second restriction). So far we have:

In	Out
C	F G

Check to see if any of the other restrictions can be applied. To do this, check to see if the antecedents of any the restrictions or their contrapositives are true. None of them are, so these are the only group assignments that are forced. The other journalists could be placed into either group (although placing one of them into one group may make further restrictions on the placement of some other yet-to-be-placed journalists.

Essentially, the diagram as it stands is compatible with the placement of each of the remaining journalists in either of the two groups. In any case, we know that G is not selected (i.e., that G must cover the political rally)—so the correct answer is choice **b**. D could either be in or out (cover either event), so choices **a** and **d** are incorrect. The same goes for E and B, ruling out choices **c** and **e**.

Question 3

The correct answer is choice **a**. By the first restriction, if B is out, then E is out (i.e., if B covers the political rally, then E also covers the political rally. By the contrapositive of the second restriction, if E is out then G is out (i.e., if E covers the political rally, then G also covers the political rally. This is answer choice **a**.

Question 4

The correct answer is choice **b**. You want to find the minimum number of journalists that can be not selected, so start by seeing if it could be that all the journalists are selected without violating any of the restrictions, and work your way up from there. Suppose all journalists are selected. The first restriction is not violated because B is selected, so the restriction does not apply. The second restriction could not be violated because E and F are selected. Same with the third restriction—it can't be violated because C is selected. The fourth restriction, however, is violated—D is selected, but F is selected as well. So it can't be that all journalists are selected (there are zero journalists not selected), and **a** is incorrect. Now move on to choice **b**.

Can there be just one journalist not selected? Use the work we just did. If D is the only journalist not selected, then none of the restrictions will be violated. So there can be just one journalist not selected (i.e., one journalist at the political rally), and **b** is the correct answer.

Since this answer explanation is particularly tricky, we rewrite it here in the original terms of the distribution game rather than in the terms of the equivalent selection game:

You want to find the minimum number of journalists that can be at the political rally, so start by seeing of there could be zero journalists assigned to the political rally without violating any of the restrictions, and work your way up from there. If there were no journalists at the political rally, they would all be at the air show. Does that violate any of the restrictions?

The first restriction is not violated because B is not at the political rally, so the restriction does not apply. The second restriction could not be violated because E and F are in fact at the air show. Same with the third restriction—it can't be violated because C is at the air show. The fourth restriction, however, is violated—D is at the air show, but by our supposition that all journalists are at the air show, F is not at the political rally. So there can't be zero journalists at the political rally, and choice **a** is incorrect. Now move on to choice **b**. Can there be just one journalist at the political rally? Use the work we just did. If D is the only journalist at the political rally, then none of the restrictions will be violated. So there can be just one journalist at the political rally, and **b** is the correct answer.

We should also note at this point that a bit of strategy might have helped. Minimum/maximum questions are often time-intensive, since you have to methodically check each number against the full set of restrictions. If you had skipped this question and saved it for the end, you would have seen that the work you did in Question 5 (showing that there can be

just one journalist not selected) would have saved you the work of checking to see if you could make choice **b** (i.e., that just one journalist is not selected) work without violating any of the restrictions.

Question 5

The correct answer is choice **e**. By the second restriction, if G is selected (if G covers the air show), then both E and F are also selected (also cover the air show). If F is selected, then C is also selected (third restriction). If E is selected, then B is also selected (contrapositive of the first restriction). And if F is selected, then D is not selected (contrapositive of the fourth restriction). So we have a full selection list:

In	Out
G E F C B	D

There are five journalists selected—i.e., covering the air show—choice **e**.

Practice Game 3

This game has groups with exact numbers, so numbers will probably drive much of the mechanics of the game. Start with a basic diagram:

$$e \qquad d \qquad b$$
$$\_ \ \_ \ \_ \qquad \_ \ \_ \qquad \_ \ \_$$

Symbolize the restrictions and try to work them into the diagram.

For the first restriction, H can be entered in the 'd' group.

For the second restriction, draw a block:

JK

For the third restriction, draw an anti-block:

L̶H̶

For the fourth restriction:

$$L(e) \rightarrow N(b)$$
$$\neq N(b) \rightarrow \neq L(e)$$

Now consider the restrictions to see what deductions can be made. For now, we note that the second restriction means that the block JK must either be in group e or group b, since there is no room in group d (H is already there). The third restriction means that L must be in either group e or group b, so make note of this in your diagram, either with arrows or crosses/parentheses:

```
      e           d        b
    _  _  _      H  _     _  _
    (L)          Ⱡ        (L)
    (JK)                  (JK)
```

Since JK seems to be an important player (it would fill up group B and nearly fill up group e), see what would happen in the two scenarios possible for JK's placement (in group e and group b). Suppose JK were in group b. Then L would have to be in group e. According to the fifth restriction, if L were in group e, then N would have to be in group b. But group b is already filled! So we know that being in group b is not really an option for the block JK, and JK must instead be in group e. So we have:

```
      e           d        b
    J  K  _      H  _     _  _
    (L)          Ⱡ        (L)
```

We have now captured the first, second, and third restrictions in our diagram. So our game has been consolidated into the diagram plus the fourth restriction:

```
      e           d        b
    J  K  _      H  _     _  _
    (L)          Ⱡ        (L)
```

$$L(e) \rightarrow N(b)$$
$$\neq N(b) \rightarrow \neq L(e)$$

Armed with this, we can turn to the questions.

Question 1

The correct answer is choice **c**. This is a "Test-the-Rules" question. The first restriction rules out **b**, since H is not on the development team. The second restriction rules out **d**, since J and K are on different teams. The third restriction rules out **a**, since L and H are on the same team. The fourth restriction rules out **e**, since L is in engineering, but N is not in branding.

Question 2

The correct answer is choice **d**. If N is on the engineering team, then by the contrapositive of the fourth restriction, L cannot be on the engineering team. So we have:

```
      e           d        b
    J  K  N      H  _     L  _
```

Scan the answer choices—choice **d** is that L is on the branding team, and so is the correct answer.

Question 3

The correct answer is choice **d**. We want all the possible students for the development team. Consider the diagram:

```
      e           d        b
    J  K  _      H  _     _  _
    (L)          Ⱡ        (L)
```

Any choice with J, L or K is definitely out: choices **c** and **e**. We have four students left: H, N, M, and I. Check to make sure each of these could be on the development team. H is definitely on the development team. If N was on the development team, no restriction would be violated as long as L was not on the engineering team (and so on the branding team, leaving I for the engineering team):

```
    e           d           b
  J K _       H N         D L
  (L)          Ł          (L)
```

This violates no restrictions. Note that we do not actually have to check if M is on the development team, because each of the three remaining answer choices contains M. So the correct answer must include H, M, N and I, and nothing else—this is choice **d**.

If we were to miss the commonality of M to the remaining answer choices, we would check whether M could be on the development team and reason as follows. If M went on the development team, then we could put I on the engineering team and N on the branding team (ensuring that the fourth restriction is met).

If I were on the development team, then again, we could N on the branding team and L on the engineering team, satisfying the remaining restriction.

Question 4

The correct answer is choice **e**. If student N and I were on the same team—that is, a block—they would have to be in group b, leaving L for group e, and M for group d:

```
    e           d           b
  J K L       H M         N I
```

Now, each of the statements in the first four answer choices is guaranteed by the diagram, so those choices must be wrong. Choice **e** states that student I is on the engineering team, which is false here, since student I is on the branding team.

Question 5

The correct answer is choice **b**. We need to check each answer choice to see if it could be true.

Start by seeing if any of the statements in the choices are true on distribution scenarios you found

to be acceptable in the course of previous work. The diagram for Question 4 rules out choices **a**, **c** and **e**. The answer to Question 2 rules out choice **d**. So we are left with **b**.

If we had not answered these prior questions, we could have referred to our up-front diagram and looked for something that cannot be true. Just by looking at our diagram, we see that K cannot be on the branding team, since it is on the engineering team. So **b** is the correct choice. Our upfront deductions directly paid off here.

```
    e           d           b
  J K _       H _         _ _
  (L)          Ł          (L)
```

We also could have taken each answer choice in turn to see if it could be true. Suppose I is on the branding team. Are there any deductions to be made, or rules violated?

```
    e           d           b
  J K _       H _         I _
  (L)          Ł          (L)
```

Again, as we already saw in Question 4, a compatible scenario did not violate any of the restrictions. So choice **a** is incorrect and we turn to choice **b**. Again, just by looking at our diagram, we recall that K cannot be on the branding team, since it is on the engineering team. So **b** is the correct choice.

Practice Game 4

Our distribution diagram will be straightforward:

```
      c           p           m
    _  _        _  _        _  _
```

We first symbolize the restrictions.

The first restriction:

~~QR~~

The second restriction:

ST

The third restriction:

$S(c) \rightarrow U(m)$
$\neq U(m) \rightarrow \neq S(c)$

In digesting the game, notice how the block ST must take up one of the three groups, leaving two groups behind. The presence of the anti-block QR means that Q and R will be distributed between the two remaining groups. And this means that the two remaining entities, V and U, will also be separated between the two remaining groups. We don't know which group is which, but the general distribution will look something like:

```
   1          2            3
  S  T      Q/R U/V      R/Q V/U
```

Question 1
The correct answer is choice **e**. This is a "Test-the-Rules" question. The first restriction rules out **a** and **d**, since Q and R are in the same group (examining the coin for **a**, and examining the pot for **d**). The second restriction rules out **c**, since S and T are in different groups. The third restriction rules out **b**, since S is examining the coin but U is not examining the mirror.

Question 2
The correct answer is choice **a**. If T examines the coin, then S and T are both examining the coin (by the first restriction). Since S is examining the coin, U is examining the mirror (by the third restriction). So we have:

```
  c        p        m
 S  T     _  _     U  _
```

Now, by the first restriction, Q and R are to be separated between groups p and m. So one of the two spots in group p will either be Q or R, and the one spot in group m will be whichever of Q and R is not in group p. Either way, the one remaining spot—in group p—will have to be filled by V. So it must be that V examines the pot—choice **a**.

Question 3
The correct answer is choice **d**. The answer is taken directly from our up-front deductions about the game. We realized that because Q and R would have to be separated (in separate groups, i.e., examining different artifacts), so would V and U have to be separated. This is choice **d**.

Note that if we had not made the up-front deductions, we could have used previous questions. The answer to Question 1 rules out **b** and **c**. The answer to Question 2 rules out choice **a**. That just leaves **d** and **e**; for each, see if the pair could examine the same artifact. We would not be forced to see what V and U together would do—they would be in one group, forcing S and T into a second group, and Q and R into a third, violating the first restriction.

Question 4
The correct answer is choice **b**. If V examines the mirror, then we know that U cannot examine the mirror (because V and U in the same group, along with S and T in the same group, would force Q and R into the same group, violating our first restriction. And according to the contrapositive of our first restriction, if U is not examining the mirror, then S is not examining the coin, which means that S (and T) are examining the pot.

Using our general diagram, we have:

```
  p          c           m
 S  T      U  R/Q      R/Q  V
```

According to this diagram, it's definitely not true that U examines the pot, because U is examining the coin. So **b** is the correct answer.

Question 5

The correct answer is choice **a**. If Q examines the pot, then again using our general diagram, we have:

```
   1        2         3
  S  T    Q  U/V    R  V/U
```

Since we are interested in who can examine the mirror, let's try the two scenarios this diagram allows for—that Group 1 is the mirror group or that group 3 is the mirror group.

```
S1
   m        p         c
  S  T    Q  U/V    R  V/U
```

```
S2
   c        p         m
  S  T    Q  U/V    R  V/U
```

We check each scenario to see if it is consistent with the restrictions. In S2, since S examines the coin, U must examine the mirror (third restriction). So S2 must be:

```
S2
   c        p       m
  S  T    Q  V    R  U
```

S1 doesn't violate any restrictions as it stands.

Now, test each answer choice. V does not examine the mirror in either scenario, so choice **a** is the answer.

Practice Game 5

The game specifies a maximum of four and minimum of three scouts per raft. So we have:

```
   f              r
  _ _ _ (_)    _ _ _ (_)
```

Now symbolize the restrictions:

The first restriction:

$$J(f) \rightarrow M(r)$$
$$M(f) \rightarrow J(r)$$

The second restriction:

~~MN~~

The third restriction:

NO

The fourth restriction can be written into the diagram.

Fifth restriction:

$$O(r) \rightarrow I(r)$$
$$I(f) \rightarrow O(f)$$

We can write K into the diagram. Since M and N must be distributed separately into the two groups, and O goes with N, the diagram looks like:

```
        f                    r
  M/NO _ _ (_)    K NO/M _ (_)
```

Since there are two scenarios listed here, go ahead and separate them to see what happens.

```
S1
        f              r
  M _ _ (_)    K N O (_)
```

```
S2
       f             r
  N O _ (_)    K M _ (_)
```

For S1: according to the first restriction, since M is in f, J must be in r, pushing the remaining entities, I and L, into f:

S1

```
        f                    r
    M  I  L  (_)      K  N  O  J
```

Is S1 consistent with the restrictions? According to the fifth restriction, if O is in the rear boat, I must be in the rear boat—but I is in the front boat. So S1 cannot be an option, and we are left only with S2:

S2

```
        f                    r
    N  O  _  (_)      K  M  _  (_)
```

What about the remaining three entities, J, L, and I? Since the consequent of the first condition is true (M is on the rear boat), and the antecedent of the fifth restriction false (O is not on the rear boat), neither the first nor fifth restrictions can affect the game. The second, third, and fourth restrictions are already satisfied. So as long as we meet our numerical restriction that there is a minimum of three and maximum of four scouts per raft, J, L, and I can appear on either raft:

```
     f                              r
N  O  _  (_)   (J, L, I)   K  M  _  (_)   (J, L, I)
```

Question 1
The correct answer is choice **b**. This is a "Test-the-Rules" question. The first restriction rules out choices **a** and **c**, since J is in the front raft but M is not in the rear raft. The second restriction rules out **d**, since M and N are on a raft together. The fourth restriction rules out choice **e**, since K is not on the rear raft.

Question 2
The correct answer is choice **d**. If J and L take different rafts, then they can be distributed in the following two ways:

```
        f                    r
    N  O  I  (_)  (I)    K  M  L  I  (_)
```

```
        f                    r
    N  O  L  (_)  (I)    K  M  J  I  (_)
```

I can be distributed to the front or rear raft for each of these two possibilities, so there are a total of four possibilities—choice **d**.

Question 3
The correct answer is choice **a**. Consider the diagram:

```
        f                              r
    N  O  _  (_)   (J, L, I)   K  M  _  (_)
```

Any list with a selection from N, O, J, L, and I—so long as no other letters appear, and so long as no more than two of J, L, and I appear—will be a partial, accurate list. If all three of J, L and I appear, then there will not be enough room on the front raft for N and O. Choice **a** gives such a partial list. Choices **b** and **e** include K, and so are incorrect. Choices **c** and **d** include all three of J, L and I, and so are incorrect.

Question 4
The correct answer is choice **d**.

```
        f                              r
    N  O  _  (_)   (J, L, I)   K  M  _  (_)
```

A quick glance at the diagram shows that O cannot be in the rear raft. All the other letters—J, K, L, I, and M—can be in rear raft.

Without the aid of the diagram, you could also note that you can use the answer to question 1 to eliminate choice **e** and the answer to question 2 to eliminate choices **b** and **c**. You can then try the two remaining answer choices and see that choice **d** results in a contradiction, since it places five people on the rear boat.

Question 5

The correct answer is choice **a**. Again, a brief glance at the diagram shows that M cannot be in the front boat.

Practice Game 6

First, the numbers: The three groups or three menus have exactly three items each. But the items to be distributed, the six menu items, can (and will have to) appear in more than one group. All menu items will be selected.

The fourth restriction is that chili appears on the dinner menu. So we can start with a diagram:

$$l \qquad d \qquad n$$
$$\underline{\ } \ \underline{\ } \ \underline{\ } \qquad \underline{C} \ \underline{\ } \ \underline{\ } \qquad \underline{\ } \ \underline{\ }$$

Let's consider the other restrictions.

The first restriction is that one menu item appears on all three menus. We'll get back to this.

The second restriction:

~~BS~~

The third restriction:

~~TN~~

Now let's consider the menu item that must appear on all three menus—this will be a major player. That item could not be the burger, because then it would appear on at least one menu with the sandwiches, violating the second restriction. The same reasoning applies to the sandwich, tacos, and nachos. So the item that appears on all three menus must either be the chili or the pizza (the two remaining menu items). This will prove to be critical information when answering the questions.

Question 1

The correct answer is choice **d**. This is a "Test-the-Rules" question. The first restriction rules out **b**, since no item appears on all three menus. The second restriction rules out **a**, since the burgers and sandwiches are on the same menu. The third restriction rules out choice **c**, since the tacos and nachos appear on the same menu. The fourth restriction rules out **e**, since chili does not appear on the dinner menu.

Question 2

The correct answer is choice **a**. We know from our up-front deductions that either chili or pizza must appear on all three menus. If chili appears on at most two menus, then pizza must appear on all three. This is choice **a**.

Question 3

The correct answer is choice **b**. If burgers appear on the lunch and dinner menus, and chili on the night menu, we have:

$$l \qquad d \qquad n$$
$$\underline{B} \ \underline{\ } \ \underline{\ } \qquad \underline{C} \ \underline{B} \ \underline{\ } \qquad \underline{C} \ \underline{\ } \ \underline{\ }$$

Since burgers and sandwiches cannot appear on the menu together, sandwiches must appear on the night menu.

$$l \qquad d \qquad n$$
$$\underline{B} \ \underline{\ } \ \underline{\ } \qquad \underline{C} \ \underline{B} \ \underline{\ } \qquad \underline{C} \ \underline{S} \ \underline{\ }$$

Let's consider our major player now—the item that appears on all three menus. If it were pizza, we would have:

$$l \qquad d \qquad n$$
$$\underline{B} \ \underline{\ } \ \underline{P} \qquad \underline{C} \ \underline{B} \ \underline{P} \qquad \underline{C} \ \underline{S} \ \underline{P}$$

But this would leave no room for T and N. So chili, not pizza, must appear three times, and we have:

$$l \qquad d \qquad n$$
$$\underline{B} \ \underline{C} \ \underline{\ } \qquad \underline{B} \ \underline{C} \ \underline{\ } \qquad \underline{C} \ \underline{S} \ \underline{\ }$$

T and N and P must take up the remaining three spots, and there are no restrictions on which item takes which spot.

Given this diagram, choice **b** is the correct answer because it can't be the case that both pizza and nachos appear on the lunch menu—there is only space for one of them.

Question 4

The correct answer is choice **a**. Since we know that either chili or pizza is the item that appears on every menu, it must be the case that either way—whether chili appears three times and therefore at least once with pizza, or whether pizza appears three times, at least once with chili—chili and pizza appear together on a menu.

We could also arrive at the answer by noticing that the answer to Question 1 rules out **c**, **d**, and **e**, and that the answer to Question 2 rules out **b**.

Question 5

The correct answer is choice **c**. If chili and nachos always appear on a menu together, then nachos must appear on the dinner menu:

$$\begin{array}{ccc} l & d & n \\ \_\ \_\ \_ & \underline{C}\ \underline{N}\ \_ & \_\ \_\ \_ \end{array}$$

Now consider the major player again, the item that appears on all three menus. We know that it must be chili or pizza. If it were chili, then the block CN would appear on all three menus (since chili would appear on all three)—leaving three spaces for the four remaining menu items yet to appear (burgers, pizza, sandwiches, tacos). So chili cannot appear three times, and instead, pizza must:

$$\begin{array}{ccc} l & d & n \\ \underline{P}\ \_\ \_ & \underline{C}\ \underline{N}\ \underline{P} & \underline{P}\ \_\ \_ \end{array}$$

B and S need to be distributed between the lunch menu and night menu, leaving two open spaces.

$$\begin{array}{ccc} l & d & n \\ \underline{P}\ \underline{B/S}\ \_ & \underline{C}\ \underline{N}\ \underline{P} & \underline{P}\ \underline{S/B}\ \_ \end{array}$$

These two spaces cannot have S or B in them (lest we violate the second restriction), nor can they have C or N in them (since either one would carry the other—i.e., they exist as a block now); nor P, since P already appears on all three menus. So the two open spaces must both have T.

$$\begin{array}{ccc} l & d & n \\ \underline{P}\ \underline{B/S}\ \underline{T} & \underline{C}\ \underline{N}\ \underline{P} & \underline{P}\ \underline{S/B}\ \underline{T} \end{array}$$

The diagram thus shows that choice **c**, which says that tacos appear on the lunch menu, must be true, and is therefore the correct answer.

Practice Game 7

There are four spots each for the Freedom and Independence, and according to the second restriction, Y is aboard the Independence. Since the first restriction means that A and C are to be separated between the Freedom and Independence, we can symbolize that information directly into the diagram as well:

$$\begin{array}{cccccc} f & & & i & & \\ \_\ \_\ \_\ \underline{A/C} & & \underline{Y}\ \_\ \_\ \underline{A/C} \\ v & & & n & & v \end{array}$$

We note the subgroups under the slots.

We symbolize the third restriction:

$$B(f) \rightarrow X(i)$$
$$\text{or } X(f) \rightarrow B(i)$$

We symbolize the fourth restriction:

$$A(i) \rightarrow Z(f)$$
$$Z(i) \rightarrow A(f)$$

Question 1

The correct answer is choice **e**. This is a "Test-the-Rules" question. Remember that the four astronauts not given in an answer choice will be aboard the Independence—a fact that will be helpful in detecting rule violations. The first restriction rules out **c**, since A and C are on the same shuttle. The second restriction rules out **a**, since Y is not aboard the Independence. The third restriction rules out choice **b**, since B is on the Freedom, but X is not on the Independence. The fourth restriction rules out **e**, since A is on the Independence, but Z is not on the Freedom.

Question 2

The correct answer is choice **e**. Start by looking for the restriction involving both B and X—the third restriction. If B and X are aboard the same shuttle, that shuttle can't be the Freedom—otherwise, the third restriction would mean that X is on the Independence. So B and X have to both be aboard the Independence. The remaining entities, V, W, and Z, have to go into the left group (the Freedom). So we have:

$$f \qquad\qquad i$$
$$\underline{V}\ \underline{W}\ \underline{Z}\ \underline{A/C} \qquad \underline{Y}\ \underline{B}\ \underline{X}\ \underline{A/C}$$
$$\quad\ \ v \qquad\qquad\quad n \qquad\ v$$

From consulting the diagram, we see that Z and B cannot be aboard the same shuttle—choice **e**.

Question 3

The correct answer is **a**. If Z is aboard the Independence, then by the contrapositive to the fourth restriction, A is on the Freedom. And if A is on the Freedom, C is on the Independence. This is choice **a**.

Question 4

The correct answer is choice **b**. If there are exactly two veterans on the Freedom, then B must be one of those veterans (since veterans A and C can't be on the same shuttle). And if B is on the freedom, then by the third restriction, X is on the Independence. This is choice **b**.

Question 5

The correct answer is choice **e**. If X is aboard the Freedom, then by the contrapositive of the third restriction, B is aboard the Independence. So the Independence will have exactly two veterans: B, and one of A or C. If the Independence has exactly two veterans, then the Freedom will have exactly one veteran, and therefore have exactly three novices. This is choice **e**.

Practice Game 8

We are told that each case is assigned at least one agent and one detective:

$$A \qquad\qquad B$$
$$\underline{\ }\ \underline{\ } \qquad \underline{\ }\ \underline{\ }$$
$$a\ \ d \qquad\ a\ \ d$$

The first restriction:

~~HI~~

The second restriction:

IJ

The third restriction:

$$K(A) \rightarrow X(B)$$
$$X(A) \rightarrow K(B)$$

The fourth restriction:

$$Y(A) \rightarrow I(A)$$
$$I(B) \rightarrow Y(B)$$

Consider the two scenarios created by the first restriction:

S1
$$A \qquad\qquad B$$
$$\underline{\ }\ \underline{I} \qquad \underline{\ }\ \underline{H}$$
$$a\ \ d \qquad\ a\ \ d$$

S2 A   B
_ $\underline{H}$ _ $\underline{I}$
a d   a d

By the second restriction, we can add in J with I. By the fourth restriction, we can put Y under case B for scenario 2, indicating that either X or Z (or both) must be assigned to A (to maintain at least one agent for each group):

S1
    A   B
_ $\underline{I}$ $\underline{J}$ _ $\underline{H}$
a d d   a d

S2
    A   B
$\underline{X/Z}$ $\underline{H}$ $\underline{Y}$ $\underline{I}$ $\underline{J}$
a d   a d d

Question 1

The correct answer is choice **a**. This is a "Test-the-Rules" question. Note that any officer not assigned to the Appleby case is assigned to the Brentwood case. The first restriction rules out **b**, since H and I are assigned the same case. The second restriction rules out choice **c**, since I and J are not assigned the same case. The third restriction rules out **d**, since K is assigned to the Appleby case, but X is not assigned to the Brentwood case. The fourth restriction rules out **e**, since Y is assigned the Appleby case, but I is not.

Question 2

The correct answer is choice **c**. If H is assigned to the Appleby case, then we must be in scenario 2. According the diagram, H and I cannot be assigned to the same case, as I is assigned to the Brentwood case.

We could also get this answer without the initial scenario diagrams by seeing what follows from H being assigned to A. By the first restriction, I must be in B, carrying J with it (by the second restriction). By

the contrapositive of the fourth restriction, Y is also in B. So we have:

    A   B
  $\underline{H}$ $\underline{J}$ $\underline{Y}$ $\underline{I}$

This is enough to see that H and I cannot be a pair in the same group.

Question 3

The correct answer is choice **b**. If exactly three detectives are assigned to the Brentwood case, then we have exactly one detective assigned to the Appleby case. Since the IJ block is comprised of two detectives, we know that block has to be assigned to the Brentwood case. This forces H over to the Appleby case, by the first restriction. This is choice **b**.

Question 4

The correct answer is choice **e**. If XY is assigned to A, then we know we are in S1 (because in S2, Y is assigned to B). Now, since XY is assigned to A, Z will be assigned to B (since we need at least one agent assigned to case B). By the contrapositive of the third restriction, K must be assigned to B, since X is in A, and we have:

S1
     A   B
$\underline{X}$ $\underline{Y}$ $\underline{I}$ $\underline{J}$ $\underline{Z}$ $\underline{H}$ $\underline{K}$
a a d d   a d d

The only item not true among the answer choices is that K is assigned to the Appleby case (since it is assigned to Brentwood case).

We could also get the answer choice without the initial scenario diagrams by seeing what follows from X and Y being in A. Since X is in A, K is in B (contrapositive of the third restriction). Since Y is in A, I is in A (fourth restriction). Since I is in A, J is in A (second restriction). Since I is in A, H is in B (first restriction). Finally, since we need at least one agent in B (and we only have two detectives at the moment), Z must go into B:

A   B

X̲ Y̲ I̲ J̲ K̲ H̲ Z̲

Question 5

The correct answer is choice **a**. First, figure out the fewest number of officers possible in Brentwood. Consulting our two scenario diagrams, the fewest number of officers will be in scenario 1, since scenario 2 guarantees Brentwood at least three officers. And in S1, H is the only officer definitely assigned to Brentwood.

Matching Games Review

In a matching game, you are given a group of entities to be matched with members of another group of entities or with some set of characteristics. The entities can be persons, places, or things, and the characteristics can be anything from shape to color to location. For example, it may be a league of soccer teams (a group of entities) assigned to wear different jersey colors (a set of characteristics).

Matching games present us with a lot of information. In sequencing, selection, or distribution games, there is usually only one set of entities to worry about—what we have been calling the domain—and the relationships between those entities, be it the order of their placement or how they are separated into groups). In matching games, however, we determine the relationships between members of two groups (e.g., students and advisors), or we determine which possible characteristics apply to each member of a group (e.g., for a set of flights, which are bound for either Chicago or Boston, and whether it's a morning, evening, or late-night departure).

For this reason, the key to mastering games is the organization of the information—and in particular, how well you can create a visual representation of the possible assignments of entities to entities or entities to characteristics. The kind of diagram you will use depends on the matching game you are working with. Think of matching games as providing you with a number of groups. Groups of two can consist of two entities (e.g., students and advisors) or an entity and a characteristic (e.g., cars and their colors). The groups of three or more usually consist of an entity and sets of characteristics (e.g., flights and their destination city and departure time).

Matching with Two Groups

If you have a game with just two groups, there are two approaches you could take—the column or the grid. In the column approach, you simply put each member of a group into a column, under which you enter the members of the other group or the assigned characteristics. For example, say you are matching students (A, B, C, D) to advisors (E, F, G, H), and are told that student A is assigned to advisors F and G, and student C does not have advisor E:

A	B	C	D
F G		E	

This diagram should remind you of our distribution diagrams. In a sense, we are distributing advisors into four groups, each group corresponding to a student. Of course, this is a distribution where there may be repeats in the groups (e.g., an advisor might advise more than one student).

In the grid approach, you draw a grid with all the members of one group across the top and all the members of the other group (or all the possible characteristics) down the side. Each box will either have a check mark, indicating a match; an ✗, indicating no match; or a blank, indicating a match is yet to be or cannot be determined. Using the student-advisor matching example from above, you could draw:

	A	B	C	D
E			✗	
F	✓			
G	✓			
H				

Or, if we were matching cars to colors:

	Car 1	Car 2	Car 3	Car 4
Red				
Blue				
Green				

Columns vs. Grids

One advantage of the column approach is that you can easily keep track of matching scenarios that work. You do not have to recreate your diagram for each new question. You simply draw a line and start a new distribution:

A	B	C	D
F G		E	
G	EF	HE	G

In addition, the column approach is often sufficient if each entity of the primary group can be matched to only one entity in the secondary group: For example, if each student can have only one advisor.

The grid approach does not allow you to easily create fresh game scenarios (e.g., when a question asks you to make a new supposition). You either have to re-draw the grid for a new game scenario, or very lightly mark the boxes in your grid and erase them as you move to a new question or scenario.

However, the grid is often extremely useful for visualizing key relationships that drive the game, especially when each primary entity can be matched to more than one secondary entity. You should experiment with both approaches for various types of questions to see which suits you better. This book usually uses the grid for its ease of demonstrating logical relationships and the application of game rules. But if you find that you can easily manage the logical relationships, it might save you more time to use the column approach.

Matching with Three or More Groups

When there are three or more groups, you again have a couple of options. First, you could draw a grid with all the entities of one group across the top, and just one row for each set of characteristics down the side. For example, if we had four flights, and had to determine for each whether it was headed for Chicago or Boston, and whether it departed in the morning, evening, or night:

	Flight 1	Flight 2	Flight 3	Flight 4
C/B				
m/e/n				

Notice that in this game, each box will have only one letter—in the top row, C or B for Chicago or Boston, and in the bottom row, m, e, or n for morning, evening, or night. Each flight can be headed for only one city and can be assigned to depart only at one time. This is indicated by the slashes. You should also keep track of what assignments aren't possible by entering a letter into a box and crossing it out.

In other games, we might have a set of characteristics that apply to a given group of entities. For example, we might have a group of four cars, and a set of three custom options for the car—spoiler, fog lamps, and performance tires—any number of which could apply to any given car. The game might specify, in addition, that each of the four cars is a Ford, Dodge, or Chevy. We might draw the following grid:

	Car 1	Car 2	Car 3	Car 4
s f p				
F/D/C				

Notice that we used slashes to indicate that only one of the three letters F, D, and C could apply to a

given car. But we take the slashes out to indicate that any number of the letters s, f, and p could apply to a given car.

We might also create a grid in which a characteristic set (in this case, the custom options) is expanded so each member of that set gets a dedicated row. In addition, if a question tells us that Car 1 is a Ford with fog lamps and performance tires and Car 3 is a Dodge that definitely lacks a spoiler, we would have a grid that looks like this:

	Car 1	Car 2	Car 3	Car 4
s			✗	
f	✓			
p	✓			
F/D/C	F		D	

It is usually a good idea to expand all characteristic sets that can be applied to more than once to a given entity in order to better visualize the matching that occurs. When the characteristic can apply only once, it is often enough to use a single row for all (as we did with the car make).

Working with Matching Rules

There are six basic kinds of rules you will encounter in matching games. Many of the rules will allow symbolization that works in concert with your diagram.

Concrete Matches

The simplest rules tell you that a particular entity is matched with another particular entity or characteristic. For example, "Car 1 is a Ford with fog lamps and performance tires." On grids, simply enter a check mark into the appropriate box. If using the column approach, just write in the letter for the characteristic(s) into the appropriate column.

Conditional Matches

Matching games sometimes present rules that take the form of conditional statements—but the components of these conditional statements are usually concrete matches. For example, you may be told that "if Car 1 has fog lamps, then Car 2 must have performance tires and a spoiler." These rules are symbolized in the usual way:

$$1 = f \rightarrow 2 = p, s$$

If you have a grid, they can also be symbolized by drawing directly into the grid:

	Car 1	Car 2	Car 3	Car 4
s				
f				
p				
F/D/C				

This shows that a check mark in 1-f requires checkmarks in both 2-s and 2-p, and that an ✗ in either 2-s or 2-p requires an ✗ in 1-f (the contrapositive).

Restricted Matches

Restricted matches are simply negative statements—a given entity definitely does NOT have a certain characteristic, or that a given entity is definitely NOT matched with another entity. For example, "Car 3 does not have a spoiler." For grids, this information is captured by an ✗ in the appropriate box. For the column approach, the symbolization is a crossed-out letter in the appropriate column.

Matching Numbers

Rules that deal with matching numbers are probably the most important of matching games. These rules take various forms. You might be told that "Car 2 has at least two custom options" or that "exactly three cars have fog lamps." This sort of information can be written next to the appropriate column or rows in order to remind you how many in that column or row are to be selected. With these two rules as examples:

	Car 1	Car 2	Car 3	Car 4	
s					
f					exactly 3
p					
F/D/C					

If you are using the column approach, it would be difficult to visually incorporate that Car 2 has "at least two" custom options. But you could incorporate the information that exactly three cars have the fog lamps by writing 3 fs next to the appropriate row:

	Car 1	Car 2	Car 3	Car 4	
s f p					f f f
F/D/C					

You would then cross out the f's as you enter them into the grid.

Similarities

A staple of the matching game is the rule that two entities or characteristics are to be similarly matched. For example, you might be told that any custom option on Car 1 will appear on Car 2 as well. Or you may be told that "the custom options on Car 1 and Car 3 are the same." Or you may be told that "any car that has fog lamps also has the performance tires." This is all crucial information for matching games. There is a particularly useful way for symbolizing these rules when using a grid: use arrows to indicate the direction of similarity. Here are the symbolizations for the example rules just presented:

Any custom option on Car 1 will appear on Car 2 as well.

Car 1 → Car 2

The contrapositive: not Car 2 → not Car 1

The custom options on Car 1 and Car 3 are the same.

Car 1 ⟷ Car 3

Any car that has fog lamps also has the performance tires.

f
↓
p

The direction of the arrows is important. Each symbol is meant to remind us that if a check mark appears in a box associated with a letter or symbol ('Car 1' or 'f'), a check mark must appear in the box associated with the other letter or symbol. As with conditional matches, these symbolizations are a visual aid for seeing how filling in one box may affect another box. This is especially apparent if we write the symbolizations directly into the diagram. For example, if we put a check mark to indicate that Car 2 has a fog lamp, we are reminded by the downward arrow to put a check mark indicating that Car 2 has performance tires:

	Car 1	Car 2	Car 3	Car 4	
s					
f		✓			exactly 3
p		✓			
F/D/C					

If it is not possible to draw arrows directly into the diagram, then draw the full symbolizations (arrows plus letters) in such a way as to best remind you of the way matching flows through the diagram.

Again, be sure to remember how the contrapositive works as well. If a box at the end of an arrow gets an ✗, then so does the box at the beginning of the arrow. If Car 2 does not have performance tires, then it cannot have fog lamps.

Differences

Another staple of the matching game is the rules that two entities or characteristics are not similarly matched. For example, you might be told that "Car 2 does not have any custom option that Car 1 has." And you may be told that "no car can have both a spoiler and performance tires." Or that "any car with a spoiler does not have performance tires." Notice that these last two rules are equivalent. They both mean that 1) if a car has a spoiler, it does not have performance tires, and 2) if a car has performance tires, it does not have a spoiler.

You can symbolize these rules as:

s → ≠ p

p → ≠ s

Sometimes, these "difference rules" can also be symbolized by a double arrow with an ✗ in the middle—any check mark one side of the arrow leads to an ✗ on the other side of the arrow. Keep in mind that this does not mean that an ✗ on one side leads to a check mark on the other. According to the rule that "no car can have both a spoiler and performance tires," it's clearly perfectly possible for a car to have neither a spoiler nor performance tires. And keep in mind that this does not mean that an ✗ on one side leads to an ✗ on the other. It's possible that a car with no performance tires still has a spoiler. These symbolizations would look like:

	Car 1	Car 2	Car 3	Car 4	
s					
f					
p					
F/D/C					

So if we are told that Car 1 has a spoiler, and we put a check mark in the appropriate box, the difference arrows immediately indicate that we need to put ✗s in certain boxes—Car 1 does not have performance tires, and car 2 does not have a spoiler:

		Car 1	Car 2	Car 3	Car 4	
s		✓	✗			
f						
p		✗				
F/D/C						

If you do not find this symbolization helpful, just stick to the regular conditional symbolizations.

Practice Game 1

Six philosophy professors—Albert, Friedman, Godfrey-Smith, Lipton, Pauly, and Varzi—each specialize in one or more areas—logic, metaphysics, and science. They are specialized according to the following conditions:

Lipton does not specialize in any area in which Varzi specializes.
Varzi specializes in logic and metaphysics.
Varzi specializes in more areas than Pauly.
Exactly three professors specialize in metaphysics.
Albert, Godfrey-Smith, and exactly two other professors specialize in science.
Pauly and Friedman share exactly one area of specialization.

1. If Albert and Friedman specialize in exactly the same areas, then each of the following statements must be true EXCEPT:
   a. Albert specializes in metaphysics.
   b. Godfrey-Smith specializes in logic.
   c. Friedman specializes in science.
   d. Lipton specializes in science.
   e. Pauly specializes in logic.

2. Which one of the following statements must be true?
   a. Pauly specializes in metaphysics.
   b. Pauly specializes in science.
   c. Albert specializes in logic.
   d. Friedman specializes in metaphysics.
   e. Friedman specializes in science.

3. If Godfrey-Smith specializes in every area in which Pauly specializes, then which one of the following statements CANNOT be true?
   a. Pauly specializes in metaphysics.
   b. Pauly specializes in logic.
   c. Godfrey-Smith specializes in metaphysics.
   d. Friedman specializes in metaphysics.
   e. Albert specializes in metaphysics.

4. Which one of the following could be a partial, accurate list of professors all of whom specialize in metaphysics?
   a. Albert, Friedman
   b. Albert, Pauly
   c. Godfrey-Smith, Pauly
   d. Albert, Lipton
   e. Albert, Friedman, Godfrey-Smith

5. If every professor who specializes in logic also specializes in metaphysics, then for how many professors are the areas of specialization fully determined?
   a. Two
   b. Three
   c. Four
   d. Five
   e. Six

Practice Game 2

A middle school computer lab receives six new computers, labeled 1 through 6, each with at least one of three programs installed on it—a math program, a reading program, and a writing program. The programs are installed according to the following conditions:

Computer 2 has the math and reading programs installed.

Computer 4 has neither the math nor writing programs installed.

Computer 5 has exactly one fewer program installed than computer 6, and does not have the writing program installed.

Computer 2 and computer 5 have exactly two programs in common.

Any computer with the writing program installed also has the reading program installed.

1. For exactly how many of the computers can it be determined exactly how many programs are installed?
   a. One
   b. Two
   c. Three
   d. Four
   e. Five

2. If the reading program is installed on exactly four computers, then each of the following must be true EXCEPT:
   a. Computer 1 has the math program.
   b. Computer 3 has the math program.
   c. Computer 3 does not have the reading program.
   d. Computer 2 does not have the writing program.
   e. Computer 1 does not have the writing program.

3. Suppose only two computers have exactly the same set of programs installed. Which one of the following statements CANNOT be true?
   a. Computer 1 has both the math and writing program.
   b. Computer 1 has both the reading and writing program.
   c. Computer 3 has both the reading and writing program.
   d. Computer 2 has both the math and writing program.
   e. Computer 3 has only the math program.

4. If at least two computers have the writing program installed, then what is the least number of computers that must have the reading program installed?
   a. One
   b. Two
   c. Three
   d. Four
   e. Five

5. Which one of the following statements must be false?
   a. Exactly four computers have the writing program.
   b. Exactly five computers have the writing program.
   c. Exactly four computers have the reading program.
   d. Exactly five computers have the reading program.
   e. Exactly five computers have the math program.

Practice Game 3

At a wedding, each of five entree options—chicken, beef, pork, fish, and vegetarian—comes with at least one side—rice, salad, or bread—according to the following restrictions:

The chicken comes with exactly one more side than the beef.
The fish comes with exactly one fewer side than the beef.
The pork comes with salad.
The pork and beef share no sides.
At least three and at most four entrees come with bread.

1. For exactly how many of the entrees can it be determined exactly how many sides each entrée comes with?
   a. One
   b. Two
   c. Three
   d. Four
   e. Five

2. If the vegetarian entrée comes with fewer sides than the beef, then how many entrees come with exactly two sides?
   a. One
   b. Two
   c. Three
   d. Four
   e. Five

3. If there are more entrees that come with rice than entrées that come with bread and entrees that come with salad, then each of the following statements must be true EXCEPT:
   a. The fish does not come with bread.
   b. The fish does not come with salad.
   c. The vegetarian entrée comes with salad.
   d. The vegetarian entrée comes with rice.
   e. The vegetarian entrée comes with bread.

4. If the fish comes with salad, then which one of the following statements must be true?
   a. The vegetarian entrée comes with salad.
   b. The vegetarian entrée comes with bread.
   c. The vegetarian entrée comes with rice.
   d. The vegetarian entrée does not come with bread.
   e. The vegetarian entrée does not come with rice.

5. If every side that comes with the vegetarian entrée also comes with the fish, then which one of the followings statements CANNOT be true?
   a. The vegetarian entree comes with exactly one side.
   b. The beef entree comes with exactly two sides.
   c. Exactly two entrees come with salad.
   d. Exactly three entrees come with salad.
   e. Exactly two entrees come with rice.

Practice Game 4

Four friends—Ross, Siddarth, Alex, and Josh—go for an adventure hike in the mountains of Scotland. Each brings a backpack with at least one of the following items: compass, extra socks, knife, and map. At least one of each item is brought on the trip. The contents of their backpacks are subject to the following restrictions:

Ross brings exactly one item.
Alex brings exactly two items.
Exactly three of the friends bring a map.
Alex does not bring every item that Siddarth brings.
Josh brings every item that Alex brings.
Anybody who brings a compass brings a map.

1. Which one of the following statements must be true?
   a. Ross does not bring extra socks.
   b. Alex does not bring extra socks.
   c. Siddarth does not bring extra socks.
   d. Josh does not bring extra socks.
   e. Josh does not bring a knife.

2. If Siddarth brings a map, then which one of the following statements CANNOT be true?
   a. Siddarth brings a compass.
   b. Siddarth brings extra socks.
   c. Alex brings extra socks.
   d. Alex brings a knife.
   e. Josh brings a compass.

3. If Alex brings a compass, then which one of the following statements could be true?
   a. Siddarth brings a compass.
   b. Siddarth brings a map.
   c. Alex brings extra socks.
   d. Josh does not bring a map.
   e. Josh brings extra socks.

4. Which one of the following statements CANNOT be true?
   a. Siddarth brings exactly one item.
   b. Siddarth brings exactly two items.
   c. Josh brings exactly one item.
   d. Josh brings exactly two items.
   e. Josh brings exactly three items.

5. If the number of backpacks containing a compass exceeds the number of backpacks containing a knife, then each of the following could be a complete and accurate list of those friends bringing extra socks EXCEPT:
   a. Josh
   b. Siddarth
   c. Alex, Josh
   d. Siddarth, Josh
   e. Alex, Siddarth

Practice Game 5

A car dealer sells four cars, labeled 1 through 4. Each car is made by one of Ford, Dodge, or Chevy. Each car comes equipped with at least one of the following three options: spoiler, fog lights, and performance tires. The cars meet the following restrictions:

Only Ford cars can have fog lights.
Car 2 has more options than car 3.
Exactly two cars have fog lights.
Car 2 is a Dodge.
Car 4 has no spoiler.

1. Which one of the following statements CAN-NOT be true?
   a. Every car with a spoiler has fog lights.
   b. Every car with a spoiler has performance tires.
   c. Every car with fog lights has performance tires.
   d. Every car with performance tires has a spoiler.
   e. All but one car with performance tires has fog lights.

2. If Car 1 is a Chevy, then which one of the following statements could be true?
   a. Car 1 has fog lights.
   b. Car 3 has performance tires.
   c. Car 3 does not have fog lights.
   d. Car 4 has performance tires.
   e. Car 4 does not have fog lights.

3. Which one of the following statements CAN-NOT be true?
   a. There are more Dodges than Chevys.
   b. There are an equal number of Dodges and Chevys.
   c. There are more Dodges than Fords.
   d. There are more Fords than Dodges.
   e. There are an equal number of Dodges and Fords.

4. If car 4 is a Dodge, then which one of the following statements could be true?
   a. Every car with performance tires has a spoiler.
   b. Every car with fog lights has a spoiler.
   c. Every car with a spoiler has fog lights.
   d. Every car with performance tires has fog lights.
   e. Every car with a spoiler has performance tires.

5. If exactly three cars have spoilers, then which one of the following statements CANNOT be true?
   a. Car 1 has exactly one option.
   b. Car 1 has exactly two options.
   c. Car 1 has exactly three options.
   d. Car 4 has exactly one option.
   e. Car 4 has exactly two options.

Practice Game 6

A street has six buildings numbered 1 to 6, three on one side and three on the other, in the following arrangement:

1   2   3

4   5   6

Each building contains a law firm, a bank, or both and each building is either a modern or historical building, but not both. The following conditions apply:

Each historical building is directly next to another historical building on the same side of the street.
Each law firm is directly across the street from a bank.
Building 3 is historical.
Building 2 contains a law firm.
Building 4 is modern.

1. If every bank is located in a historical building, then which one of the following statements MUST be true?
   a. Building 2 contains a bank.
   b. Building 3 contains a law firm.
   c. Building 1 is historical.
   d. Building 5 is modern.
   e. Building 6 contains a bank.

2. If exactly three of the six buildings are modern, then which one of the following statements must be true?
   a. At least one bank is located in a historical building.
   b. At least one bank is located in a modern building.
   c. At least one law firm is located in a modern building.
   d. Exactly one bank is located in a historical building.
   e. Exactly one bank is located in a modern building.

3. If every bank is located in a modern building, then what is the maximum number of modern buildings that contain only law firms?
   a. Zero
   b. One
   c. Two
   d. Three
   e. Four

4. If every historical building contains only a law firm, then which one of the following statements must be true?
   a. Building 4 is modern and contains a bank.
   b. Building 4 is modern and contains a law firm.
   c. Building 5 is modern and contains both a bank and law firm.
   d. Building 6 is modern and contains a bank.
   e. Building 6 is modern and contains both a bank and law firm.

5. Which one of the following statements CANNOT be true?
   a. Building 6 is modern and building 5 is historical.
   b. Both buildings 1 and 4 are modern.
   c. Building 3 is historical and building 4 is modern.
   d. Building 4 is modern and building 5 is historical.
   e. Both buildings 5 and 6 are historical.

Practice Game 7

Six skydivers—three male (A, B, and C) and three female (D, E, and F)—each deploy a parachute in exactly one of four colors: red, green, orange, or purple. The parachute colors meet the following restrictions:

No two males deploy the same color parachute, and no two females deploy the same color parachute.

A has a green parachute.

D's parachute is neither orange nor purple.

If B has a red or orange parachute, then E has a green parachute.

Exactly two parachutes are orange.

1. Which one of the following statements CAN-NOT be true?
   a. Both B and D have a red parachute.
   b. C has a red parachute and F has a green parachute.
   c. C has a purple parachute and E has a green parachute.
   d. E has a purple parachute and F has an orange parachute.
   e. E has an orange parachute and F has a purple parachute.

2. If E has a red parachute, then which one of the following statements must be true?
   a. There are exactly two purple parachutes.
   b. There are exactly two red parachutes.
   c. There are exactly two green parachutes.
   d. There is exactly one green parachute.
   e. There are no red parachutes.

3. If B and E have the same color parachute, then which one of the following statements CAN-NOT be true?
   a. F has a green parachute.
   b. D has a red parachute.
   c. D has a green parachute.
   d. C has an orange parachute.
   e. B has a purple parachute.

4. If there is exactly one green parachute, then which one of the following is a complete and accurate list of the colors any one of which could be the color of F's parachute?
   a. Orange
   b. Purple
   c. Red
   d. Orange, red
   e. Orange, purple

5. If C's parachute is purple, then for exactly how many of the six skydivers is the color of his or her parachute determined?
   a. Two
   b. Three
   c. Four
   d. Five
   e. Six

Practice Game 8

Five whiskey critics—H, I, J, K and L—are each to taste at least one of the following three scotches: Talkisker, Glenfiddich, and Macallan. They taste according to the following restrictions:

H tastes the Talisker and the Macallan.
H tastes fewer scotches than K.
Exactly three critics taste the Talisker.
If I tastes the Macallan, then J tastes both the Talisker and the Glenfiddich.
There are no scotches L tastes that I does not taste.

1. For exactly how many of the critics can it be determined exactly which scotches he or she tastes?
   a. One
   b. Two
   c. Three
   d. Four
   e. Five

2. If L tastes the Macallan, then each of the following statements could be true EXCEPT:
   a. I tastes the Glenfiddich.
   b. I tastes the Talkisker.
   c. J tastes the Talkisker.
   d. J tastes the Macallan.
   e. L tastes the Glenfiddich.

3. If exactly two critics taste the Glenfiddich, then each of the following must be true EXCEPT:
   a. I tastes the Macallan.
   b. J tastes the Glenfiddich.
   c. J tastes the Talikser.
   d. J tastes the Macallan.
   e. L tastes the Macallan.

4. If I tastes the Talikser, then each of the following statements could be true EXCEPT:
   a. I tastes the Macallan.
   b. I tastes the Glednfiddich.
   c. J tastes the Glenfiddich.
   d. J tastes the Macallan.
   e. L tastes the Glenfiddich.

5. If every critic who tastes the Glenfiddich also tastes the Talisker, then for exactly how many of the critics can it be determined exactly which scotches he or she tastes?
   a. One
   b. Two
   c. Three
   d. Four
   e. Five

Setup, Answers, and Explanations

Practice Game 1

We have six professors—A, F, G, L, P, V—each of whom will be assigned one to three specialties—l, m, and s. The matching can be done in a grid:

	A	F	G	L	P	V
l						
m						
s						

Now symbolize the restrictions and work them into the diagram.

The first restriction is that L and V share no specialties:

$$L \leftarrow \text{✗} \rightarrow V$$

(We would draw this into the diagram, but we are about to see that we can fully determine L and V.)

The second is concrete information that V specializes in l and m. We can immediately apply the first restriction to see that L does not specialize in l or m. So L must specialize in s; and since s specializes in s, V cannot specialize in s. So we have:

	A	F	G	L	P	V
l				✗		✓
m				✗		✓
s				✓		✗

The third restriction is that V has more specialties than P. Since V has exactly two specialties, this means that P has exactly one specialty. The fourth restriction is that exactly three professors specialize in metaphysics. The fifth is that G and A specialize in science and that exactly four professors in total specialize in science. We can work this information into the diagram:

	A	F	G	L	P	V
l				✗		✓
m (ex. 3)				✗		✓
s (ex. 4)	✓		✓	✓		✗

(ex. 1)

The sixth restriction is that P shares exactly one specialty with F. Since P has exactly one specialty, this means that we can draw an arrow from P to F: any specialty that P has, F will have. (Note: this does not mean that F will have only one specialty).

So we have:

	A	F	G	L	P	V
l				✗		✓
m (ex. 3)				✗		✓
s (ex. 4)	✓		✓	✓		✗

(ex. 1)

Now, see if any other deductions can be made. We know that exactly four professors specialize in science and we have identified three of them. Can we identify the fourth? If we check P's s-box, then we will have to check F's s-box as well—that is, if P specializes in s, then F must specialize in s. But then we will have exactly 5 professors specializing in science. So P can't specialize in s, meaning that F must specialize in s, yielding:

	A	F	G	L	P	V
l				✗		✓
m (ex. 3)				✗		✓
s	✓	✓	✓	✓	✗	✗

(ex. 1)

No other deductions seem obvious, so we can move on to the questions.

Question 1

The correct answer is choice **b**. We start by seeing what deductions follow from the new information, which can be symbolized A ↔ F, and entered into the diagram as follows:

	A	F	G	L	P	V
l				✗		✓
m (ex. 3)				✗		✓
s	✓	✓	✓	✓	✗	✗

(ex. 1)

By looking at the diagram, the way the arrows work together should help us realize that whatever P specializes in, F and A will specialize in them as well. This means that if P specializes in m, so will F and A. But that would mean that at least four professors specialize in m, contradicting the fourth restriction (written into our diagram, that row m has exactly three, not four, check marks). So we know that P does not specialize in m, meaning that P specializes in l. According to the arrows, p specializing in l means s that F and A will specialize in l.

So we have:

	A	F	G	L	P	V
l	✓	✓		✗	✓	✓
m (ex. 3)				✗	✗	✓
s	✓	✓	✓	✓	✗	✗

Now, what further deductions can be made? We only have three boxes left for row m, from which two must have check marks (since exactly three must have check marks, and one check mark already appears under V). Could G have a check mark? If it did, then to keep exactly three check marks for row m, one of A and F must have a check mark, and the other would have an ✗—but the bidirectional arrow between A and F would prevent this.

In other words, G can't specialize in m, because then we would either have just two professors (V and G) specializing in m, or else four professors (A, F, V, and G) specializing in m. So G cannot specialize in m, meaning that A and F must specialize in m:

	A	F	G	L	P	V
l	✓	✓		✗	✓	✓
m (ex. 3)	✓	✓	✗	✗	✗	✓
s	✓	✓	✓	✓	✗	✗

G may or may not specialize in l.

Now compare the answer choices against the diagram. All but **b** must be true (we cannot deduce that G specializes in logic, nor that G does not specialize in logic)—so **b** is the correct answer.

Question 2

The correct answer is choice **e**. Compare the answer choices to the initial diagram.

	A	F	G	L	P	V
l				✗		✓
m (ex. 3)				✗		✓
s	✓	✓	✓	✓	✗	✗

(ex. 1)

The only thing appearing on that diagram is that F specializes in s.

Question 3

The correct answer is choice **a**. Start by seeing what follows from the new information that G specializes in every area in which P specializes—that is, that P → G, entered into the diagram as follows:

	A	F	G	L	P	V
l				✗		✓
m (ex. 3)				✗		✓
s	✓	✓	✓	✓	✗	✗

(ex. 1)

The arrows taken together mean that whatever P specializes in, both F and G must specialize in. So if P specializes in m, then F and G must, meaning that at least four professors specialize in m. So P cannot specialize in m, meaning that P specializes in l and that G and F also, therefore:

	A	F	G	L	P	V
l		✓	✓	✗	✓	✓
m (ex. 3)				✗	✗	✓
s	✓	✓	✓	✓	✗	✗

(ex. 1)

Now compare the answer choices to this diagram. Since P cannot specialize in m, choice **a** must be the correct answer.

Question 4

The correct answer is choice **a**. Notice that we are looking for a partial, accurate list of professors all of whom specialize in m. In other words, the correct answer choice will be all or part of a list which could be a list of all and only those professors who specialize in metaphysics. If an answer choice includes a professor who could not specialize in m, it would be incorrect. That rules out choice **d**, since L does not specialize in metaphysics.

	A	F	G	L	P	V
l				✗		✓
m (ex. 3)				✗		✓
s	✓	✓	✓	✓	✗	✗

(ex. 1)

And if an answer choice includes a set of professors who couldn't all specialize in metaphysics at the same time, then that answer choice is incorrect. Choice **b** is incorrect because if P specializes in m, then so does F. Then we would have A, P, F, and V specializing in m, violating the fourth restriction.

Choice **c** is incorrect for a similar reason—we would have G, P, F, and V specializing in m. Choice **e** is incorrect because we would have A, F, G, and V specializing in m, again violating the fourth restriction.

Choice **a** is correct because we could have A, F, and V specializing in m, while G, L, and P do not specialize in m.

Question 5

The correct answer is choice **d**. Start by seeing what follows from the new information, that if a professor specializes in l, that professor also specializes in m:

l
↓
m

We could incorporate this into the diagram:

	A	F	G	L	P	V
l				✗		✓
m (ex. 3)				✗		✓
s	✓	✓	✓	✓	✗	✗

(ex. 1)

By now, we should have an inkling that trying to work out P's specialties will be helpful. Given the new information, P cannot specialize in l, since P would then also specialize in m (and P is limited to one specialty). So P must specialize in m, meaning that F also specializes in m:

	A	F	G	L	P	V
l				✗	✗	✓
m (ex. 3)		✓		✗	✓	✓
s	✓	✓	✓	✓	✗	✗

Note that we now have all three check marks we need in row m, so we can finish row m:

	A	F	G	L	P	V
l				✗	✗	✓
m (ex. 3)	✗	✓	✗	✗	✓	✓
s	✓	✓	✓	✓	✗	✗

Now remember what the ✗ at the end of an arrow means—that there must be an ✗ at the beginning of that arrow (since if there was a check mark at the beginning of the arrow, there must be a check mark at the end of the arrow; this is essentially an application of the contrapositive). So, A and G must not specialize in l:

	A	F	G	L	P	V
l	✗		✗	✗	✗	✓
m (ex. 3)	✗	✓	✗	✗	✓	✓
s	✓	✓	✓	✓	✗	✗

F could either specialize in l, or not specialize in l without violating any restrictions.

This means that five professors—A, G, L, P, and V—have their specialties fully determined. This is choice **d**.

Practice Game 2

We have six computers: 1, 2, 3, 4, 5, and 6—each of which will have one to three of the following programs installed: m, r, w. The matching can be done in a grid:

	1	2	3	4	5	6
m						
r						
w						

Now symbolize the restrictions and work them into the diagram.

The first restriction tells us that 2 will have m and r. The second tells us that 4 will not have m or w, and must therefore have r:

	1	2	3	4	5	6
m		✓		✗		
r		✓		✓		
w				✗		

The third restriction tells us that 6 has exactly one more program than 5, meaning that either 5 has one program and 6 has two, or 5 has two and 6 has three. The fourth restriction settles this for us; since computers 5 and 2 have exactly two programs in common, computer 5 must have two programs (and so computer 6 has three). Furthermore, since according to the third restriction, 5 cannot have w, those two programs must be m and r. So we have:

	1	2	3	4	5	6
m		✓		✗	✓	✓
r		✓		✓	✓	✓
w				✗	✗	✓

Finally, the fifth restriction tells us that if a computer has the writing program, it also has the reading program. This can be symbolized as:

r
↑
w

The contrapositive is:

≠ r
↓
≠ w

We can draw the arrow directly into the diagram:

	1	2	3	4	5	6
m		✓		✗	✓	✓
r	↑	✓		✓	✓	✓
w				✗	✗	✓

All the information from the restrictions has been captured in this diagram, and we can now just refer to this diagram as we tackle the questions.

Question 1

The correct answer is choice **c**. The work here is pretty much done already. Consulting the diagram, we see that three computers—3, 4, and 5—are fully determined on the grid, and three—1, 2, and 3—are not. This is choice **c**. To double-check this, see if you can put checks and ✗'s into each of the columns for 1, 2, and 3, without violating the restrictions. For example, imagine putting a check into m1, m3, and w2, and then an ✗ into the same—no matter what, as long as the arrow from w to r is satisfied, either one (checks into all three and ✗'s into all three) lead to acceptable tables—note that as long as each computer has at least 1 check mark, and the arrow is satisfied, all the restrictions of the game are satisfied (because they are all built into this diagram already).

Question 2

The correct answer is choice **d**. Consider the diagram. If the reading program is installed on exactly four computers, then we can cross out the r-box for 1 and 3. And if we do this, because of the arrow, we can cross out the w-box for 1 and 3 as well. And if we do this, that leaves the m-box for 1 and 3 to be checked (since each computer must have at least one program.

This leaves us with:

	1	2	3	4	5	6
m	✓	✓	✓	✗	✓	✓
r	↑ ✗	✓	✗	✓	✓	✓
w	✗		✗	✗	✗	✓

The only answer choice not given in this diagram is that computer 2 does not have a writing program; it is left undetermined whether computer 2 has a writing program. So the correct answer is **c**.

Question 3

The correct answer is choice **a**. Start by consulting the diagram to see what the new information means.

	1	2	3	4	5	6
m		✓		✗	✓	✓
r	↑		✓		✓	✓	✓
w				✗	✗	✓

Since only two computers can have exactly the same set of programs, every column must be different from every other column (when fully determined with ✗'s and check marks), save for one set of two columns. 4, 5, and 6 are set already. What about column 2? Column 2 can either have an ✗ in the W-box or a check in the W-box. Either way, it will be identical with either column 5 or column 6. Therefore, columns 1 and 3 need to be different from all of the other columns and also need to be different from each other. Now we need to figure out what can go into columns 1 and 3. We have three of the seven vertical patterns instantiated in 4, 5, and 6:

$$
\begin{array}{ccc}
✗ & ✓ & ✓ \\
✓ & ✓ & ✓ \\
✗ & ✗ & ✓
\end{array}
$$

The remaining four possible patterns are:

✗	✓	✓	✗
✗	✗	✗	✓
✓	✗	✓	✓

But notice that the first and third patterns violate the arrow—the w-box would be checked while the r-box is ✗'d. So we only have the following patterns which are to describe columns 1 and 3 (one pattern each):

✓	✗
✗	✓
✗	✓

Now compare each answer choice to this set. In either case, computer 1 (as well as computer 3) cannot have both a math and writing program (check marks in the top and bottom row). This is choice **a**. Computer 1 could have the right-hand pattern, making **b** incorrect. Computer 3 could have the right-hand pattern, making **c** incorrect. Computer 2 could have a check mark in the writing-box, making **d** incorrect. Computer 3 could have the left-hand configuration, making **e** incorrect.

Question 4

The correct answer is choice **d**. Consult the diagram.

	1	2	3	4	5	6
m		✓		✗	✓	✓
r		✓		✓	✓	✓
w				✗	✗	✓

We want to enter at least one more check mark into the w-row, and see what the least number of check marks in the r-row there could be. If we enter a check mark into w1 or w3, then the arrow indicates that we would have a check mark in r1 or r3, respectively. This would produce at least five check marks in row r. But if we put a check mark in w2, and no other box in the w-row, then we would only have to produce a check mark in r2, where there is already a check mark.

Therefore, it is possible to have only four check marks in row r, and the correct answer is four, choice **d**.

Question 5

The correct answer is choice **b**. Compare each answer choice against our diagram. The diagram doesn't seem to prevent four computers from having the writing program—6 already has it, and it seems 1, 2, and 3 could have it. So **a** is incorrect. But since there are ✗-marks in two of the six w-boxes, it can't be that five computers have the writing program—so choice **b** is correct.

Practice Game 3

We have five entrees—C, B, P, F, V—each of which can come with one or more of three sides, salad (s), bread (b), or rice (r). The matching can be done in a grid:

	C	B	P	F	V
s					
b					
r					

Now symbolize the restrictions and work them into the diagram.

The first restriction is that C has exactly one more side than B. This means that either B has two sides and C has three, or B has one side and C has two. The second restriction says that F has exactly one less side than B. This means that either F has one side and B has two, or F has two sides and B has three. The only way these two restrictions can both be true is if B has two sides—meaning that C has three sides and F has one. So we have:

	C	B	P	F	V
s	✓				
b	✓				
r	✓				

ex. 2   ex. 1

The third restriction is that P comes with s. The fourth restriction is that P and B share no sides:

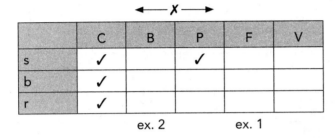

$$B \longleftarrow\!\!\!\!\textbf{\textit{X}}\!\!\!\!\longrightarrow P$$

So we have:

	C	B	P	F	V
s	✓		✓		
b	✓				
r	✓				

ex. 2   ex. 1

This means that an **X** must appear in the s-row under B: B does not come with s. However, we know that B must come with two sides, so we now know which sides B comes with: b and r. And since P and B share no sides, this means that P cannot come with b or r—so P must only come with s. So we have:

	C	B	P	F	V
s	✓	✗	✓		
b	✓	✓	✗		
r	✓	✓	✗		

ex. 1

Finally, the fifth restriction says that three or four entrees come with bread:

	C	B	P	F	V
s	✓	✗	✓		
b (3-4)	✓	✓	✗		
r	✓	✓	✗		

ex. 1

Question 1

The correct answer is choice **d**. According to the diagram, C, B, and P are fully determined with respect to the sides that accompany each. F and V are not determined. For example, F might come with salad, or not come with salad; and V might come with bread or not come with bread—and all these cases are compatible with the restrictions. So the correct answer is that the exact number of sides can be determined for three entrees (C, B, and P)—choice **c**.

Question 2

The correct answer is choice **a**. If the vegetarian entrée comes with fewer sides than the beef, then since the beef comes with two sides, the vegetarian entrée must come with one side. So we have:

	C	B	P	F	V
s	✓	✗	✓		
b (3-4)	✓	✓	✗		
r	✓	✓	✗		

ex. 1   ex. 1

We can see that C comes with three sides, and each of P, F, and V come with exactly 1 side. Only B comes with exactly two sides—so the correct answer is that one entrée comes with exactly two sides. This is choice **a**.

Question 3

The correct answer is choice **c**. If there are more entrees that come with rice than entrees that come with bread and entrees that come with salad, then since we know that the bread must come with at least three entrees, we know that the rice must come with four entrees (it cannot come with five entrees, since we know it does not come with the pork). Glancing at the diagram, this means that the rice must come with both the fish and vegetarian entrée. But then, since the fish comes with exactly one entrée, we know that the fish does not come with the salad or bread.

So we have:

	C	B	P	F	V
s	✓	✗	✓	✗	
b (3-4)	✓	✓	✗	✗	
r	✓	✓	✗	✓	✓

Finally, since we must have 3-4 check marks in the b-row, we see that the V must come with b:

	C	B	P	F	V
s	✓	✗	✓	✗	
b (3-4)	✓	✓	✗	✗	✓
r	✓	✓	✗	✓	✓

The only paring that is not given in this diagram is that V comes with s—and that is choice **c**.

Question 4

The correct answer is choice **b**. If F comes with s, then we know that F cannot come with b or r:

	C	B	P	F	V
s	✓	✗	✓	✓	
b (3-4)	✓	✓	✗	✗	
r	✓	✓	✗	✗	

ex. 1

But since we know that 3-4 check marks must appear in the b-row, this means that V must come with b:

	C	B	P	F	V
s	✓	✗	✓	✓	
b (3-4)	✓	✓	✗	✗	✓
r	✓	✓	✗	✗	

ex. 1

Among the answer choices, the only information that appears in this diagram is that V comes with b— answer choice **b**.

Question 5

The correct answer is choice **d**. We can symbolize the new information that every side that comes with the vegetarian entrée also comes with the fish as:

$V \rightarrow F$

Contrapositive: not $F \rightarrow$ not V

Or written into the diagram:

	C	B	P	F	V
s	✓	✗	✓		
b (3-4)	✓	✓	✗		
r	✓	✓	✗		

ex. 1

The arrow combined with the note that F has exactly one check mark should give us pause. Since every time we have a check mark under V, we must have a check mark in F, the arrow means that we can have at most one check mark under V (which means we have exactly one check mark under V, since every entrée has at least one side). Further, since there must be three to four checkmarks in row b, F must have a checkmark in row b—for if it didn't, then V couldn't have a checkmark in row b either, and we wouldn't have 3-4 checkmarks in row b. Since F must have exactly one checkmark, it must have ✗-marks in row s and row r—meaning that V must have ✗-marks in row s and row r, leaving a checkmark for V in row b:

	C	B	P	F	V
s	✓	✗	✓	✗	✗
b (3-4)	✓	✓	✗	✓	✓
r	✓	✓	✗	✗	✗

ex. 1   ex. 1

Choice **d** is the only answer choice inconsistent with this diagram—exactly two, not three, entrees come with salad.

Practice Game 4

We are asked to match each of four people—R, S, A, and J—to one or more of four items, c, e, k, m:

	R	S	A	J
c				
e				
k				
m				

The first, second, and third restrictions can be incorporated into the diagram:

	R	S	A	J
c				
e				
k				
m (ex. 3)				

ex. 1   ex. 2

The fourth restriction can be symbolized with a 'difference arrow':

	R	S	A	J
c				
e				
k				
m (ex. 3)				

ex. 1   ex. 2

← X →

It can also be symbolized with regular conditionals:

$$S \to \neq A$$
$$A \to \neq S \text{ [the contrapositive]}$$

The fifth and sixth restrictions can be symbolized with one-way similarity arrows:

	R	S	A	J
c				
e				
k				
m (ex. 3)				

ex. 1   ex. 2

← X →   →

The fifth restriction can also be symbolized with a regular conditional:

$$A \to J$$
$$\neq J \to \neq A \text{ [contrapositive]}$$

And the sixth restriction:

$$c \to m$$
$$\neq m \to \neq c$$

Now we make deductions. We see that row m will contain exactly three check marks. Since S and A have a difference arrow, it can't be that two of those three checkmarks are in the S-box and A-box. So at most one of those two will have a check mark in row m (in fact, exactly one of those two will have a check mark in row m). This means that both R and J must have a check mark in row m. Furthermore, since R has a check mark in row m, and since R only has one item, all the other boxes in R's column must be X's:

	R	S	A	J
c	X			
e	X			
k	X			
m (ex. 3)	✓			✓

ex. 2

← X →   →

Question 1

The correct answer is choice **a**. This is directly given in the diagram—according to the diagram, Ross does not bring extra socks.

Question 2

The correct answer is choice **b**. If S brings m, then since row m must have exactly three checkmarks, A does not bring m (this is also apparent from the difference arrow: A does not bring any item S brings):

	R	S	A	J
c	✗			
e	✗			
k	✗			
m (ex. 3)	✓	✓	✗	✓

ex. 2

← ✗ → ⟶

Glancing at the arrows, we see that since A does not bring m, he cannot have brought c either. This leaves A to bring e and k (since he must bring two items).

At this point, we have:

	R	S	A	J
c	✗		✗	
e	✗		✓	
k	✗		✓	
m (ex. 3)	✓	✓	✗	✓

ex. 2

← ✗ → ⟶

Glancing at the arrows again, we see that these two checkmarks, in kA and eA, lead us to put checkmarks in kJ and eJ, and ✗-marks in kS and eS. That is, we see that J must bring e and k, and S cannot bring either e or k:

	R	S	A	J
c	✗		✗	
e	✗	✗	✓	✓
k	✗	✗	✓	✓
m (ex. 3)	✓	✓	✗	✓

ex. 2

← ✗ → ⟶

Now we compare the answer choices against this diagram. According to the diagram, S may or may not bring c, so **a** is incorrect. S definitely does not bring e, so **b** is the correct answer. A in fact brings e and k, so **c** and **d** are incorrect, and J may or may not bring c, so **e** is incorrect.

Question 3

The correct answer is choice **e**. If A brings c then as the one-way arrows indicate, A brings m and J brings c:

	R	S	A	J
c	✗		✓	✓
e	✗			
k	✗			
m (ex. 3)	✓		✓	✓

ex. 2

← ✗ → ⟶

Since A must bring exactly two items, we have:

	R	S	A	J
c	✗		✓	✓
e	✗		✗	
k	✗		✗	
m (ex. 3)	✓		✓	✓

ex. 2

← ✗ → ⟶

And since whatever A has, S cannot (the difference arrow), we have:

	R	S	A	J
c	✗	✗	✓	✓
e	✗		✗	
k	✗		✗	
m (ex. 3)	✓	✗	✓	✓

ex. 2

← ✗ →　　→

Now compare the answer choices against this diagram. S brings neither c nor m, so choices **a** and **b** are incorrect. A does not bring e, so **c** is incorrect. J brings m, so **d** is incorrect. But J may or may not bring e, so choice **e** is correct.

Question 4

The correct answer is choice **c**. Consult the diagram:

	R	S	A	J
c	✗			
e	✗			
k	✗			
m (ex. 3)	✓			✓

ex. 2

← ✗ →　　→

Glance at each answer choice and compare it to the diagram to see if anything quickly strikes you as impossible. Looking at S's column, you don't immediately see that he can't bring one or can't bring two items. So choices **a** and **b** can be set aside for the moment. Looking at J's column, you might immediately see that J brings anything A brings, and that A brings exactly two items—so J can't bring just one item. So choice **c** is correct.

If you missed this and your quick glance at the answer choices didn't yield the answer, then go through each choice more systematically. Take each answer and check if it seems that a scenario could

be constructed consistent both with that answer and the restrictions. Use prior work. The diagram from question 2 shows that at most likely, S could either bring exactly one item or exactly two items.

	R	S	A	J
c	✗		✗	
e	✗	✗	✓	✓
k	✗	✗	✓	✓
m (ex. 3)	✓	✓	✗	✓

ex. 2

← ✗ →　　→

Using this table, we can test two scenarios—one in which S brings c (a total of exactly two items) and one in which S does not bring c (a total of exactly one item). Both seem consistent with the restrictions, so we move on to answer choice **c**. If J brings exactly one item, then since we already know he brings m, he cannot bring c, e, or k:

	R	S	A	J
c	✗			✗
e	✗			✗
k	✗			✗
m (ex. 3)	✓			✓

ex. 2

← ✗ →　　→

The one-directional arrow tells us that A cannot bring c, e, or k either:

	R	S	A	J
c	✗		✗	✗
e	✗		✗	✗
k	✗		✗	✗
m (ex. 3)	✓			✓

ex. 2

← ✗ →　　→

But then there is no way that A can bring exactly two items. So it can't be that J brings exactly one item—choice **c**.

Question 5

The correct answer is choice **e**. If the number of c checkmarks is greater than the number of k checkmarks, then there must be either two or three c checkmarks (we already know that R does not have a c). If it is three, then each of S, A and J will bring c. But following the arrow, this will mean that each of S, A, and J will also bring m—and this will exceed the cap of three checkmarks for row m.

	R	S	A	J
c	✗	✓	✓	✓
e	✗			
k	✗			
m (ex. 3)	✓	✓	✓	✓

ex. 2

← ✗ → ⟶

So this diagram is not possible, and there must be exactly two checkmarks in row c. The two checkmarks cannot be under S and A, since again, that would result in four checkmarks for row m. So one must be under J, and the other must be under one of S or A. We can see what happens for both scenarios:

S1

	R	S	A	J
c	✗		✓	✓
e	✗			
k	✗			
m (ex. 3)	✓			✓

ex. 2

← ✗ → ⟶

S2

	R	S	A	J
c	✗	✓		✓
e	✗			
k	✗			
m (ex. 3)	✓			✓

ex. 2

← ✗ → ⟶

For S1, we can follow the arrows to fill in mA and cross out cS and mS. To keep column A at exactly two items, we also cross out eA and kA:

S1

	R	S	A	J
c	✗	✗	✓	✓
e	✗		✗	
k	✗		✗	
m (ex. 3)	✓	✗	✓	✓

ex. 2

← ✗ → ⟶

For S2, we follow the arrows to put a checkmark in mS and ✗-mark in cA. To keep row m at exactly three checkmarks, we put an ✗ in mA.

S2

	R	S	A	J
c	✗	✓	✗	✓
e	✗			
k	✗			
m (ex. 3)	✓	✓	✗	✓

ex. 2

← ✗ → ⟶

Then, to keep column A at exactly two checkmarks, we fill in the remaining spots in that column, eA and kA. This leads to checkmarks in eJ and kJ, and ✗-marks in eS and kS:

S2

	R	S	A	J
c	✗	✓	✗	✓
e	✗	✗	✓	✓
k	✗	✗	✓	✓
m (ex. 3)	✓	✓	✗	✓

ex. 2

← X → →

This determines the entire diagram. We now compare each answer choice against the two scenarios to see if that choice could be a list of all those bringing e's. Choices **a**, **b**, and **d** are made possible in S1. Choice **c** is made possible in S2. Choice **e** is not possible in either scenario: in S1, Alex does not have extra socks and in S2, Siddarth does not have extra socks.

So **e** is the correct answer.

Practice Game 5

We have four cars, labeled 1 to 4, and two sets of characteristics to be assigned to each. The first set is options—each car has one or more the following options: spoiler (s), fog lights (f), and performance tires (p). The second is each car is one of Ford, Dodge, or Chevy. We diagram the matching with a grid:

	1	2	3	4
s				
f				
p				
F/D/C				

The first restriction says that only Fords can have fog lights. We symbolize this as:

$$f \rightarrow F$$

This indicates that if a car has fog lights, it must be a Ford.

And the contrapositive:

$$\neq F \rightarrow \neq f$$

The second restriction says that car 2 has more options than car 3. So car 2 must have either two or three options, and car 3 must have either one or two options. We can write that information into the diagram, along with the information that one is greater than the other (see below).

The third restriction says that exactly two cars have fog lights. Note that in the diagram, the fourth restriction is that car 2 is a Dodge and the fifth that car 4 has no spoiler—this can all be directly incorporated into the diagram, which now looks like:

	1	2	3	4
s				✗
f (ex. 2)				
p				
F/D/C		D		

2 or 3 > 1 or 2

$$f \rightarrow F \ [\neq F \rightarrow \neq f]$$

Now for the deductions: Since car 2 is a Dodge and only Fords can have fog lamps, we know that car 2 cannot have f. Since car 2 cannot have fog lamps, it must have two options rather than three (which must be s and p). This means that car 3 must have exactly one option.

The diagram is now:

	1	2	3	4
s		✓		✗
f (ex. 2)		✗		
p		✓		
F/D/C		D		

ex. 1

We also note that since there are exactly two fog lamps and only Fords can have fog lamps, there must be at least two Fords.

Question 1

The correct answer is choice **a**. Compare each answer choice to the diagram. Since car 2 has a spoiler but no fog lights, it can't be that every car with a spoiler has fog lights, and choice **a** is the correct answer. The rest of the answer choices are each compatible with this diagram. In particular, choice **e** is incorrect because it could be the case that every car with performance tires with the exception of car 2 also has fog lights.

Question 2

The correct answer is choice **d**. If car 1 is a Chevy, then it cannot have f, and so cars 3 and 4 must have f (and be Fords). Since car 3 has f, it cannot have s or p:

	1	2	3	4
s		✓	✗	✗
f (ex. 2)	✗	✗	✓	✓
p		✓	✗	
F/D/C	C	D	F	F

ex. 1

Now compare each answer choice to the diagram. Since car 1 does not have fog lights, the statement in choice **a** can't be true, making **a** incorrect. Since car 3 does not have performance tires, the statement in choice **b** can't be true, making **b** incorrect.

Since car 3 does have fog lights, the statement in choice **c** can't be true, making **c** incorrect. Since, according to the diagram, car 4 may or may not have performance tires, choice **d** is the correct answer. Since car 4 has fog lights, the statement in choice **e** can't be true, making **e** incorrect.

Question 3

The correct answer is choice **c**. We realized in our deductions that since there are exactly two cars with fog lamps, and only Fords have fog lamps, there must be at least two Fords. We already know one car is a Dodge. There could be more Dodges than Chevys if there were no Chevys, so choice **a** is incorrect. There could be an equal number of Dodges and Chevys if there were one Chevy in addition to the Dodge, making choice **b** incorrect (we saw this in the diagram for Question 2). There could not be more Dodges than Fords, because that would require three Dodges (since there are two Fords), meaning there would be five cars, not four— so **c** is the correct answer. There could be more Fords than Dodges if there were one Dodge and one Chevy, so **d** is incorrect (again, we saw this in the diagram for Question 2). And there could be an equal number of Dodges and Fords if there were an additional Dodge and no Chevy's, so choice **e** is incorrect.

Question 4

The correct answer is choice **e**. If car 4 is a Dodge, then it cannot have fog lights and thus must have performance tires:

	1	2	3	4
s		✓		✗
f (ex. 2)		✗		✗
p		✓		✓
F/D/C		D		D

ex. 1

Since there are exactly two cars with fog lights, we now know that these two must be cars 1 and 3 (which must be Fords). Since car 3 has exactly one option, it cannot have a spoiler or performance tires:

	1	2	3	4
s		✓	✗	✗
f (ex. 2)	✓	✗	✓	✗
p		✓	✗	✓
F/D/C	F	D	F	D

ex. 1

Now compare each answer choice to the diagram. Choice **a** is incorrect because car 4 has performance tires but no spoiler. Choice **b** is incorrect because car 3 has fog lights but no spoiler. Choice **c** is incorrect because car 2 has a spoiler but no fog lights. Choice **d** is incorrect because cars 2 and 4 have performance tires but no fog lights. Choice **e** is correct because there is no car that definitely has a spoiler but no performance tires: car 2 has both, cars 3 and 4 lack spoilers, and car 1 could have both a spoiler and performance tires (or performance tires and no spoiler, or neither performance tires nor a spoiler).

Question 5

The correct answer is choice **a**. If exactly three cars have spoilers, then those three must be cars 1, 2, and 3. If car 3 has a spoiler, it does not have fog lights or performance tires. And if car 3 does not have fog lights, then cars 1 and 4 must have fog lights and be Fords:

	1	2	3	4
S	✓	✓	✓	✗
f (ex. 2)	✓	✗	✗	✓
P		✓	✗	
F/D/C	F	D		F

ex. 1

Now compare the answer choices to this diagram. Car 1 has at least two options (s and f), so it can't have exactly one option and **a** is the correct answer. The other choices are incorrect since they are compatible with the diagram (they could be true). Depending

on whether it has performance tires, car 1 could have two or three options, making choices **b** and **c** incorrect. And depending on whether it has performance tires, car 4 could have two or three options, making choices **d** and **e** incorrect.

Practice Game 6

Since this game uses a set of entities (buildings) that have a particular spatial configuration, and since their spatial relationships will figure into the game rules, the diagram should use this spatial configuration. For each building, 1 through 6, it is to be determined whether it is historical (H) or modern (M), and whether it contains a law firm (l), bank (b), or both. Write the letters under each number as matches are determined. The third, fourth, and fifth restrictions all give specific information, so write this in:

```
1       2       3
        l       H
4       5       6
M
```

Symbolize the first restriction as:

H next to H

Symbolize the second restriction as:

```
l       b
↓       ↑
b       l
```

This reminds us that if we have a law firm (l), there must be a bank (b) across the street. Keep in mind that this does not mean that every bank has a law firm across the street from it.

Also, keep the contrapositives in mind:

```
b̶       l̶
↓       ↑
l̶       b̶
```

Now make deductions by applying the first and second restrictions to the diagram. Since 3 is H, 2 must be H. Since 2 is l, 5 must be b. Also, since 4 is M, 5 and 6 are either both H (to satisfy the 'H next to H' rule) or both M. These seem to exhaust the immediate deductions that can be made.

The diagram is now:

1	2	3
	l H	H
4	5	6
M	b	

Question 1

The correct answer is choice **c**. If every bank is located in a historical building, then building 5 must be H. But we must also consider the contrapositive, that if a building is not historical (i.e., is modern), then it cannot have a bank (and therefore must have a law firm). This means that building 4 has an l:

1	2	3
	l H	H
4	5	6
b̶l M	b H	

Since building 4 has an l, building 1 must have a b, and therefore—according to the supposition of this question—be located in a historical building:

1	2	3
b H	l H	H
4	5	6
b̶l M	b H	

Finally, since 5 is H, 6 must also be H (to satisfy the 'H next to H' rule):

1	2	3
b H	l H	H
4	5	6
b̶l M	b H	H

Now compare the answer choices to this diagram. Choice **c**, that building 1 is historical, is the only choice given in this diagram. The other choices give statements that could be false without contradicting this diagram. Note that choice **e** is incorrect because building 6 could contain a law firm or bank. The question stem says that every bank is located in a historical building, not that every historical building contains a bank (the two are not the same). This goes for choice **a** as well.

Question 2

The correct answer is choice **b**. Since we already have one modern building, we must place two more M's into the diagram. If one of those M's were placed under building 1, then we would have an M under one of buildings 5 and 6, and an H under the other. But either way, we would violate the restriction that 'H next to H'—the H on the 4-5-6 side of the street would not be adjacent to any other H. So both M's must be placed under buildings 5 and 6, making building 1 H:

1	2	3
H	l H	H
4	5	6
M	b M	M

Now scan the answer choices for something given in this diagram. Choice **b** says that one bank must be in a modern building, and we know this must be true since building 5 is a modern building containing a bank. The other choices all show statements that could be false. In particular, choice **e** is incorrect because it could be that there is another modern building containing a bank.

Question 3

The correct answer is choice **b**. This question requires playing with the diagram to see how to maximize the number of modern buildings containing law firms. The first step, however, is to see what follows from the fact that every bank is located in a modern building (and the contrapositive that every historical building lacks a bank and contains a law firm). Given this information, building 5 must be modern, and buildings 2 and 3 must contain a law firm and no bank (since they are historical):

1	2	3
	~~b~~l H	~~b~~l H
4	5	6
M	b M	

Since building 3 contains a law firm, building 6 must contain a bank (by the second restriction), and therefore, by the new supposition, must be modern (you could also note that building 6 has to be modern because there is no historical building next to it):

1	2	3
	~~b~~l H	~~b~~l H
4	5	6
M	b M	b M

Now, we are looking to maximize the number of modern buildings containing only a law firm (no bank). So buildings 2 and 3 are out because they are historical, and buildings 5 and 6 are out because they contain banks. So we must focus on buildings 1 and 4. If building 4 contain a law firm, then building 1 contains a bank (by the second restriction), leaving building 4 as the only possible modern building containing only a law firm. And if building 1 contains a law firm, then building 4 would contain a bank (by the second restriction), leaving building 1 to be the only possible modern building containing only a law firm. So the maximum number of modern buildings containing only a law firm is one—choice **b**.

Question 4

The correct answer is choice **d**. If every historical building contains only a law firm, then buildings 2 and 3 contain a law firm and no bank. Further, the contrapositive of this new information—that if a building contains a bank, it is modern—tells us that building 5 is modern:

1	2	3
	~~b~~l H	~~b~~l H
4	5	6
M	b M	

The second restriction gives us that building 6 contains a bank—and again, by the contrapositive of the new supposition, is modern (or since 5 is modern, 6 must be as well, to satisfy the 'H next to H' rule):

1	2	3
	~~b~~l H	~~b~~l H
4	5	6
M	b M	b M

Finally, by the contrapositive of the second restriction, we know that 5 and 6 don't contain l's (since 2 and 3 don't contain b's).

1	2	3
	~~b~~l H	~~b~~l H
4	5	6
M	b ~~l~~ M	b ~~l~~ M

Scan the answer choices for information given in this diagram. Choice **d**, that building 6 is modern and contains a bank, is given in this diagram; therefore, that is the correct answer.

Question 5

The correct answer is choice **a**. Consider each answer choice in turn. If building 6 were modern and building 5 historical, then the first restriction would be violated: building 5 would not have any adjacent historical building. The other choices represent possibilities that are consistent with the restrictions.

Practice Game 7

Since the set of characteristics to be assigned to the six skydivers are such that only one can be assigned to each skydiver, it may be better to use the column-approach rather than a grid:

m								
		A	B	C		D	E	F	
r/g/o/p									r/g/o/p

The double-line indicates the division between male and female.

The first restriction tells us that we will need different colors for each of the group A, B, C, and for each of the group D, E, F. We will have to keep this in mind: to make sure you don't forget, write this down next to your diagram or circle it. We have included "r/g/o/p" for each of the two groups, male and female, so that as we assign colors we can cross the appropriate letter out and keep track of what colors are available for that group.

The second restriction tells us that A is green, and the third that D is not orange or purple, meaning that D is red or green. This information can be put into the diagram:

m								
		A	B	C		D	E	F	
r/g/o/p		g				r/g			r/g/o/p

The fourth restriction can be symbolized:

B = r or o → E = g
E ≠ g → B ≠ r and ≠ o [the contrapositive]

The fifth restriction tells us that there must be exactly one orange parachute in the male group and exactly one in the female group. We will have to keep

this information in mind, and note it by writing '1 o' under each group.

So we have:

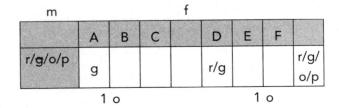

B = r or o → E = g
E ≠ g → B ≠ r and ≠ o [the contrapositive]

Question 1

The correct answer is choice **b**. Take each answer in turn, and check to see if it can be ruled out by any deductions, or seems to be possible (i.e., can be worked into an assignment of colors to skydivers consistent with the rules).

Choice **a** assigns r to B and D:

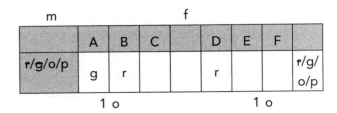

B = r or o → E = g
E ≠ g → B ≠ r and ≠ o [the contrapositive]

This means that E = g (by the fourth condition), and that C and F = o (by the fifth):

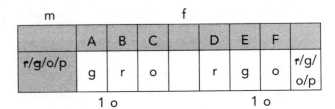

B = r or o → E = g
E ≠ g → B ≠ r and ≠ o [the contrapositive]

This assignment does not seem to contradict any game rules, so move on to test the next answer choice.

If C = r, then by the fifth restriction, B = o; and if F = g, then D cannot be G and D must be r, leaving o for E:

	A	B	C		D	E	F	
r/g/o/p	g	o	r		r	o	g	r/g/o/p

1 o   1 o

B = r or o → E = g
E ≠ g → B ≠ r and ≠ o [the contrapositive]

But this contradicts the fourth restriction: B = o, but E is ≠ g. So the statement in **b** cannot be true, and **b** is the correct answer.

If you found yourself stuck on this question, or find that you take too much time for these types of questions in general (in which you need to do a lot of work with each answer choice to see if it represents an acceptable scenario), then it might be a useful strategy to return to this question after you have done the other questions. In this case, you would have seen that choice **c** can be ruled out by Question 5, and that choices **d** and **e** can be ruled out by Question 4.

Question 2

The correct answer is choice **c**. If E has a red parachute, then D must have a green one. Since E is not green, by the contrapositive of the fourth restriction, B is not red or orange; and since g is taken in the male group, B must be p:

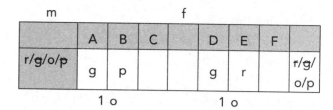

	A	B	C		D	E	F	
r/g/o/p	g	p			g	r		r/g/o/p

1 o   1 o

B = r or o → E = g
E ≠ g → B ≠ r and ≠ o [the contrapositive]

The fifth restriction puts o in C and F:

	A	B	C		D	E	F	
r/g/o/p	g	p	o		g	r	o	r/g/o/p

1 o   1 o

B = r or o → E = g
E ≠ g → B ≠ r and ≠ o [the contrapositive]

Now compare the answer choices to this diagram. Choice **c** is correct, as the diagram shows that there are exactly two green parachutes.

Question 3

The correct answer is choice **a**. Look at the fourth restriction, which governs the relationship between E and B. If B is r or o, E and B cannot have the same color. So B cannot be r or o; and g is already taken in the male group; so B must be p. This means that E must be p, since B and E have the same color:

	A	B	C		D	E	F	
r/g/o/p	g	p			r/g	p		r/g/o/p

1 o   1 o

B = r or o → E = g

E ≠ g → B ≠ r and ≠ o [the contrapositive]

By the fifth restriction, we can fill in the remaining spaces with o:

m				f				
	A	B	C		D	E	F	
r/g/o/~~p~~	g	p	o		r/g	p	o	r/g/ o/~~p~~
		1 o					1 o	

B = r or o → E = g

E ≠ g → B ≠ r and ≠ o [the contrapositive]

Now look at the answer choices to see which is contradicted by this diagram. Choice **a** is contradicted: the diagram shows that F has an orange parachute, not a green one. So **a** is the correct answer.

Question 4

The correct answer is choice **e**. If there is exactly one green parachute, then the female group cannot have a green parachute, since the male group already has one (A is green).

So D must be r:

m				f				
	A	B	C		D	E	F	
r/g/o/p	g				r			r/g/ o/p
		1 o					1 o	

B = r or o → E = g

E ≠ g → B ≠ r and ≠ o [the contrapositive]

Furthermore, E cannot be green; and so by the contrapositive of the fourth restriction, B cannot be red or orange, and so must be purple. This leaves orange for C (by the fifth restriction). E and F are then left with orange and purple (since red is taken and green is forbidden). The assignment of o and p to E and F could go either way:

m				f				
	A	B	C		D	E	F	
r/g/o/p	g	p	o		r	o/p	o/p	r/g/ o/p
		1 o					1 o	

B = r or o → E = g

E ≠ g → B ≠ r and ≠ o [the contrapositive]

According to this diagram, then, F could be either orange or purple, and could not be any other color. Therefore, **e** is the correct answer.

Question 5

The correct answer is choice **e**. If C's parachute is purple, then B must be orange (by the fifth restriction). Since B is orange, the fourth restriction tells us that E is green. Since E is green, green is not an option for D, and D must be red. This leaves orange for F, and we have:

m				f				
	A	B	C		D	E	F	
r/g/o/p	g	o	p		r	g	o	r/g/ o/p
		1 o					1 o	

B = r or o → E = g

E ≠ g → B ≠ r and ≠ o [the contrapositive]

This shows us that all six skydivers have their parachute colors determined—choice **e**.

Practice Game 8

This game has 5 critics—H, I, J, K, and L—matched up to 1–3 of t, g, and m:

	H	I	J	K	L
t					
g					
m					

The first restriction puts t and m under H. The second says that H tastes fewer scotches than K—so H must taste two and K must taste all three. The third restriction says that exactly three critics taste the Talisker—this can be noted in the diagram:

	H	I	J	K	L
t (ex. 3)	✓			✓	
g	✗			✓	
m	✓			✓	

The fourth restriction can be symbolized:

I = m → J = t and g
J ≠ t or J ≠ g → I ≠ m [the contrapositive]

This can also be symbolized by drawing arrows directly into the diagram:

	H	I	J	K	L
t (ex. 3)	✓			✓	
g	✗			✓	
m	✓			✓	

The fifth restriction essentially says that whatever L tastes, I tastes as well. This can be symbolized by drawing yet another arrow into the diagram:

	H	I	J	K	L
t (ex. 3)	✓			✓	
g	✗			✓	
m	✓			✓	

One deduction that can be immediately made is that since only three critics taste the Talisker, L cannot taste the Talisker; for if L did, then I would also taste the Talisker and there would be a total of four critics (H, I, K, L) tasting the Talisker.

So the final diagram looks like:

	H	I	J	K	L
t (ex. 3)	✓			✓	✗
g	✗			✓	
m	✓			✓	

Question 1

The correct answer is choice **b**. Consulting the initial diagram, we see that only H and K are fully determined with respect to exactly which scotches they do or do not taste—so two, choice **b**, is the correct answer.

Question 2

The correct answer is choice **b**. Follow the arrows. If L tastes m, then so does I. If I tastes m, then J tastes t and g. We have:

	H	I	J	K	L
t (ex. 3)	✓		✓	✓	✗
g	✗		✓	✓	
m	✓	✓		✓	✓

Since there must be exactly three critics tasting Talisker, we can also put an ✗ for t under I:

	H	I	J	K	L
t (ex. 3)	✓	✗	✓	✓	✗
g	✗		✓	✓	
m	✓	✓		✓	✓

Now compare the answer choices to this diagram, looking for one that contradicts the diagram.

Choice **b** contradicts the diagram—I does not taste the Talisker—and so choice **b** is the correct answer.

Question 3

The correct answer is choice **d**. First, note the new information, that exactly two critics taste g, in the diagram. Then start by seeing how many different ways exactly two critics might taste g, and see what follows. There is already one checkmark in row g (under K), so we must place exactly one more. If we were to place the checkmark under L, we would also have to place one under I, resulting in three checkmarks for row g. So we can put an ✗ under L:

	H	I	J	K	L
t (ex. 3)	✓		✓	✓	✗
g (ex. 2)	✗			✓	✗
m	✓			✓	

Since there are now two ✗-marks under L (i.e., L tastes neither t nor g), we can put a check mark in row m under L. Following the arrows, that check mark results in a check mark in row m under I, which in turn results in check marks under J for rows t and g:

	H	I	J	K	L
t (ex. 3)	✓		✓	✓	✗
g (ex. 2)	✗		✓	✓	✗
m	✓	✓		✓	✓

The numerical constraints in row t (exactly three checkmarks) and row g (exactly two checkmarks) are now met, so we can put ✗-marks in those rows under I:

	H	I	J	K	L
t (ex. 3)	✓	✗	✓	✓	✗
g (ex. 2)	✗	✗	✓	✓	✗
m	✓	✓		✓	✓

Now compare the answer choices to the diagram and look for a statement that could be false.

According to the diagram, the statement that J tastes m, could either be true or false—and so choice **d** is the correct answer.

Question 4

The correct answer is choice **a**. If I tastes t, then since exactly three critics taste t, J cannot taste t.

So we have:

	H	I	J	K	L
t (ex. 3)	✓	✓	✗	✓	✗
g	✗			✓	
m	✓			✓	

Since there is an ✗ at the end of the arrow, in row t under J, there must be an ✗ in row m under I:

	H	I	J	K	L
t (ex. 3)	✓	✓	✗	✓	✗
g	✗			✓	
m	✓	✗		✓	

Further, if I doesn't taste m, then L cannot taste m. This means that L must taste g, and so I must taste g:

	H	I	J	K	L
t (ex. 3)	✓	✓	✗	✓	✗
g	✗	✓		✓	✓
m	✓	✗		✓	✗

Now compare the answer choices to this diagram and look for one contradicted by the diagram. Choice **a**—that I tastes the Macallan—contradicts the diagram, and so is the correct answer.

Question 5

The correct answer is choice **d**. Start by incorporating the new information into the diagram (which essentially says that if a critic tastes g, that critic also tastes t, along with the contrapositive, that if a critic doesn't taste t, then he doesn't taste g), and seeing what follows:

	H	I	J	K	L
t (ex. 3)	✓			✓	✗
g	✗			✓	
m	✓			✓	

Since L does not taste t, L cannot taste g (an application of the contrapositive of our new arrow). This means that L tastes m. Following the arrows, I tastes m, and therefore J tastes t and g:

	H	I	J	K	L
t (ex. 3)	✓		✓	✓	✗
g	✗		✓	✓	✗
m	✓	✓		✓	✓

We now have three checkmarks in row t, so I does not taste t. Again applying the contrapositive of our new arrow, we see that I cannot taste g:

	H	I	J	K	L
t (ex. 3)	✓	✗	✓	✓	✗
g	✗	✗	✓	✓	✗
m	✓	✓		✓	✓

The only remaining box concerns whether J tastes m. J could either taste m or not taste m, without violating any rules of the game. So there are exactly four critics—H, I, K, and L for whom it's determined exactly which scotches he or she tastes. This is choice **d**.

CHAPTER 7

Hybrid Games Review

So far, you have looked at sequencing, selection, distribution, and matching games. Each game type has its own diagramming techniques as well as its own usual set of condition types. Mastering these games has required learning these techniques and rules and getting a feel for the kind of game mechanics specific to each game type.

But learning each individually is not enough; the makers of the LSAT love to combine game types to produce hybrid logic games. Never fear—you already have the tools you need to solve these games. You just need to practice recognizing what's familiar in these games, dissecting them into their component game types, and applying the relevant techniques.

First, recall that each game-type has a certain preferred set of diagramming techniques:

GAME TYPE	DIAGRAMMING TECHNIQUES
Sequencing	A sequence of slots
Selection	List of entities, entities listed on a grid (for cross-group domains), slots for a group of known size
Distribution	Columns for each group, sets of slots for groups of known size
Matching	Grid for matching, column-approach

You will want to use one or all of the diagramming techniques specific to the game types that make up the hybrid game you are considering. Most LSAT hybrid games include a heavy sequencing component, so you will most often want to start by trying a sequencing diagram or technique.

In particular, a high proportion of sequencing-based hybrids will be matching/sequencing hybrids in which you are asked to both sequence a group of entities and match them to characteristics or another group of entities. For these games, it's often useful to modify a matching grid to include a "matching" of entities to sequencing spots. For example, suppose you are asked to sequence five entities (A, B, C, D, and E) and match them to one of three possible characteristics (X, Y, and Z).

You could set this up by drawing the following diagram:

	1	2	3	4	5
A/B/C/D/E					
X					
Y					
Z					

If a high proportion of the information concerns the direct matching of characteristics to entities, then you might consider a regular matching grid instead of, or in addition to, a sequencing diagram:

	A	B	C	D	E
X					
Y					
Z					

Another popular sequencing-based hybrid is the selection/sequencing game. In this game, you are asked to select a group of entities from a larger domain and sequence them. In a selection/sequencing hybrid diagram, list the sequence of spots and write out the symbols for the entities that will be selected for each spot. For example, a band must select four of six songs

(entities A, B, C, D, E, and F) to put on a set-list (sequence) for their next concert:

$$\underline{}\ \underline{}\ \underline{}\ \underline{}\quad (A\ B\ C\ D\ E\ F)$$
$$1\ \ 2\ \ 3\ \ 4$$

While the diagram for these games is fairly straightforward, some of the rules can be a bit tricky. In particular, beware of rules that combine selection and sequencing elements, such as:

> If both are selected, X precedes Y.
> If both are selected, Y precedes Z.

These two rules work a bit differently than similar rules in regular sequencing games. In a regular sequencing game, you might join the sequence strings X—Y and Y—Z into X—Y—Z. If you do this, you might infer that X—Z. Although this would be a valid inference for a regular sequencing game, it's not necessarily the case in a selection/sequencing game—if Y is not selected, Z could come before X.

There are many possible game-type combinations that produce a hybrid game, but, in general, you should do two things when approaching hybrids. First, try to break down the game into its component game types and diagram accordingly. Second, keep in mind that although many of the rules will work the same way as they did for the regular game types, some rules will not, so make sure that you fully understand the mechanics of the rule you are considering and be especially wary of hybrid rule types that are thrown your way.

Practice Game 1

A wine-tasting group tours six wineries—Domaine Chandon, V. Sattui, Piccetti, Mumm, Artesa, and Black Stallion. At each winery, at least one of three wine types is tasted: white wine, red wine, and sparkling wine. The tasting is subject to the following restrictions:

> The group stops at V. Sattui either immediately before or immediately after Piccetti, and stops at Domain Chandon before V. Sattui.
>
> The group stops at Domaine Chandon either immediately before or immediately after Artesa.
>
> The group tastes sparkling wine and red wine at Mumm, and stops at Mumm first.
>
> The group tastes white wine at exactly four wineries.
>
> The group tastes more wine types at V. Sattui than at Piccetti, and more wine types at the last winery than at the first winery at which they stop.

1. Which one of the following could be the list of wineries in order from the first winery at which the group stops to the last?
   a. Mumm, Domaine Chandon, Artesa, Black Stallion, V. Sattui, Piccetti
   b. Mumm, Artesa, Domain Chandon, Black Stallion, Piccetti, V. Sattui
   c. Domaine Chandon, Artesa, Mumm, Piccetti, V. Sattui, Black Stallion
   d. Mumm, Piccetti, V. Sattui, Black Stallion, Domaine Chandon, Artesa
   e. Mumm, Domaine Chandon, Black Stallion, Artesa, Piccetti, V. Sattui

2. If the group stops at two wineries at which red wines are tasted before stopping at any wineries at which white wines are tasted, then which one of the following statements must be true?
   a. They taste red wine at Black Stallion.
   b. They taste white wine at Domaine Chandon.
   c. They taste red wine at Artesa.
   d. They taste white wine at Piccetti.
   e. They taste red wine at V. Sattui.

3. If the group stops at Black Stallion before Artesa, then which one of the following statements must be true?
   a. Artesa is third on the tour.
   b. Domaine Chandon is third on the tour.
   c. Domain Chandon is fourth on the tour.
   d. V. Sattui is fifth on the tour.
   e. Piccetti is fifth on the tour.

4. If the group stops at two wineries in between stopping at Piccetti and stopping at Black Stallion, then which one of the following statements must be true?
   a. They taste red wine and sparkling wine at V. Sattui.
   b. They taste white wine and red wine at Piccetti.
   c. They taste red wine and sparkling wine at Artesa.
   d. They taste white wine and sparkling wine at Domaine Chandon.
   e. They taste white wine and red wine at Black Stallion.

5. If the group tastes the exact same types of wine at the last stop and second to last stop, then each of the following statements could be true EXCEPT:
   a. They taste the same number of wine types at the first and third stops on the tour.
   b. They taste the same number of wine types at the second and third stops on the tour.
   c. They taste the same number of wine types at the second and fourth stops on the tour.
   d. They taste the same number of wine types at the third and fourth stops on the tour.
   e. They taste the same number of wine types at the fourth and fifth stops on the tour.

Practice Game 2

The top five photos in a photo competition are ranked first through fifth. Each photo is either color or black and white, and each was submitted by exactly one of five photographers: A, B, C, D, and E. The highest ranked photo is the first place photo. The ranking meets the following conditions:

D's photo places second.
The fifth place photo is color.
A's photo is ranked higher than E's.
E's and B's photos are black and white.

1. Which one of the following could be a list of photographers in order from the one whose photo placed first to the one whose photo placed fifth?
   a. A, B, E, D, C
   b. B, D, E, A, , C
   c. A, D, B, E, C
   d. A, D, E, C, B
   e. A, D, C, B, E

2. Which one of the following statements CAN-NOT be true?
   a. The fourth place photo is black and white.
   b. The fourth place photo is color.
   c. The third place photo is black and white.
   d. The third place photo is color.
   e. The second place photo is color.

3. If the third place photo is color, then each of the following must be true EXCEPT:
   a. The first place photo is black and white.
   b. The first place photo is B's photo.
   c. The second place photo is color.
   d. The second place photo is D's photo.
   e. The third place photo is color.

4. Each of the following could be true EXCEPT:
   a. A's photo is ranked immediately above or immediately below B's.
   b. A's photo is ranked immediately above or immediately below D's.
   c. D's photo is ranked immediately above or immediately below B's.
   d. B's photo is ranked immediately above or immediately below C's.
   e. B's photo is ranked immediately above or immediately below E's.

5. If there is exactly one photo ranked in between B's photo and C's photo, then which one of the following statements must be true?
   a. B's photo ranks fourth.
   b. A's photo ranks third.
   c. E's photo ranks third.
   d. B's photo ranks first.
   e. A's photo ranks first.

Practice Game 3

Five songs are to be selected from eight (H, I, J, K, L, M, N, O) to be burned into tracks on a mix CD. The tracks are ordered according to the following conditions:

> If both are selected for the CD, song H precedes song J.
> If both are selected for the CD, song K precedes song L.
> If the fourth track is song I, then the first track is song J.
> Either song H or song K must be on the CD.
> Song N is the third track.

1. Which one of the following could be the list of tracks in order from first to last?
   a. J, L, N, I, K
   b. M, H, N, I, J
   c. J, O, N, H, I
   d. M, K, N, L, I
   e. M, L, N, O, J

2. Which pair cannot precede song N on the CD?
   a. M and K
   b. J and L
   c. O and H
   d. J and K
   e. I and L

3. If the fourth track is song I, then each of the following statements could be true EXCEPT:
   a. The second track is song L.
   b. The second track is song K.
   c. The fifth track is song L.
   d. The fifth track is song K.
   e. The fifth track is song M.

4. If song H is on the CD, then each of the following statements could be true EXCEPT:
   a. Song H immediately precedes song I.
   b. Song J immediately precedes song O.
   c. Song N immediately precedes song I.
   d. Song K immediately precedes song N.
   e. Song L immediately precedes song I.

5. If song L precedes song J on the CD, then each of the following statements could be true EXCEPT:
   a. The fourth track is song K.
   b. The fourth track is song H.
   c. The fourth track is song J.
   d. The second track is song K.
   e. The fifth track is song J.

Practice Game 4

For a local magazine's article on the best of the seven restaurants in a neighborhood, A, B, C, D, E, F and G, the top four are chosen by popular vote and then only those four are ranked by a food critic. The highest ranking is the first place ranking. The final ranking is consistent with the following conditions:

> C is ranked second.
> If A or B make the top four, so does E.
> If E makes the top four, F does not.
> If both make the top four, D is ranked above G.
> If both make the top four, G is ranked above C.

1. Which one of the following could be the list of the top four restaurants, in order from first to last (top to bottom)?
   a. F, C, A, D
   b. A, C, G, E
   c. E, C, F, B
   d. B, E, A, C
   e. B, C, E, A

2. If C is ranked above D in the top four, then which one of the following statements must be true?
   a. E is not in the top four.
   b. A is not in the top four.
   c. G is not in the top four.
   d. B is in the top four.
   e. B is not in the top four.

3. Which one of the following cannot be in the top four?
   a. A
   b. B
   c. D
   d. E
   e. F

4. If A is in the top four, which one of the following statements cannot be true?
   a. E is ranked above G.
   b. E is ranked above A.
   c. B is ranked above C.
   d. A is ranked above D.
   e. G is ranked above A.

5. Which two restaurants cannot both make the top four?
   a. D and G
   b. E and A
   c. B and E
   d. G and E
   e. D and B

Practice Game 5

On Halloween, a group of six children approach the scary house at the end of the street. The group consists of a ghost, witch, zombie, vampire, mummy, and devil. One at a time, each says trick-or-treat to the kind lady who lives there. Not one for tricks, she gives each one or more of the following types of treats—chocolate, hard candy, licorice—depending on how much she likes their costumes. The trick-or-treating proceeds according to the following restrictions:

> The devil receives more types of treats than the ghost.
> The zombie goes before the vampire, but after the witch.
> The ghost goes before the zombie.
> The first child to approach the house gets all three treat types.
> The devil goes fifth.
> The kind lady does not hand out hard candy to two children in a row, nor does she hand out chocolate to two children in a row.

1. Which one of the following could be a list of the children by costume, in order from the first to approach the house to the last?
   a. Mummy, ghost, witch, devil, zombie, vampire
   b. Witch, zombie, mummy, ghost, devil, vampire
   c. Ghost, zombie, witch, mummy, devil, vampire
   d. Mummy, ghost, witch, zombie, devil, vampire
   e. Witch, ghost, mummy, vampire, devil, zombie

2. Which one of the following statements CANNOT be true?
   a. The first child gets more types of treats than the second.
   b. The second child gets more types of treats than the third.
   c. The third child gets more types of treats than the fourth.
   d. The fifth child gets more types of treats than the sixth.
   e. The fourth child gets more types of treats than the third.

3. If the sixth child is the mummy and gets chocolate, then each of the following statements could be true EXCEPT:
   a. The mummy gets hard candy.
   b. The mummy gets licorice.
   c. The devil gets hard candy.
   d. The vampire gets chocolate.
   e. The zombie gets hard candy.

4. If the ghost gets chocolate, then which one of the following statements must be true?
   a. The mummy goes first.
   b. The witch goes second.
   c. The ghost goes second.
   d. The vampire goes fourth.
   e. The zombie goes fourth.

5. If the vampire goes fourth, then which one of the following statements must be true?
   a. The zombie gets licorice.
   b. The vampire gets licorice.
   c. The devil gets licorice.
   d. The ghost gets licorice.
   e. The mummy gets licorice.

Practice Game 6

An architectural tour of a college grounds will include exactly five of seven major landmarks: the chapel, the library, the dining hall, the fountain, the bridge, the porters lodge, and the senior common room. The tour is subject to the following conditions:

If the dining hall is on the tour, then the fountain and bridge are on the tour.
The second stop on the tour is either the porters lodge or the bridge.
If both are selected for the tour, the library comes before the dining hall.
The chapel is fourth on the tour.
If all three are selected for the tour, both the senior common room and the fountain come before the bridge.

1. Which one of the following could be a list of the landmarks toured, from first to last?
   a. Library, bridge, dining hall, chapel, porters lodge
   b. Dining hall, porters lodge, fountain, chapel, bridge
   c. Bridge, porters lodge, chapel, senior common room, library
   d. Dining hall, bridge, fountain, chapel, library
   e. Porters lodge, senior common room, fountain, chapel, bridge

2. If the dining hall is on the tour, then each of the following statements could be true EXCEPT:
   a. The senior common room is on the tour.
   b. The fountain is on the tour.
   c. The bridge is on the tour.
   d. The library is on the tour.
   e. The porters lodge is on the tour.

3. If the bridge is toured before the senior common room, then which of the following is a complete and accurate list of the landmarks any one of which could be the third landmark on the tour?
   a. Library, porters lodge
   b. Library, porters lodge, bridge
   c. Library, bridge, senior common room
   d. Library, bridge, porters lodge, senior common room
   e. Library, bridge, dining hall, senior common room

4. If the library and dining hall are both on the tour, then which one of the following statements must be true?
   a. The fountain is toured before the chapel.
   b. The bridge is toured before the dining hall.
   c. The bridge is toured before the fountain.
   d. The library is toured before the bridge.
   e. The senior common room is toured before the dining hall.

5. If the library is not on the tour, then each of the following must be on the tour EXCEPT:
   a. Porters lodge
   b. Bridge
   c. Chapel
   d. Fountain
   e. Senior common room

Practice Game 7

Eight friends—Bock, Karla, Michael, Smita, Praveen, Gary, Lauren, and Cynthia—are planning a weekend trip to the lake. They carpool using three cars, each departing at a different time, and each carrying at least one and at most three people. The carpool meets the following restrictions:

Michael must ride with Karla, and Praveen must ride with Smita.
Gary departs first and Michael departs last.
Smita and Lauren do not ride together.
Bock either rides with Karla or with Praveen.
If Lauren departs first, then Cynthia departs last.
Bock does not depart immediately after Smita.

1. Each of the following statements could be true EXCEPT:
   a. Smita departs before Bock.
   b. Cynthia departs before Lauren.
   c. Bock departs before Praveen.
   d. Gary departs before Karla.
   e. Cynthia departs before Bock.

2. If Smita departs neither first nor last, then which one of the following statements must be true?
   a. Michael rides with Lauren.
   b. Smita rides with Bock.
   c. Lauren rides with Gary.
   d. Cynthia rides with Karla.
   e. Cynthia rides with Bock.

3. If Lauren and Cynthia do not ride together, then each of the following statements could be true EXCEPT:
   a. Bock departs before Cynthia.
   b. Smita departs before Karla.
   c. Smita departs before Cynthia.
   d. Praveen departs before Bock.
   e. Praveen departs before Lauren.

4. Which one of the following is a complete and accurate list of the people any one of which could be in the car that departs first?
   a. Gary, Smita, Cynthia
   b. Gary, Praveen, Smita, Cynthia
   c. Gary, Praveen, Smita, Lauren, Cynthia
   d. Gary, Praveen, Smita, Cynthia, Bock
   e. Gary, Praveen, Smita, Lauren, Cynthia, Bock

5. If the carpool does not have to meet the restriction that that Smita and Lauren do not ride together, then each of the following statements could be true EXCEPT:
   a. Cynthia departs first.
   b. Bock departs second.
   c. Bock departs third.
   d. Lauren departs third.
   e. Smita departs third.

Practice Game 8

A circus consists of two tents, A and B, each with three rings, numbered 1 to 3. Five animals—a horse, an elephant, a tiger, a lion, and a monkey—perform simultaneously. Each animal performs in exactly one of the six rings, and each ring contains at most one animal. Consecutively-numbered rings are adjacent to one another. The performances proceed according to the following conditions:

The monkey performs in a ring numbered 1.
The lion and tiger both perform in tent B.
The elephant performs in a lower-numbered ring than both the lion and the horse.
The elephant and the tiger perform in the same tent.

1. Each of the following statements could be true EXCEPT:
   a. The monkey performs in tent A.
   b. The horse performs in tent B.
   c. The elephant performs in a ring numbered 2.
   d. The lion performs in a ring numbered 2.
   e. The horse performs in a ring numbered 3.

2. If the tiger is in a ring numbered 3, then each of the following statements must be true EXCEPT:
   a. The monkey performs in tent A, ring 1.
   b. The elephant performs in tent B, ring 1.
   c. The ring in which the lion performs is adjacent to the ring in which the elephant performs.
   d. The ring in which the tiger performs is adjacent to the ring in which the lion performs.
   e. The ring in which the horse performs is adjacent to the ring in which the monkey performs.

3. Which one of the following is a complete and accurate list of the animals any one of which could perform in tent B, ring 2?
   a. Elephant
   b. Elephant, lion
   c. Elephant, tiger, horse
   d. Elephant, tiger, lion
   e. Tiger, horse, lion

4. Which one of the following statements could be true?
   a. There is no performance in tent A, ring 3.
   b. There is no performance in tent A, ring 1.
   c. There is no performance in tent B, ring 3.
   d. The elephant performs in tent A.
   e. The horse performs in tent B.

5. If the tiger performs in a lowered-number ring than the elephant, then which one of the following rings must be empty?
   a. Tent A, ring 1
   b. Tent A, ring 2
   c. Tent A, ring 3
   d. Tent B, ring 2
   e. Tent B, ring 3

Setup, Answers, and Explanations

Practice Game 1

This game has elements of sequencing and matching. The first, second, and third rules provide fairly informative sequencing information, so make the primary diagram a sequencing diagram, with a grid for matching wine-types to the sequence spots (1–6) and the wineries that will be matched to those spots:

	1	2	3	4	5	6
D/V/P/M/A/B						
w						
r						
s						

The first and second restrictions give you the following joint sequence string:

D/A—V/P

The third restriction gives you concrete information, which can be entered into the diagram and you can enter the fifth restriction into the diagram as a note:

	1	2	3	4	5	6
D/V/P/M̶/A/B	M					
w(ex. 4)						
r	✓					
s	✓					

The sixth restriction tells you that the number of checkmarks in column 6 will be greater than column 1—so there must be three under 6 and exactly two under 1. It also tells you that the number of checkmarks under V will be greater than the number under P. This tells us that spot 6 cannot be P, but we still need to keep this information noted next to the diagram:

	1	2	3	4	5	6
D/V/P/M̶/A/B	M					P̶
w (ex. 4)	✗					✓
r	✓					✓
s	✓					✓

D/A—V/P

#V > #P

Also note that given the sequence string D/A—V/P, neither V nor P can be in spots 2 or 3 (they would leave no room for D/A to their left), and neither D nor A could be in spots 5 or 6 (they would leave no room for V/P to their right):

	1	2	3	4	5	6
D/V/P/M̶/A/B	M	V̶ P̶	V̶ P̶		D̶ A̶	D̶ A̶ P̶
w (ex. 4)	✗					✓
r	✓					✓
s	✓					✓

D/A—V/P

#V > #P

Can we make any further deductions? The sequencing information is fairly rich, so see what options you have for adding the remaining winery B into the sequence. Since spot 1 has M, we just consider spots 2–6. If B comes before D/A—V/P, then we know that P comes before V, so that P is not in spot 6: B—D/A—PV. If B comes in between D/A and V/P, then we again we know that P comes before V, so that P is not in spot 6: D/A—B—PV. If B comes after D/A—V/P, then we have D/A—V/P—B.

So we have three options:

B—D/A—PV

D/A—B—PV

D/A—V/P—B

Question 1

The correct answer is choice **b**. This is a "Test-the-Rules" question. The first restriction rules out choice **d**, since Picceti and V. Sattui precede Domain Chandon. The second restriction rules out choice **e**, since Domaine Chandon and Artesa are not immediately adjacent on the itinerary. The third restriction rules out choice **c**, since Mumm is not the first winery. The fifth restriction rules out choice **a**, since it would mean that three wine-types are tasted at Piccetti (this requires the deductions we already made—that since two wine-types are tasted in spot 1 as per the third restriction, three are tasted in spot 6).

Question 2

The correct answer is choice **d**. The new information means that we need to fit two checkmarks in the r-row before any checkmarks occur in the w-row. Since exactly four spots will have checkmarks in the w-row (by the fourth restriction), we need to fit two r-row checkmarks under spots 1 and 2:

D/V/P/M̶/A/B	1	2	3	4	5	6
	M	V̶ P	V̶ P		D̶ A	D̶ A P
w (ex. 4)	✗	✗	✓	✓	✓	✓
r	✓	✓				✓
s	✓					✓

D/A—V/P

#V > #P

Now scan the answer choices to see if you can find a statement that must be true. Since P cannot appear in spots 1, 2, or 3, it must appear in 4, 5, or 6—and each of 4, 5, and 6 has a checkmark in the w-row. So choice **d** is the correct answer, that the group must taste white wine at Piccetti.

We could also use the three sequence strings to systematically check each answer choice to see if the statement in that answer choice could be false.

Again, the three strings are:

B—D/A—PV

D/A—B—PV

D/A—V/P—B

These three possible sequence strings can be placed into spots 2–6. If we use D/A—B—PV, Black Stallion will be in spot 4, and there is no requirement that red wine is tasted in spot 4—so choice **a** is incorrect. If we use D/A—B—PV, Domaine Chandon could be in the spot 2, where no white wine is tasted—so choice **b** is incorrect. If we use D/A—B—PV, then Artesa could be in spot 3, and there is no requirement that red wine is tasted in spot 4—so **c** is incorrect. If we use D/A—V/P—B, then V. Sattui could be in spot 4 and there is no requirement that red wine is tasted in spot 4—so choice **e** is incorrect.

Question 3

The correct answer is choice **e**. If B—A holds, then we must be using the sequence string B—D/A—PV, and our diagram will look like:

D/V/P/M̶/A/B	1	2	3	4	5	6
	M	B	D/A	A/D	P	V
w (ex. 4)	✗					✓
r	✓					✓
s	✓					✓

#V > #P

Scan the answer choices to see which is given in the diagram—choice **e**, that P is in spot 5, is given by in diagram.

Question 4

The correct answer is choice **a**. Check each of the three possible sequence strings to see which one allows there to be two letters in between P and B:

B—D/A—PV
D/A—B—PV
D/A—V/P—B

Only B—D/A—PV allows there to be two letters between P and B. So again, we have the following diagram:

D/V/P/M̶/A/B	1	2	3	4	5	6
	M	B	D/A	A/D	P	V
w (ex. 4)	✗					✓
r	✓					✓
s	✓					✓

D/A—V/P
#V > #P

Only the information in choice **a**—r and s are tasted at V—is given in this diagram, so **a** is the correct answer.

Question 5

The correct answer is choice **e**. The number of checkmarks under spot 5 is the same as the number under spot 6—namely, all three of w, r, and s are checked. If spot 5 has three checkmarks, P can't be in spot 5, because by the fifth restriction, it must have less checkmarks than V. So, two of our three possible sequence strings are ruled out (namely B—D/A—PV and D/A—B—PV, which both have P in spot 5), and we have the sequence string D/A—V/P—B. But again, since P is not spot 5, we can further determine this: D/A—PV—B.

D/V/P/M̶/A/B	1	2	3	4	5	6
	M	D/A	A/D	P	V	B
w (ex. 4)	✗				✓	✓
r	✓				✓	✓
s	✓				✓	✓

1 or 2

#V > #P

Finally, we have noted that P must have one or two checkmarks, since it must have fewer checkmarks than V.

Now scan the answer choices to see which one is inconsistent with this diagram. Choice **e** is inconsistent with the diagram, since the fifth spot has three checkmarks, and the fourth can have at most two checkmarks—so choice **e** is the correct answer.

Practice Game 2

This game has a sequencing element (each photo is ranked first through fifth), and matching element (each photo is either black and white or color). Three of the four restrictions give sequencing information, so make the primary diagram a sequencing diagram, with a row for the sequence spots (1–5) and the photographers (A through E) will be matched to those spots. Since there are only two options for the matching (color or black and white), and each photo/spot can only be matched to one of the two options (each photo is only color or only black and white, not both), we can use an unexpanded grid:

	1	2	3	4	5
A/B/C/D/E					
c/bw					

The first and second restrictions can be incorporated into the diagram:

	1	2	3	4	5
A/B/C/D̶/E		D			
c/bw					c

The third restriction can be symbolized: A—E

The fourth restriction can be symbolized: E = bw, B = bw.

Notice that since spot 5 must contain a color photo, it cannot contain E or B—that leaves C and A. But now consider the sequencing information: E must come after A, so A can't be last.

Therefore, C is fifth:

	1	2	3	4	5
A/B/~~C~~/~~D~~/E		D			C
c/bw					c

A——E

E = bw, B = bw

We need to place A——E and B in spots 1, 3, and 4. There are three ways to do this:

B——A——E

A——B——E

A——E——B

Notice that whatever the case, spot 4 will contain either E or B, and therefore be a black and white photograph. All in all, we have:

	1	2	3	4	5
A/B/~~C~~/~~D~~/E		D			C
c/bw				bw	c

B——A——E

A——B——E

A——E——B

E = bw, B = bw

All three possible scenarios for A, B, and E were placed under the grid to show how you might be flexible with your notations, but if it is confusing, just keep in mind that the real sequence string is A——E, and B must float somewhere on this string.

Question 1

The correct answer is choice **c**. This is a "Test-the-Rules" question. The first restriction rules out choice **a**, since D is not second. The second restriction does not rule out anything by itself, but in combination with the fourth restriction, it does. Choice **d** violates a combination of these two restrictions: the fifth spot

must be color, but B is black and white (and so can't be fifth). Similarly, for choice **e**, the fifth spot must be color, but E is black and white (and so can't be fifth). Finally, the third restriction rules out choice **b**, since A is not ranked higher than E.

Question 2

The correct answer is choice **b**. Scan the choices for something that contradicts our diagram. Since spot 4 must be black and white, choice **b**, which says that the fourth place photo must be color, is the correct answer.

Question 3

The correct answer is choice **c**. If the third place photo is color, the third place photo cannot be E or B. Therefore, it must be A and the sequence scenario in play here is B——A——E):

	1	2	3	4	5
A/B/~~C~~/~~D~~/E	B	D	A	E	C
c/bw	bw		c	bw	c

B——A——E

A——B——E

A——E——B

E = bw, B = bw

Compare the answer choices against the diagram to see which one is not given by the diagram. The second place photo, D, could be either color or black and white, so **c** is the correct answer. The other choices all give statements that are in fact true in this diagram and so are incorrect.

Question 4

The correct answer is choice **a**. Check each answer to see if it could be accommodated by the initial diagram and the restrictions (in particular, since the answer choices deal with sequencing, the three sequencing scenarios).

	1	2	3	4	5
A/B/C̶/D̶/E		D			C
c/bw				bw	c

B—A—E
A—B—E
A—E—B
E = bw, B = bw

In all three of the sequencing scenarios, A cannot be immediately adjacent to B. When we plug B—A—E into the diagram, we see that B is isolated from all other letters (including A) by D. When we plug either A—B—E or A—E—B into the diagram, we see that A is isolated from all other letters (including B) by D. So, A cannot be immediately next to B, and choice **a** is the correct answer. The other choices represent sequencing statements that are made possible by at least one of the three sequencing scenarios.

Question 5

The correct answer is choice **e**. See which of the three sequencing scenarios is compatible with there being exactly one letter in between B and C. Only the second, A—B—E, allows this:

	1	2	3	4	5
A/B/C̶/D̶/E	A	D	B	E	C
c/bw			bw	bw	c

B—A—E
A—B—E
A—E—B
E = bw, B = bw

You could also produce this sequence just by noting that if C is fifth, then B has to be third (since there is one space in between them), which forces A into the first spot and E into fourth spot (to keep A ranked higher than E). Now scan the answer

choices for a statement guaranteed by this diagram. According to the diagram, A ranks first, so choice **e** is correct. The other choices all present statements that are false according to this diagram, and so are incorrect.

Practice Game 3

This game combines an element of selection (five of eight songs) and sequencing (ordering those five songs into tracks on a CD). Given the mix of sequencing and selection rules, be prepared to use both diagrams:

$$\underline{\quad}\ \underline{\quad}\ \underline{\quad}\ \underline{\quad}\ \underline{\quad}\quad (H\ I\ J\ K\ L\ M\ N\ O)$$
$$1\quad 2\quad 3\quad 4\quad 5$$

Now symbolize the restrictions:

If selected, H—J
If selected, K—L
I = 4 → J = 1
Contrapositive: J ≠ 1 → I ≠ 4
H or K

The firth restriction can be entered into the diagram:

$$\underline{\quad}\ \underline{\quad}\ \underline{N}\ \underline{\quad}\ \underline{\quad}\quad (H\ I\ J\ K\ L\ M\ N\ O)$$
$$1\quad 2\quad 3\quad 4\quad 5$$

There are no obvious upfront deductions to be made, so move on to the questions. Note, however, that H and K appear in the first, fourth, and fifth restrictions, so they might be key players in the game.

Question 1

The correct answer is choice **d**. This is a "Test-the-Rules" question. The first restriction rules out choice **c**, since H does not precede J. The second restriction rules out choice **a**, since K does not precede L. The third restriction rules out choice **b**, since I is fourth but J is not first. The fourth restriction rules out choice **e**, since neither H nor K are selected.

Question 2

The correct answer is choice **b**. If both J and L preceded N, then all the other songs go after N. Since H or K must be selected, either the first or the second restriction will have to be in effect. Either way, H or K must be placed after J and N, and so at least one of these two restrictions would be violated.

Question 3

The correct answer is choice **a**. If the fourth track is song I, then by the third restriction, the first track must be song J. This means that H cannot be on the CD, because if it were, it would have to precede J (the first restriction), but J is the first track. Since H is not on the CD, K must be on the CD (the fourth restriction).

So we have:

J _ N I _ (H̶ K̲ L M O)
1 2 3 4 5

Now consider each answer choice. If L is second, then K must be fifth—but this would violate the second restriction. So K cannot be second—choice **a**.

Question 4

The correct answer is choice **c**. If H is selected, then J could not be first, since that would violate the first restriction. But if J is not first, then by the contrapositive of the third restriction, I is not fourth. Since I cannot be fourth, N—which is third—cannot immediately precede I.

Question 5

The correct answer is choice **a**. We are supposing that L and J are selected and that L—J. We know from Question 2 that L and J cannot both precede N.

Therefore, we get three possibilities:

S1

_ L N J _
1 2 3 4 5

S2

_ L N J _
1 2 3 4 5

S3

_ _ N L J
1 2 3 4 5

Since K must precede L if it is on the CD, these three scenarios show that K cannot be fourth (the latest it could appear would be the second track). So choice **a** is correct.

Practice Game 4

This game combines an element of selection (four of seven restaurants) and sequencing (ranking those four restaurants). Since there are a number of sequencing rules and a number of selection rules, you will likely have to use both diagrams:

_ _ _ _ (A B C D E F G)
1 2 3 4

The first restriction can be entered into the diagram:

_ C _ _ (A B C D E F G)
1 2 3 4

Now symbolize the other restrictions:

A or B → E
Contrapositive: ≠E → ≠A and ≠B

E → ≠F
Contrapositive: F → ≠E
E̶F̶
If ranked, D—G
If ranked, G—C

Notice that these last two are not regular sequence strings—they each require that the given elements are selected first. For this reason, it doesn't make sense to combine them into a joint sequence string (D—G—C), unless you keep in mind that all three elements are required for this string to hold. This is because you would lose the information that each one separately requires both elements to first be selected (e.g., if you write D—G—C, you might think that D—C is a restriction, but this is not required as long as G is not selected).

Now try to digest the action of this game. The first thing to do is consider the conditional selection statements in relation to each other. The two statements (the second and third restrictions) can be strung together via E:

$$F \rightarrow \neq E \rightarrow \neq A \text{ and } \neq B$$

So if F is chosen, A, E, and B are not. A lot has been excluded from the top four here, so let's see where this goes. C is chosen regardless, so that only leaves D and G, and we have:

$$\underline{\quad} \quad \underline{C} \quad \underline{\quad} \quad \underline{\quad} \qquad (\cancel{A} \, B \, \underline{D} \, \cancel{E} \, \cancel{F} \, \underline{G})$$
$$\,1 \quad\; 2 \quad\; 3 \quad\; 4$$

A or B → E
≠E→≠A and ≠B
If ranked, D—G
If ranked, G—C

But consider the last two restrictions. G cannot be first, since D must go before G. However, G cannot be third or fourth because G must go before C. F cannot be first because then D and G would be third or fourth, but this cannot be, since G must go before C. And D cannot be first, since that would force G to go after C. So we must conclude that F cannot be chosen no matter what!

Therefore, our initial diagram looks like this:

$$\underline{\quad} \quad \underline{C} \quad \underline{\quad} \quad \underline{\quad} \qquad (A \, B \, D \, E \, \cancel{F} \, G)$$
$$\,1 \quad\; 2 \quad\; 3 \quad\; 4$$

Move on to the questions.

Question 1

The correct answer is choice **e**. This is a "Test-the-Rules" question. The first restriction rules out choice **d**, since C is not ranked second. The second restriction rules out choice **a**, since A is chosen for the top four, but E is not. The third restriction rules out choice **c**, since both E and F are chosen for the top four. The fifth restriction rules out choice **b**, since G is not ranked above C (given that both are chosen for the top four).

Question 2

The correct answer is choice **c**. This question requires either remembering our up-front deductions or looking for rules that involve C and D. The last two restrictions together imply that if all three of D, G, and C are selected for the top four, then their relative ordering must be D—G—C. This ordering is contradicted by the ordering given in the question stem, C—D, and so all three of D, G, and C cannot be chosen—and since C and D are chosen, that means that G cannot be chosen.

At this point, you might note that what is really going on here is that D and G cannot both be chosen, since C must be chosen.

Question 3

The correct answer is choice **e**. We already figured out in our initial deductions that F cannot be chosen for the top four.

Question 4

The correct answer is choice **a**. You could take each answer choice in turn to see if the accompanying statement is possible or not. Consider the first answer choice: if G is chosen, then given the fifth restriction, it must be ranked first, since it is ranked above C, and C is ranked second. But if G is first, then nothing can be ranked above it, including E, so **a** is the correct answer.

Question 5

The correct answer is choice **a**. We already saw in Question 2 that D and G cannot both be selected together, since then the sequence must be D—G—C, which would not be possible given that C is second.

Practice Game 5

This game has a sequencing element relating to the order in which the children (G, W, Z, V, M, and D) approach the kind lady and a matching element—each child gets between one and three treats (c, h, and l). Since most of the restrictions give sequencing information, make the primary diagram a sequencing diagram for the order of approach (1–6) and rows for matching treat types to the children (or rather, costumes):

	1	2	3	4	5	6
G/W/Z/V/ M/D						
c						
h						
l						

The first restriction can be symbolized:

D>G

The second and third restrictions can be joined into the following sequence string:

W—Z—V
←G⊣

The fourth and fifth restrictions can be entered directly into the diagram:

	1	2	3	4	5	6
G/W/Z/V/M/D̶					D	
c	✓					
h	✓					
l	✓					

The sixth restriction can be shortened to:

No hh or cc

So cross out c and h for column 2, leaving l for column 2. The diagram and notations now look like:

	1	2	3	4	5	6
G/W/Z/V/M/D̶					D	
c	✓	✗				
h	✓	✗				
l	✓	✓				

W—Z—V
←G⊣
No hh or cc
D>G

Question 1

The correct answer is choice **d**. This is a "Test-the-Rules" question. The second restriction rules out choice **c**, since the witch does not come before the zombie. The second restriction also rules out choice **e**, since the zombie does not come before the vampire. The third restriction rules out choice **b**, since the ghost does not come before the zombie. The fifth restriction rules out choice **a**, since the devil is not fifth.

Question 2

The correct answer is choice **b**. Compare each answer choice to the initial diagram to see which one is contradicted by the diagram/notations. Choice **b** is correct because according to the diagram, spot 2 has exactly one checkmark, meaning that for it to have more checkmarks than spot 3, spot 3 would have to not have any checkmarks—contradicting the game condition that each child gets at least one candy-type. The rest of the answer choices provide statements that are consistent with the diagram.

Question 3

The correct answer is choice **a**. Start by incorporating the new information, that 6 = M and gets c, into the diagram:

	1	2	3	4	5	6
G/W/Z/V/M/Đ					D	M
c	✓	✗				✓
h	✓	✗				
l	✓	✓				

W—Z—V
←G⊣
No hh or cc
D>G

	1	2	3	4	5	6
G/W/Z/V/M/Đ	W	G	Z	V	D	M
c	✓	✗			✗	✓
h	✓	✗		✗	✓	✗
l	✓	✓			✓	

W—Z—V
←G⊣
No hh or cc
D>G

Since the last two spots are taken, we can try to fit the sequence string into spots 1–4. Z must be in spot 4 and V in spot 5. G cannot be in spot 1, because G must have either 1 or 2 checkmarks to have fewer checkmarks than D, and spot 1 has three checkmarks. So G is in spot 2, leaving W for spot 1. We also note that the restriction against adjacent h's or c's means that D cannot get c:

	1	2	3	4	5	6
G/W/Z/V/M/Đ	W	G	Z	V	D	M
c	✓	✗			✗	✓
h	✓	✗				
l	✓	✓				

W—Z—V
No hh or cc
D>G
←G⊣

Since we know that D has more checkmarks than G, it must have two checkmarks in the remaining two rows in that column, rows h and l. Since there is a checkmark in row h under column 5 now, columns 4 and 6 cannot have a checkmark in that row (by the sixth restriction):

Now scan the answer choices for a statement that contradicts this diagram. Choice **a** is the correct answer because according to the diagram, the mummy in fact does not get hard candy.

Question 4

The correct answer is choice **e**. Start by trying to place the ghost. We know from previous work that the ghost cannot be in spot 1, since spot 1 has three checkmarks and the ghost can have at most two checkmarks (due to the restriction that D>G). If the ghost gets chocolate, then according to the initial diagram, the ghost cannot be in spot 2 either, since the child in spot 2 does not get chocolate. To fit Z and V to the right of G, as required by the joint sequence string,

W—Z—V
←G⊣

G must be in spot 3. This pushes Z into spot 4 and V into spot 6, leaving M and W to be distributed into spots 1 and 2:

	1	2	3	4	5	6
G/W/Z/V/M/Đ	M/W	W/M	G	Z	D	V
c	✓	✗	✓	✗		
h	✓	✗				
l	✓	✓				

W—Z—V
←G⊣
No hh or cc
D>G

We have added the information that the ghost gets chocolate, and what follows from that (by the sixth restriction), that Z cannot get chocolate. Now, scan the answer choices for a statement guaranteed by this diagram. Choice **e**—that the zombie goes fourth—is given in the diagram, and so choice **e** is the correct answer.

Question 5

The correct answer is choice **d**. If the vampire goes fourth, then given the sequence string W, X, and G must go into spots 1–3. From previous work we know that G cannot go into spot 1. To keep Z to the right of G, G must therefore go into spot 2. This pushes Z into spot 3 and W into spot 1. The remaining spot, spot 6, goes to M:

	1	2	3	4	5	6
G/W/Z/V/M/Đ	W	G	Z	V	D	M
c	✓	✗				
h	✓	✗				
l	✓	✓				

W—Z—V
←G⊣
No hh or cc
D>G

There do not seem to be any other immediate further deductions to be made, so see if there is an answer choice that is guaranteed by this diagram. Choice **d**—that the ghost gets licorice—is given in the diagram.

Practice Game 6

This game combines an element of selection (five of seven landmarks) and sequencing (ordering those five landmarks into a tour). There is only one pure

selection rule (the first one), so go ahead and start with a sequencing diagram and use a selection list when necessary.

$$\underline{\quad}\ \underline{\quad}\ \underline{\quad}\ \underline{\quad}\ \underline{\quad}$$
$$1\quad 2\quad 3\quad 4\quad 5$$

Using abbreviations for the landmarks, the selection list is: C L D F B P S

Now symbolize the restrictions:

D → F and B
Contrapositive: ≠F or ≠B → ≠D

The second restriction:

2 = P or 2 = B
If selected, L—D
If selected, S//F—B

The fourth restriction can be written into the diagram:

$$\underline{\quad}\ \underline{\quad}\ \underline{\quad}\ \underline{C}\ \underline{\quad}$$
$$1\quad 2\quad 3\quad 4\quad 5$$

At this point, there are a couple of routes to take. The second restriction provides two distinct scenarios, so we could see what follows from each:

S1
$$\underline{\quad}\ \underline{P}\ \underline{\quad}\ \underline{C}\ \underline{\quad}$$
$$1\quad 2\quad 3\quad 4\quad 5$$

S2
$$\underline{\quad}\ \underline{B}\ \underline{\quad}\ \underline{C}\ \underline{\quad}$$
$$1\quad 2\quad 3\quad 4\quad 5$$

For the second scenario, we note that the restriction S//F—B means that we can't have both F and S on the tour—there wouldn't be enough room to the left of B. We can note this next to the scenario:

S1

$\underline{}$ $\underline{P}$ $\underline{}$ $\underline{C}$ $\underline{}$
1   2   3   4   5

S2

$\underline{}$ $\underline{B}$ $\underline{}$ $\underline{C}$ $\underline{}$
1   2   3   4   5
(≠S or ≠F)

Unfortunately, not much else seems to follow from the restrictions. At this point, you could either make two sub-scenarios for each of S1 and S2, depending on whether D is selected, or you could move to the questions.

Question 1

The correct answer is choice **b**. This is a "Test-the-Rules" question. The first restriction rules out choice **a**, since the dining hall is on the tour, but the fountain is not. The second restriction rules out choice **e**, since neither the porters lodge nor the bridge are second. The third restriction rules out choice **d**, since the library is not before the chapel. The fourth restriction rules out choice **c**, since the chapel is not fourth in the tour.

Question 2

The correct answer is choice **a**. If D is selected, then according to the first restriction, F and B are both selected. So we have selected D, F, B, and C.

At this point, you could either try to fill out the scenarios based on this information, or try out the answer choices. If we try out the answer choices, we would start with the first answer choice. If we try to select S for the tour, then we have filled our five slots with D, F, B, C, and S, and therefore by the second restriction, B would have to be second on the tour. But this is not possible since according to the fifth restriction, S and F need to precede B. So S cannot be selected for the tour and **a** is the correct answer.

If we had instead tried to use the scenarios, we could have reasoned as follows. Again, we have

selected D, F, B, and C. Consider how this selection plays out in our two scenarios.

In S1, since P is selected, we have all five letters selected:

S1

$\underline{}$ $\underline{P}$ $\underline{}$ $\underline{C}$ $\underline{}$ (D, F, B)
1   2   3   4   5

In S2, B is already selected, so we have room for one more:

S2

$\underline{}$ $\underline{B}$ $\underline{}$ $\underline{C}$ $\underline{}$ (D, F, one more)
1   2   3   4   5
(≠S or ≠F)

Notice, however, that we have noted that at least one of S or F can't be on the tour—and since F is on the tour, S cannot be:

S2

$\underline{}$ $\underline{B}$ $\underline{}$ $\underline{C}$ $\underline{}$ (D, F, one more)
1   2   3   4   5
(≠S)

Now compare each answer choice against the two scenarios to see which statement is forbidden by both. S is not chosen on either scenario, so the correct answer is **a**.

Question 3

The correct answer is choice **d**. If the bridge is toured before the senior common room (B—S), then we cannot have S//F—B. So, F cannot be on the tour (because by the fifth restriction, S//F—B would have to hold). Now, scanning the restrictions, we see that by the contrapositive of the first restriction, since F is not on the tour, D is not on the tour.

$\underline{C}$ $\underline{L}$ $\cancel{D}$ $\cancel{F}$ $\underline{B}$ $\underline{P}$ $\underline{S}$

This leaves L and P to be selected—so C, L, B, P, and S are on the tour. Only C is restricted to the fourth spot, so the list of letters that could be in spot 4 is: L, B, P, S. To double-check this, see if the other restrictions actually restrict the ordering. The first and third restrictions are irrelevant because D is not selected. The second restriction can be satisfied whether B or P is in spot 4 (since the other can be in spot 2). The fourth restriction is taken into account, and the fifth restriction is irrelevant because F is not selected. So, the correct answer is choice **d**.

Question 4

The correct answer is choice **b**. We know that both L and D are selected for the tour, and that L—D. Since D is selected, we know that F and B are selected. That gives us our five landmarks: L, D, F, B, and C. This means we are in scenario 2:

S2

$$\underline{} \quad \underline{B} \quad \underline{} \quad \underline{C} \quad \underline{} \quad (L—D, F$$
$$1 \quad 2 \quad 3 \quad 4 \quad 5$$

Compare each answer choice to see which statement must be true on this diagram. F could go in spot 5, with L in spot 1 and D in spot 3—so choice **a** is incorrect. The furthest left D could go in spot 3, since there must be room for L to its left and spot 2 is taken. So, B must come before D—this is choice **b**, the correct answer.

Question 5

The correct answer is choice **e**. This question requires either testing each answer choice in turn to see if it could be off the tour if the library is also off the tour, or pushing our deductions a bit further.

Let's first see if we can make some more deductions. We are looking for the landmark that could be off the tour. Since five of seven landmarks are selected, two will be left out. The question already tells us that L is left out, so that accounts for one of the two. So, both F and B must be selected, because if either one is not

selected, D cannot be selected either (by the contrapositive of the first restriction), and that would mean a total of three landmarks are not selected for the tour. If the other landmark not selected is P, then we would have C, D, F, B, and S on the tour; and since P would not be selected, B must be second; but then we not have room for S and F before B, as would be required by the fifth restriction, so P must be selected.

So we have:

$$\underline{C}\text{Ł}D\underline{F}\underline{B}PS$$

This means that either D or S must be the other landmark (besides L) left off the tour. Since landmark D is not an answer choice, landmark S must be the other one left off the tour—this is answer choice **e**.

You could also try to make further deductions using the scenarios. If L is not selected, we have two scenarios:

S1

$$\underline{} \quad \underline{P} \quad \underline{} \quad \underline{C} \quad \underline{} \quad (D\ F\ B\ S)$$
$$1 \quad 2 \quad 3 \quad 4 \quad 5$$

S2

$$\underline{} \quad \underline{B} \quad \underline{} \quad \underline{C} \quad \underline{} \quad (D\ P\ S/F)$$
$$1 \quad 2 \quad 3 \quad 4 \quad 5$$
$$(\neq S\ \text{or}\ \neq F)$$

(We wrote S/F in our list of letters to be selected from in S2 to remind us that both cannot be selected).

We recall from the initial digestion of the game that it seemed that the presence or absence of D might play a major role in the mechanics of the game. So, let's see what D's presence or absence means for each of S1 and S2.

In S1, if D is present, F and B must be (by the first restriction). So we would have:

S1.1

$$\underline{} \quad \underline{P} \quad \underline{} \quad \underline{C} \quad \underline{} \quad (D,\ F,\ B)$$
$$1 \quad 2 \quad 3 \quad 4 \quad 5$$

If D was absent, the remaining three letters would have to be F, B, and S:

S1.2

$\underline{}$ $\underline{P}$ $\underline{}$ $\underline{C}$ $\underline{}$ (F B S)
1   2   3   4   5

In S2, D and P and exactly one of S or F must be selected. By the first restriction, since D is selected, F must be selected (rather than S).

So we have:

S2

$\underline{}$ $\underline{B}$ $\underline{}$ $\underline{C}$ $\underline{}$ (D P F)
1   2   3   4   5
($\neq$S or $\neq$F)

Now see which of the landmarks in the answer choices fails to appear on at least one of the three scenarios, S1.1, S1.2, and S2. Only S fails to appear (in S1.1 and S2), and so choice **e** is the correct answer. P, B, C, and F all appear on all three scenarios and so choices **a** through **d** are incorrect.

Practice Game 7

This game combines elements of distribution and sequencing. We are to distribute eight friends (B, K, M, S, P, G, L, and C) into three cars, and then sequence those groups from first to third. The main action of the game is the distribution—the first, second, and fourth restrictions are strictly distribution rules. We can consider the whole game a distribution game in which the groups to be distributed happen to be labeled first, second, and last—or 1, 2, and 3. Essentially, it is a distribution game in which some of the rules, questions, and answer choices are couched in sequencing terms.

Since the second restriction says that M is third and G is first, we start our diagram like this:

$\underline{G}$ $\underline{}$ $\underline{}$ $\underline{}$ $\underline{}$ $\underline{}$ $\underline{M}$ $\underline{}$ $\underline{}$
   1   2   3

The first restriction says that M and K form a block and P and S form a block:

$\underline{G}$ $\underline{}$ $\underline{}$ $\underline{}$ $\underline{}$ $\underline{}$ $\underline{M}$ $\underline{K}$ $\underline{}$
   1   2   3
PS

The third restriction says that L and S form an anti-block:

~~LS~~

The fourth restriction says that B is either with K or P:

BK or BP

The fifth restriction says:

L = 1 → C = 3
C ≠ 3 → L ≠ 1

The sixth can just be noted:

B not immediately after S.

Now try to make some deductions. Since PS form a block, we can see that the diagram allows for two scenarios, one in which PS is in 1, and one in which PS is in 2:

S1:

$\underline{G}$ $\underline{P}$ $\underline{S}$ $\underline{}$ $\underline{}$ $\underline{}$ $\underline{M}$ $\underline{K}$ $\underline{}$
   1   2   3

S2:

$\underline{G}$ $\underline{}$ $\underline{}$ $\underline{P}$ $\underline{S}$ $\underline{}$ $\underline{M}$ $\underline{K}$ $\underline{}$
   1   2   3

The fourth restriction tells us that B is either with K or P. In S1, this means B is in car 3, and the remaining letters, C and L, must be in car 2 because of the fifth restriction:

S1:

$$\underline{G}\ \underline{P}\ \underline{S} \qquad \underline{C}\ \underline{L}\ \underline{} \qquad \underline{M}\ \underline{K}\ \underline{B}$$
$$\quad 1 \qquad\qquad 2 \qquad\qquad 3$$

In S2, B is either in car 2 or car 3. But if we consider the sixth restriction—that B does not depart immediately after S—we realize that B cannot be in car 3:

S2:

$$\underline{G}\ \underline{}\ \underline{} \qquad \underline{P}\ \underline{S}\ \underline{B} \qquad \underline{M}\ \underline{K}\ \underline{}$$
$$\quad 1 \qquad\qquad 2 \qquad\qquad 3$$

Now consider the fifth restriction. If L is in 1, then C must be in 3; so we cannot have both L and C in 1, which means that L and C must be distributed between 1 and 3:

S2:

$$\underline{G}\ \underline{L/C}\ \underline{} \qquad \underline{P}\ \underline{S}\ \underline{B} \qquad \underline{M}\ \underline{K}\ \underline{C/L}$$
$$\quad 1 \qquad\qquad 2 \qquad\qquad 3$$

With these scenarios in mind, we can turn to the questions.

Question 1

The correct answer is choice **c**. Check each answer choice against the scenario diagrams. In neither S1 nor S2 is B in a car that departs before P, so **c** is the correct answer. Even if we hadn't made the scenarios, we can still see that there's no room for P and S in car 3, so the latest that P could be is car 2. But we can also see that B has to go with either MK of SP, so it can never fit in car 1. Therefore, B cannot go before P.

Question 2

The correct answer is choice **b**. If S departs neither first nor last, then S must depart in car 2, and we must

be in S2. Scan for an answer choice that is guaranteed by S2—S and B ride in the same car, car 2, which his choice **b**.

Question 3

The correct answer is choice **d**. If C and L are not in the same car, we must again be in S2. Scan for an answer choice that contradicts S2. P and B leave at the same time on S2, so the statement that P departs before B cannot be true, and therefore **d** is the correct answer.

Question 4

The correct answer is choice **c**. We are looking for all the letters that appear in car 1, on either scenario. In S1, G, P and S appear in car 1. In S2, G, L and C appear in car 1. Altogether, G, P, S, L and C can appear in car 1. This is choice **c**. Even if you didn't see this, you could cross out **d** and **e** because you know that B can't be in car 1, and you can cross out **a** since you've seen situations where P is in car 1.

Question 5

The correct answer is choice **e**. Normally, we would redo the deductions and diagramming, except without the third restriction. But, you might have noticed that we in fact never used the third restriction. The fact that Smita and Lauren do not ride together was completely irrelevant to the scenarios generated in the initial diagramming. So, we just have the same two scenarios:

S1:

$$\underline{G}\ \underline{P}\ \underline{S} \qquad \underline{C}\ \underline{L}\ \underline{} \qquad \underline{M}\ \underline{K}\ \underline{B}$$
$$\quad 1 \qquad\qquad 2 \qquad\qquad 3$$

S2:

$$\underline{G}\ \underline{L/C}\ \underline{} \qquad \underline{P}\ \underline{S}\ \underline{B} \qquad \underline{M}\ \underline{K}\ \underline{C/L}$$
$$\quad 1 \qquad\qquad 2 \qquad\qquad 3$$

Each of the statements is true in at least one of the scenarios except for the statement that Smita departs third—she must either depart first or second. Therefore, the correct answer is **e**.

Practice Game 8

This game combines elements of distribution and sequencing. The five animals—H, E, T, L, and M—are to be distributed into two tents, A and B, and then sequenced from ring 1 to ring 3 (with one empty ring). However, we can consider this a matching game at core—each of the five animals is to be matched to a letter (A or B) and a number (1 to 3), at most one for each letter-number combination. So we can set up a grid with numbers along the top and letters down the side, and try to place the animals into the grid. That is, we want to place the letters H, E, T, L, and M into this grid:

	1	2	3
A			
B			

The first restriction says that M performs in ring 1, and the second that L and T are in tent B:

	1	2	3	
A				
B				L, T

M

The third restriction states that E is in a lower-numbered ring than L and H:
E—L//H

We start by noting that if E—L//H, E can't be in ring 3, and neither L nor H can be in ring 1:

	1	2	3	
A				
B				L, T

M Ł H̶   Ɇ

Now let's look at the fourth restriction:

E and T perform in the same tent.

Since, by way of the second restriction, we already know that T performs in tent B, we now also know that E performs in tent B. Since each tent has three rings, and E, L, and T must all perform in tent B, the tent is now closed to M and H, who must perform in tent A. Adding this information to our grid, we have:

	1	2	3	
A				M, H
B				E, L, T

M Ł   Ɇ

Notice that according to the grid, M must be in tent A and also in ring 1, so the position of M has been determined and we now have:

	1	2	3	
A	M			H
B				E, L, T

Ł   Ɇ

No other deductions can be made from the information, so we can turn to the questions.

Question 1

The correct answer is choice **b**. We know that each of the three rings in tent B is occupied by one of E, L, or T, so H must perform in tent A, making choice **b** false and the correct answer. Again, since E, L, and T occupy all of tent B, M must perform in tent A, making choice **a** true, and incorrect. Looking at ring 2, we see that there are no restrictions on E or L performing there, so choices **c** and **d** could be true, and so these answer choices are incorrect. While H is limited to tent A, it can perform in either ring 2, or ring 3, so choice **e** can be true, and is incorrect.

Question 2

The correct answer is choice **e**. The new information tells us that T performs in a ring numbered three, but we also know that T performs in tent B, so combining these pieces of information, we know that T must perform in tent B, ring 3. Let's add this to the grid:

	1	2	3	
A	M			H
B			T	E, L

t̶   E̶

Now, using the third restriction:

E—L//H

We know that E occupies a lower numbered ring than L, and since they have to occupy the two remaining spots in tent B, rings 1 and 2, E must occupy ring 1 and L must occupy ring 2. Now we have:

	1	2	3	
A	M			H
B	E	L	T	

t̶   E̶

No further deductions can be made, so we turn to the answer choices. Our grid tells us that M must perform in tent A, ring 1, and so choice **a** is incorrect. Similarly, we know that E must perform in tent B, ring 1 so choice **b** is incorrect. The grid also makes clear that E and T perform in rings adjacent to L so choices **c** and **d** are incorrect. We cannot, however, determine whether H performs in tent A, ring 2 or in tent A, ring 3, so while choice **e** may be true, it may also be false, and so choice **e** is the correct answer.

Question 3

The correct answer is choice **d**. Looking at our grid again:

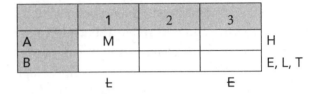

	1	2	3	
A	M			H
B				E, L, T

t̶   E̶

We know that H must perform in tent A. This allows us to eliminate any answer choice that includes H, so choices **c** and **e** are incorrect and can be eliminated. The three remaining choices include only E, L, and T. Let's start with the choice that includes them all, choice **d**. Here, building scenarios, will be an effective way to determine if any one of E, L, or T can be eliminated from tent B, ring 2.

The third restriction prevents L from occupying ring 1, but either T or E may fill that spot. Let's try them both, beginning with E:

S1

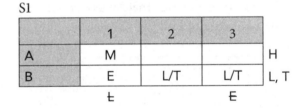

	1	2	3	
A	M			H
B	E	L/T	L/T	L, T

t̶   E̶

In S1, after E occupies ring 1, L or T can occupy ring 2, as there are no restrictions against either. Let's now look at what happens when T is in ring 1:

S2

	1	2	3	
A	M			H
B	T	E	L	

t̶   E̶

In S2, after T fills ring 1, E and L are left to fill rings 2 and 3, but because of the third restriction, E cannot occupy ring 3 and must then occupy ring 2, leaving ring 3 for L. Taken together these scenarios show that E, L, or T can occupy tent B, ring 2, and so choice **d** is correct. Choices **a** and **b**, while accurate, are only partial lists and so are incorrect answer choices.

Question 4

The correct answer is choice **a**. Check each statement against the grid:

	1	2	3	
A	M			H
B				E, L, T
	Ŀ		E	

Since we know that M occupies tent A, ring 1 and the only other performer in tent A is H, H must occupy either ring 2 or ring 3, so choice **a** could be true, and you could circle it and move on, but let's examine the remaining choices. Choice **b** is false, because we know that M performs in tent A, ring 1. Since there are three rings and three performers for tent B, each ring must have a performer, so choice **c** is false and incorrect. By the fourth restriction we know that E performs in the same tent as T, and since the second restriction tells us T performs in tent B, E must also perform in tent B, so choice **d** is false and incorrect. We know that E, L, and T must each occupy one of the three rings in tent B, leaving no open rings in tent B for H, so choice **e** is false and incorrect.

Question 5

The correct answer is choice **b**. The new information can be noted as:

$$T—E$$

We can combine this new information with what we already have in the third restriction to get:

$$T—E—L//H$$

There are two key pieces of information to be culled from this: first, it determines the order of tent B. We know that E, L, and T occupy all the rings in tent B, and now we know that T is in a lower-numbered ring than E, and E is in a lower-numbered ring than L, so the order must be, T—E—L. Let's put that into the grid:

	1	2	3	
A	M			H
B	T	E	L	
	Ŀ		E	

The second piece of information relates to the placement of H. We know that though H is in tent A, and E in tent B, but E must be in a lower-numbered ring, and since we know that E is in ring 2, H must occupy ring 3, in tent A. So now we have:

	1	2	3
A	M		H
B	T	E	L
	Ŀ		E

Now check the answer choices against the grid. Tent A, ring 1 is occupied by M, so choice **a** is incorrect. Tent A, ring 3 is occupied by H, so choice **c** is incorrect. Tent B, ring 2 is occupied by E, so choice **d** is incorrect. Tent B, ring 3 is occupied by L, so choice **e** is incorrect. Only tent A, ring 2 remains open, and so choice **b** is the correct answer.

Practice Set 1

Game 1

Seven students—Betty, Carl, Diane, Earl, Fran, Greg, and Hugo—are to be assigned to exactly one of two class sections, a morning section and an afternoon section, according to the following restrictions:

Each section must have a minimum of three students and a maximum of four students:

If Greg is in the morning section, Carl is in the afternoon section.
Betty and Carl must be in the same section.
Diane is in the afternoon section.
Earl and Fran cannot be in the same section.

1. If exactly four students are in the afternoon section, then those four students could be:
   a. Carl, Betty, Earl, Hugo
   b. Diane, Greg, Fran, Hugo
   c. Diane, Carl, Hugo, Earl
   d. Diane, Greg, Earl, Fran
   e. Diane, Betty, Fran, Hugo

2. If Betty is in the morning section, which one of the following must be true?
   a. Exactly three students are in the morning section.
   b. Exactly four students are in the morning section.
   c. Hugo is in the morning section.
   d. Diane and Greg are in the same section.
   e. Earl and Greg are in the same section.

3. Which one of the following could be a complete and accurate list of the students in the morning section?
   a. Betty, Carl, Diane, Greg
   b. Betty, Diane, Earl, Fran, Greg
   c. Diane, Earl, Fran, Greg, Hugo
   d. Betty, Carl, Earl, Fran, Greg, Hugo
   e. Betty, Carl, Diane, Earl, Fran, Greg

4. If Carl is in the afternoon section, which pair of students could be in the morning section?
   a. Fran, Greg
   b. Diane, Fran
   c. Betty, Earl
   d. Betty, Fran
   e. Fran, Earl

5. If Greg is not in the afternoon section, which student must be in the morning section?
   a. Earl
   b. Betty
   c. Carl
   d. Hugo
   e. Fran

Game 2

Eight paintings, identified by letter—I, J, K, L, M, N, O, and P—are to be hung in a house. The house has 4 rooms; one painting is to go into room 1, two paintings into room 2, two paintings into room 3, and three paintings into room 4, according to the following conditions:

> Painting J goes in room 3.
> Painting M cannot go in the same room as painting N.
> Painting K must go in the same room as painting L.
> If Painting O goes in room 2, then painting M goes in room 4.

1. Which one of the following is a complete and accurate distribution of paintings into the rooms of the house?
   a. Room 1: I
      Room 2: K, L
      Room 3: O, J
      Room 4: M, P, N
   b. Room 1: I
      Room 2: O, P
      Room 3: M, J
      Room 4: N, K, L
   c. Room 1: M
      Room 2: N, I
      Room 3: J, P
      Room 4: O, K, L
   d. Room 1: N
      Room 2: M, J
      Room 3: O, P
      Room 4: K, L, I
   e. Room 1: P
      Room 2: K, N
      Room 3: M, J
      Room 4: O, L, I

2. If painting M is placed in room 2, then which of the following is a complete and accurate list of all the other paintings that could be placed in room 2?
   a. I
   b. I, P
   c. P, N
   d. I, P, O
   e. P, K, L

3. If painting O is placed in the same room as painting N, then which of the following is a complete and accurate list of all the rooms in which M could be placed?
   a. Room 4
   b. Rooms 1, 3
   c. Rooms 2, 3, 4
   d. Rooms 1, 3, 4
   e. Rooms 1, 2, 3, 4

4. If painting O is placed in room 2, which one of the following statements could be true?
   a. Painting P is placed in room 4.
   b. Painting I is placed in room 3.
   c. Painting I is placed in room 4.
   d. Painting L is placed in room 2.
   e. Painting K is placed in room 1.

5. The placement of all eight paintings can be determined if which of the following statements is true?
   a. Painting K is in room 2, M in room 1, and N in room 4.
   b. Paintings O and P are in room 2, and painting I is in room 1.
   c. Paintings O, N, and I are in room 4.
   d. Paintings I and P are in room 2, and painting O in room 1.
   e. Paintings K and L are in room 2, and panting I in room 4.

Game 3

An airport is building seven terminals—A, B, C, D, E, F, and G—over the course of seven years. Due to the airport design, the terminals must be built one at a time, at the rate of one terminal per year and must be built according to the following restrictions:

Terminal C is built in year 2.
If Terminal F is built in year 4, Terminal B must be built after Terminal G.
Terminal A must be built in year 3 or year 7.
Terminal E must be built in the year immediately before or after the year Terminal D is built.

1. Which one of the following is an acceptable schedule for building the terminals, starting in year 1 and ending in year 7?
a. B, C, A, F, G, E, D
b. B, C, F, D, E, G, A
c. G, C, E, D, F, A, B
d. F, D, E, C, G, B, A
e. F, C, D, B, G, E, A

2. If Terminal G is built in year 7, then any of the following could be true EXCEPT:
a. Terminal B is built in year 1.
b. Terminal F is built in year 6.
c. Terminal E is built in year 5.
d. Terminal F is built in year 4.
e. Terminal D is built in year 5.

3. If Terminal F is built in year 4, which of the following is a complete and accurate list of the years in which Terminal E could be built?
a. 5, 6
b. 5, 6, 7
c. 1, 3, 5, 7
d. 2, 5, 6, 7
e. 3, 5, 6, 7

4. Which of the following is a complete and accurate list of the terminals that could be built in year 1?
a. B, F, G
b. A, D, G
c. B, E, F, G
d. B, G
e. B, C, F

5. If Terminal F is built in year 4, then there are exactly how many acceptable orders in which the terminals could be built?
a. One
b. Two
c. Three
d. Five
e. Six

Game 4

Seven friends—Helen, Ian, Jack, Kate, Lorna, Matt, and Nick—sit in the same row in a movie theater. They take seats 1 through 7, where seat 1 is the left-most seat, according to the following conditions:

Jack sits to the right of Helen but to the left of Matt.
Kate sits in between Ian and Lorna.
If Jack sits to the left of Nick, then Kate sits to the left of Jack.
If Nick sits to the left of Jack, then Lorna sits to the left of Kate.

1. Which one of the following could be an accurate ordering of the friends, from left to right?
   a. I, N, K, H, L, J, M
   b. H, J, L, M, K, I, N
   c. I, K, H, M, N, J, L
   d. H, L, N, I, J, M, K
   e. I, K, H, L, J, N, M

2. If Jack sits in seat 6, which one of the following is a complete and accurate list of the friends who could sit in seat 5?
   a. I, H
   b. I, N, H
   c. K, H, M, N
   d. I, N, H, J, L
   e. I, K, H, M, N

3. Which one of the following cannot be true?
   a. Kate sits in seat 2
   b. Matt sits in seat 5
   c. Jack sits in seat 2
   d. Lorna sits in seat 7
   e. Helen sits in seat 1

4. Which one of the following is the lowest numbered seat in which Matt could sit?
   a. One
   b. Three
   c. Four
   d. Five
   e. Six

5. If Kate sits to the left of Lorna, which one of the following could be true?
   a. Ian sits in seat 3
   b. Matt sits in seat 4
   c. Nick sits in seat 3
   d. Helen sits in seat 4
   e. Jack sits in seat 3

Game 5

Of seven books—A, B, C, D, E, F, and G—at most four will be chosen for a reading list, according to the following set of restrictions:

If A is chosen, C will not be chosen.
If B is chosen, E will be chosen.
If A is not chosen, then either F or G must be chosen.
If both F and G are chosen, then E is not chosen and D is chosen.

1. Which one of the following could be a complete and accurate list of the books chosen for the reading list?
   a. C, D
   b. F, G, A
   c. A, B, F, D
   d. C, A, B, E
   e. A, B, E, F

2. Which one of the following could be true?
   a. None of A, F, or G is chosen
   b. C is chosen, and neither F nor G is chosen
   c. F, G, and B are chosen
   d. B and E are not chosen, and A is chosen
   e. D is not chosen, and F and G are chosen

3. If neither F nor G is chosen, which one of the following cannot be true?
   a. Both B and E are chosen
   b. Both C and E are chosen
   c. Both B and D are chosen
   d. A, D, and E are chosen
   e. A, B, D, and E are chosen

4. If C is chosen but F is not chosen, which one of following must be chosen?
   a. Book B
   b. Book G
   c. Book E
   d. Book D
   e. Book A

5. If B and G are chosen, which one of the following must be true?
   a. A is chosen
   b. C is not chosen
   c. F is not chosen
   d. A is not chosen
   e. D is chosen

Game 6

At least five and at most seven cars are to be selected for a car show from a set of nine cars, including two red antique cars, three red modern cars, one white antique car, and three white modern cars. The cars are to be selected according to the following conditions:

Exactly two antique cars are selected.
At least three and at most four red cars are selected.
If the white antique car is selected, at least two white modern cars are selected.
Either the white antique car or at least two red modern cars must be selected.

1. Which one of the following could be a complete and accurate list of the cars selected for the show?
   a. One white antique car, one white modern car, one red antique car, two red modern cars
   b. One white antique car, two white modern cars, three red modern cars
   c. One red modern car, two red antique cars, and two white modern cars
   d. One red antique car, one white antique car, two white modern cars, three red modern cars
   e. Two red antique cars, three red modern cars, and one white modern car

2. If exactly one red antique car is selected, then which one of the following must be true?
   a. At least three white cars are selected.
   b. At most four modern cars are selected.
   c. Exactly three red cars are selected.
   d. Exactly three modern cars are selected.
   e. Exactly four white cars are selected.

3. Each of the following could be true EXCEPT:
   a. Exactly three white modern cars are selected.
   b. Exactly four white cars are selected.
   c. Exactly one white car is selected.
   d. Exactly one red modern car is selected.
   e. Exactly five modern cars are selected.

4. If the white antique car is not selected, then which of the following must be true?
   a. Exactly three modern cars are selected.
   b. Exactly four red cars are selected.
   c. At most four modern cars are selected.
   d. At most three red cars are selected.
   e. At least two white cars are selected.

5. If exactly five cars are selected, then which one of the following is a partial, accurate list of the cars in the show?
   a. White antique car
   b. Three red modern cars
   c. Two red modern cars, one white modern car
   d. Two white modern cars
   e. Two white cars

Game 7

The five houses in a neighborhood—Q, R, S, T, and V—have each been outfitted with at least one of three security features: guard dog, fence, and alarm system. Any house can have more than one feature, and the following conditions hold:

House Q has a guard dog and fence.
House S has a fence.
House Q and House R have exactly two features in common, and House R does not have an alarm
   system.
House V has at least one more feature than House S.
House T has exactly one more feature than House R.

1. The exact number of features can be determined for how many of the five houses?
   a. One
   b. Two
   c. Three
   d. Four
   e. Five

2. If exactly four houses have an alarm system, then how many houses have exactly three features?
   a. One
   b. Two
   c. Three
   d. Four
   e. Five

3. If every house with a fence but one also has an alarm system, then all of the following statements must be true EXCEPT:
   a. House Q has an alarm system.
   b. House V has a fence.
   c. House S has a guard dog.
   d. House R has a guard dog.
   e. House T has a fence.

4. If houses R and S have exactly the same features, which of the following is a complete and accurate list of all houses that could have an alarm system?
   a. T
   b. T, V
   c. Q, S
   d. Q, T, V
   e. Q, T, R, S

5. If House V does not have a guard dog, then which one of the following statements must be true?
   a. House S has more features than House R.
   b. House Q has more features than House S.
   c. House Q has more features than House R.
   d. House V has the same number of features as House T.
   e. House R has more features than House V.

Game 8

Six ships—D, E, F, G, H, and I—arrive at port, one at a time. Three ships are from Portland, two from Seattle, and one from Vancouver. The ships are either cargo or military, but not both. They arrive according to the following conditions:

Ships F and H are the last two to arrive, not necessarily in that order.
Ships G, D, and E arrive after ship I.
The second ship to arrive is a cargo ship from Portland.
At least two military ships are from Portland.
The first ship to arrive is a cargo ship.

1. Which of the following could be an accurate list of the ships in the order in which they arrive, from first to last?
   a. I, G, E, F, D, H
   b. G, I, D, E, H, F
   c. I, D, G, H, F, E
   d. I, E, D, G, F, H
   e. E, D, G, I, H, F

2. Which one of the following cannot be true?
   a. Ship D is from Portland.
   b. Ship I is from Portland.
   c. Ship H is from Vancouver.
   d. Ship F is from Seattle.
   e. Ship G is from Seattle.

3. If four cargo ships arrive before all military ships, then which one of the following must be true?
   a. Ship H is from Portland.
   b. Ship F is from Seattle.
   c. Ship I is from Vancouver.
   d. Ship D is from Portland.
   e. Ship D is from Vancouver.

4. If ship E and ship F are separated by exactly two ships in the arrival sequence and are both from Seattle, then the following must be true EXCEPT:
   a. Ship I is from Vancouver.
   b. Ship H is from Portland.
   c. Ship H is a military ship.
   d. Ship G is a cargo ship.
   e. Ship D is from Portland.

5. If all the ships from any given city arrive consecutively, then which one of the following cannot be true?
   a. A Seattle ship is cargo.
   b. A Seattle ship is military.
   c. A Portland ship is military.
   d. The Vancouver ship is military.
   e. The Vancouver ship is cargo.

Answer Explanations

Game 1

In this distribution game, there are two sections, morning and afternoon; according to the first restriction, each must have three or four students. Note that each of the seven students is assigned to exactly one of two groups, and so this could be treated like a selection game. However, the fourth rule places a student in a specific group, making this game different from most selection games. Since there are only seven students and each is assigned to exactly one section, one section must have three students and the other must have four students.

We can now set up our basic diagram, labeling the morning section (M) and afternoon section (A):

$$M \qquad\qquad A$$
$$\_\ \_\ \_\ (\_) \quad \_\ \_\ \_\ (\_)$$

We draw three slots in each section and the fourth slot in parentheses to indicate that there may be a fourth student in that section.

We can symbolize our entities by lowercase letters: b, c, d, e, f, g, and h.

We now symbolize the restrictions. The second restriction says that if Greg is in the morning section, Carl is in the afternoon section.

We can symbolize this as:

$$g(M) \longrightarrow c(A)$$

We remember to find the contrapositive: If Carl is not in the afternoon section, Greg is not in the morning section. Since there are only two sections and each student must be assigned to one of them, we can state this more directly: If Carl is in morning section, Greg is in the afternoon section.

We can symbolize this as:

$$c(M) \longrightarrow g(A)$$

The third restriction says that Betty and Carl must be in the same section.

We can symbolize this:

$$cb$$

The fourth restriction says that Diane is in the afternoon section. We can add that directly into our diagram:

$$M \qquad\qquad A$$
$$\_\ \_\ \_\ (\_) \quad \underline{d}\ \_\ \_\ (\_)$$

The fifth restriction says that Earl and Fran cannot be in the same section. We can symbolize this:

$$ef$$

We can also symbolize this directly into our diagram, where the slash means "or":

$$M \qquad\qquad A$$
$$\_\ \_\ \_\ (\_) \quad \underline{d}\ \_\ \_\ (\_)$$
$$e/f \qquad\qquad e/f$$

Note that Carl appears in both the second and third restriction. The second rule says that if Greg is in the morning section, Carl is in the afternoon section. But since Carl and Betty must be in the same section, according the third restriction, this means that if Greg is in the morning section, both Betty and Carl must be in the afternoon section:

$$g(M) \longrightarrow c(A) \text{ and } b(A)$$

This symbolization can replace the original symbolization of the second restriction. Note the new contrapositive:

$$c(M) \text{ or } b(M) \longrightarrow g(A)$$

Now we can start looking at our (symbolized) restrictions, and apply them directly to the diagram. For this game, we use scenarios. To begin, we might try to find a strong clue with which to divide the game into different possible scenarios. The third restriction says that Betty and Carl must be in the same section. Our eye should gravitate to that symbolization because blocks force entities together. So, there are two possible scenarios, one in which c and b are in A, and another in which c and b are in M.

Scenario 1

$$M \qquad\qquad A$$
$$\underline{}\ \underline{}\ \underline{}\ (\underline{}) \qquad \underline{d}\ \underline{b}\ \underline{c}\ (\underline{})$$
$$\text{e/f} \qquad\qquad \text{e/f}$$

Scenario 2

$$M \qquad\qquad A$$
$$\underline{b}\ \underline{c}\ \underline{}\ (\underline{}) \qquad \underline{d}\ \underline{}\ \underline{}\ (\underline{})$$
$$\text{e/f} \qquad\qquad \text{e/f}$$

Now the second restriction comes into play. The contrapositive version of our revised second restriction dictates that if b and c are in M, then g is in A. Likewise, b and c must be in A if g is in M. Therefore, in scenario 1, where b and c are in A, g must go into the morning section. And finally, in scenario 1, h must be in M because placing h in A would cause e and f to be together in M, which the fifth restriction does not allow. Therefore, M must have three students and A must have four in scenario 1. In scenario 2, g is the afternoon section. There are no other restrictions in play. We do not know where to place h, so we can draw h between the two sections. Thus, our scenarios are:

Scenario 1

$$M \qquad\qquad A$$
$$\underline{g}\ \underline{h}\ \underline{} \qquad\qquad \underline{d}\ \underline{b}\ \underline{c}\ \underline{}$$
$$\text{e/f} \qquad\qquad \text{e/f}$$

Scenario 2

$$M \qquad\qquad A$$
$$\underline{b}\ \underline{c}\ \underline{}\ (\underline{}) \qquad \underline{d}\ \underline{g}\ \underline{}\ (\underline{})$$
$$\text{e/f} \qquad (\text{h}) \qquad \text{e/f}$$

We should note that instead of creating scenarios, you might also have chosen to proceed directly to the questions after symbolizing the restrictions and filling out the initial diagram. We provide both methods for each answer explanation that follows—you will have to see which method suits you better and saves you the most time.

Question 1

The correct answer is choice **b**. This question is a standard "Test-the-Rules" question. The second restriction rules out choice **e**. It implies that both Greg and Carl must be in the morning section, but the second restriction says that if Greg is in the morning section, Carl is in the afternoon section. Choice **e** is also ruled out by the third restriction, because Betty is present but Carl is missing. The third restriction also rules out choice **c** because it includes Carl, but not Betty. The fourth restriction rules out choice **a**, since it does not include Diane. The fifth restriction rules out choice **d**, since it includes both Earl and Fran.

Another method for answering this question is to refer to the scenarios diagram. Simply look at the afternoon section part of the two scenarios, and test each answer choice against it. Choice **a** cannot work because in the first scenario, c and b are in A, while h is in M, and second scenario does not have c and b in A. Choice **b** is correct: in scenario 2, the afternoon section contains Diane and Greg, and can contain Fran and Hugo. You can immediately stop and move on to the next question.

Question 2

The correct answer is choice **d**. This is a standard "supposition" question. One method for answering this question is to start making a chain of inferences. If Betty is in the morning section, then by the third restriction, Carl is also in the morning section. If Carl is in the morning section, then by the contrapositive of the second restriction, Greg is in the afternoon section. Filling out this information in the diagram, coupled with the information in fourth and fifth restrictions, gives us:

$$
\begin{array}{cc}
\text{M} & \text{A} \\
\underline{b} \ \underline{c} \ \underline{\ } \ (\underline{\ }) & \underline{d} \ \underline{g} \ \underline{\ } \ (\underline{\ }) \\
\ \ \ \ {}_{e/f} \ \ \ \ {}_{(h)} & \ \ \ {}_{e/f}
\end{array}
$$

Note that the scenario we created based on the information from the question stem is exactly the same as scenario 2 from our pre-question diagramming. Therefore, you could go straight to scenario 2 and use the following reasoning to consider each answer choice.

Choice **a** is incorrect because the morning section could have four students (e.g., b, c, f, h). Choice **b** is incorrect for the same reason—the morning section could have three students (e.g., b, c, e). Choice **c** is incorrect because Hugo could either be in the morning section or the afternoon section. Choice **e** is incorrect because Earl and Greg do not have to be in the same section—e.g., the afternoon section might contain d, g, and f, while the morning section contains b, c, e, and h. Choice **d** is correct because if Betty is in the morning section, Diane and Greg must both be in the afternoon section.

Question 3

The correct answer is choice **d**. First, we need to understand the question. We want a list of all the students who, given the restrictions, might be in the morning section. If any rule prevents a student from being in the morning section, that student cannot be on the list.

Any entity that appears in the morning section of either of our scenarios must appear on the list. We see that b, c, e, f, g, and h all appear somewhere under M, but d never does. Therefore, the correct choice is **d**.

A word of caution: you might be tempted to think that since Diane is the only student directly placed into the afternoon section, this answer choice is obvious. But it is entirely possible that some other entity is also, indirectly, restricted from the morning section. For example, if there was an additional restriction that Carl was in the morning section, then by the second restriction, Greg must be in the afternoon section and would not appear on our list.

We could also answer this question without the aid of the scenarios, by using information from previous questions. The answer to Question 1 tells us that b, c and e have to be present in the correct answer. This eliminates answer choices **a**, **b** and **c**. We also know that d has to be in the afternoon section, so it can't show up on this list. That eliminates answer choice **e** and we're only left with choice **d**.

Question 4

The correct answer is choice **a**. This is a supposition question, so we could start by making a chain of inferences. If c is in A, then b is also in A, by the third restriction. By the fourth restriction, d is in A. So b, c, and d are in A. By fifth restriction Earl or Fran must be in the afternoon section, and so we have filled our maximum number of slots in that section (which is four slots, by the first restriction). So the remaining entities—g and h—must be in the morning section. Entering this information into a diagram, we have:

$$
\begin{array}{cc}
\text{M} & \text{A} \\
\underline{g} \ \underline{h} \ \underline{\ } & \underline{d} \ \underline{b} \ \underline{c} \ \underline{\ } \\
\ \ \ \ {}_{e/f} & \ \ \ \ {}_{e/f}
\end{array}
$$

Note that this is just scenario 1 from our pre-question diagramming. We can now test our answer choices. Choice **b** is wrong because d cannot be in the morning section. Choices **c** and **d** are wrong because they separate b from c. Choice **e** is wrong because it places e and f together. This leaves choice **a** as the only possible correct answer.

Question 5

The correct answer is choice **d**. If Greg is not in the afternoon section, he must be in the morning section. The contrapositive version of our revised second restriction dictates that if g is in the morning section, b and c must be in the afternoon section. We also know that h must be in the morning section because placing h in the afternoon section would put e and f together.

$$
\begin{array}{cc}
\text{M} & \text{A} \\
\underline{g}\ \underline{h}\ \underline{\ } & \underline{d}\ \underline{b}\ \underline{c}\ \underline{\ } \\
\text{e/f} & \text{e/f}
\end{array}
$$

Note that this is just scenario 1 from our pre-question diagramming. We can now quickly and easily test our answer choices. Choices **a** and **e** are incorrect because e and f could be in either the morning or afternoon sections. Choices **b** and **c** are incorrect because b and c must be in the afternoon section. Hugo is the only other student who must be in the morning section—this is choice **d**.

Also note that if you ran out of time and couldn't diagram, you could eliminate two answers because they are interchangeable. Here, choices **a** and **e** must be incorrect. Earl and Fran appear only in the fifth restriction. Neither one could be the correct answer, since they would both have to be correct. Now you only have three possible answers, which improves your odds of guessing correctly.

Game 2

In this grouping game, eight paintings are to be placed in four rooms. So, there are four groups (the four rooms) into which eight entities (the paintings) are to be distributed and the number of entities in each group are specified. Since we know the specific numbers involved, the game should be diagrammed as follows:

$$
\begin{array}{cccc}
1 & 2 & 3 & 4 \\
\underline{\ } & \underline{\ }\ \underline{\ } & \underline{\ }\ \underline{\ } & \underline{\ }\ \underline{\ }
\end{array}
$$

We now symbolize our restrictions and, if possible, work them into the diagram. We can write J directly into room 3.

$$
\begin{array}{cccc}
1 & 2 & 3 & 4 \\
\underline{\ } & \underline{\ }\ \underline{\ } & \underline{J}\ \underline{\ } & \underline{\ }\ \underline{\ }
\end{array}
$$

We symbolize the second restriction as an MN block that is crossed out (M̶N̶), the third restriction as a KL block, and the fourth restriction and its contrapositive as follows:

$$
O = 2 \longrightarrow M = 4
$$
$$
M \neq 4 \longrightarrow O \neq 2
$$

Now we look to see if there are any obvious deductions, connections, or insights to be made. Since K and L go together, they cannot fit into room 1 (since there is one space), or room 3 (since one of the two spaces is already filled with J). If any other painting is placed in room 2, KL must appear in room 4.

For this game, we will illustrate the approach of creating scenarios only when they might appear useful for particular questions.

Question 1

The correct answer is choice **c**. This question is a standard "Test-the-Rules" question. The first restriction rules out choice **d**, since J is not in room 3. The second restriction rules out choice **a**, since M and N are both in room 4. The third restriction rules out choice **e**, since K and L are not in the same room. The fourth restriction rules out choice **b**, since O is in room 2, but M is not in room 4.

Question 2

The correct answer is choice **b**. Start by seeing what deductions can be made from the new information that M is placed in Room 2. Since M is in room 2, there is no room for the KL block in room 2, so K and L must be in Room 4. Further, according to the contrapositive of the fourth restriction, since M is not in room 4, O is not in room 2. According to the second restriction, N cannot be in room 2, because M is in room 2.

This leaves us with the following diagram:

(I, P, O, N)
1   2   3   4
_ M _ J _ K L _
   (O, N)

The "(I, P, O, N)" note is written to remind us that these four paintings still need to be distributed into the four remaining spots. From this diagram, we can determine which paintings besides M can be in placed in room 2. We have I, P, O, and N remaining to be placed, but O and N are banned from room 2. So I and P are the only paintings which can be placed in room 2. This is answer choice **b**. Choice **a** is incorrect because it does not include P as a possibility. You can also tell that choice **a** is incorrect because it includes only one of two interchangeable elements. Paintings I and P are not involved in any restrictions, so anything that applies to one (including being a candidate for room 2) must apply to the other. Choice **c** is incorrect because it violates the second restriction: if N appeared in room 2, M and N would both appear in Room 2. Choice **d** is incorrect because it violates the fourth restriction: O is in room 2, but M is not in room 4 (it is in room 2, as specified by the question stem). Choice **e** is incorrect because it violates the fourth restriction. It may not at first appear that the fourth restriction is violated, since both K and L appear in the answer choice. But note that the answer choice is supposed to be a list of the possible candidates for room 2—and if K appears in room 2, L cannot (and vice-versa), since there are only two spots in room 2 and M is filling one of them. So neither K nor L should appear on the list we want.

Question 3

The correct answer is choice **d**. Start by seeing what deductions can be made from the information that O and N go into the same room. Since O and N are now a 2-entity block, like K and L, the same reasoning applies to them as to K and L: the ON block must go either in room 2 or room 4. Since we have two scenarios, draw each out and see where they lead.

Scenario 1
1   2   3   4
_ O N J _ _ _ _

Scenario 2
1   2   3   4
_ _ _ J _ O N _

Notice that the room for the KL block can now be determined for each scenario. In scenario 1, KL must go in room 4, and in scenario 2, KL must go in room 2. Further, notice that the fourth restriction will apply to scenario 1: since O is in room 2, M must be in room 4. And the second restriction will give us more information about scenario 2: since N is in room 4, M cannot be.

So our diagram will now look like:

Scenario 1
(I, P)
1   2   3   4
_ O N J _ K L M

Scenario 2
(I, P, M)
1   2   3   4
_ K L J _ O N _
                        (M)

Now we want to determine where M can be placed. In scenario 1, M is placed in room 4. In scenario 2, M is free to float into rooms 1 or room 3. So M can be placed exactly in room 1, 3, and 4, which is answer choice **d**.

Question 4

The correct answer is choice **b**. Start by seeing what deductions follow from the new information that O is placed in room 2. If O is in room 2, then the fourth condition kicks in, and M must be placed in room 4. Since O is in room 2, the KL block has no place to go but room 4 as well.

So our diagram now looks like:

```
(N, I, P)
1       2       3       4
_       O _     I _     K L M
```

N, I, and P can float into any spot, since the only restriction on N (that it is not in same room as M) is satisfied no matter what, and I and P have no restrictions on them. Now, consider each answer choice.

Choice **a** is incorrect because there is no room for P in room 4. Choice **c** is incorrect because there is no room for I in room 4. Choice **d** is incorrect because painting L is in room 4. And choice **e** is incorrect not only because we already know that painting K is in room 4, but also because it could never be in room 1—the KL block would be broken. Therefore, the correct answer is choice **b**.

Question 5

The correct answer is choice **b**. This is a difficult question, which must be answered by trying each statement individually to see which deductions can be made. For choice **a**, M is in room 1, N is in room 4, and since K is in room 2, so is L.

So we have:

```
(O, I, P)
1       2       3       4
M       K L     I _     N _ _
```

No restrictions are made on I and P, so they are interchangeable, and the distribution cannot be fully determined, so choice **a** is incorrect.

Let's turn to choice **b**. If O is in 2, then M must be in 4, by the fourth restriction. Since room 2 is filled, K and L also must be in room 4.

So we have:

```
1       2       3       4
I       O P     I _     M K L
```

N must then be in Room 3, and we have a fully determined distribution. So the correct answer is **b**. We can circle the answer and move on to the next question.

For the sake of illustration, we note that the remaining answer choices have the following deductions/diagrams.

For choice **c**, since O and N are in room 4, K and L are in room 2. P and M are left to float and so the distribution is not determined.

```
(P, M)
1       2       3       4
_       K L     I _     O N I
```

For choice **d**, since I and P are in room 2, K and L are in room 4. M and N are left to float between rooms 3 and 4, so the distribution is not determined.

```
(M, N)
1       2       3       4
O       I P     I _     K L _
```

For choice **e**, we have K and L in room 2, which means O cannot be in room 2. The contrapositive of the fourth restriction is that if O is not in room 2, then M is not in room 4. We also know that M and N are not in the same room. No further deductions assigning a painting to a room can be made.

(M, N, O, P)

~~MN~~

1	2	3	4
_	K L	I _	I _ _

(~~M~~)

Game 3

This is a standard sequencing game, so you should draw and label seven slots for each terminal:

1	2	3	4	5	6	7

Now symbolize the clues. Since we are told that Terminal C is built in year 2, C can be written directly into the diagram. The other restrictions can be noted above the diagram, such as A = 3 or 7; Terminal E must be built in the year immediately before or after the year Terminal D; and if Terminal F is built in year 4, Terminal B must be built after Terminal G (along with the contrapositive):

A = 3 or 7

D/E

F = 4 $\longrightarrow$ G–B

B–G $\longrightarrow$ F ≠ 4

_	C	_	_	_	_	_
1	2	3	4	5	6	7

~~D/E~~

We look for any deductions or connections to be made, but the years and terminals mentioned do not appear in multiple restrictions, so it is difficult to come up with any immediate insights. Notice, however, that since E and D must be side by side, neither can be built in year 1 (since C occupies year 2). You could mark this by crossing out E and D underneath slot 1.

Now we turn to the questions.

Question 1

The correct answer choice is **b**. This question is a standard "Test-the-Rules" question. The first restriction rules out choice **d**, since C is in year 4. The second restriction rules out choice **a**, since F is in 4, but B is before G instead of after G. The third restriction rules out choice **c**, since A is in year 6. The fourth restriction rules out choice **e**, since D and E are not built in consecutive years.

Question 2

The correct answer is choice **d**. Start by inputting the new information about G into the diagram. And since G occupies 7, we know that A occupies 3. The contrapositive of the second restriction says that if B is before G, F will not be in year 4. Since G is in the last year, B must be before year G, so F cannot be in year 4:

D/E

F = 4 $\longrightarrow$ G–B

B–G $\longrightarrow$ F ≠ 4

_	C	A	_	_	_	G
1	2	3	4	5	6	7
~~D/E~~			F			

Now that we've made all possible deductions, we look for answer choices that don't work in our diagram. The only answer choice with an impossible option is **d**.

Question 3

The correct answer is choice **b**. Start by inputting the new information about Terminal F into the diagram.

A = 3 or 7

D/E

F = 4 $\longrightarrow$ G–B

B–G $\longrightarrow$ F ≠ 4

_	C	_	F	_	_	_
1	2	3	4	5	6	7
~~D/E~~						

Now let's divide our diagram into scenarios, one with A built third and the other with A built seventh:

Scenario 1

D/E

F = 4 —→G–B

B–G —→F ≠ 4

_	C	A	F	_	_	_
1	2	3	4	5	6	7

~~D/E~~

Scenario 2

D/E

F = 4 —→G–B

B–G —→F ≠ 4

_	C	_	F	_	_	A
1	2	3	4	5	6	7

~~D/E~~

Now we turn to the D/E block. Let's see how that block works in our two scenarios. In scenario 1, we see that the D/E block can occupy years 5/6 or 6/7:

Scenario 1

F = 4 —→GB

BG —→F ≠ 4

_	C	A	F	_	_	_
1	2	3	4	5	6	7
				D/E	D/E	

_	C	A	F	_	_	_
1	2	3	4	5	6	7
					D/E	D/E

And we know that if F is in 4, G must come before B, so we can finish the diagram with two possibilities:

G	C	A	F	_	_	B
1	2	3	4	5	6	7
				D/E	D/E	

G	C	A	F	B	_	_
1	2	3	4	5	6	7
					D/E	D/E

Now we turn to scenario 2. The D/E block can also only occupy years 5/6:

_	C	_	F	_	_	A
1	2	3	4	5	6	7
				D/E	D/E	

And again, G must come before B:

G	C	B	F	_	_	A
1	2	3	4	5	6	7
				D/E	D/E	

Note that the placement of G and B in all three scenarios is superfluous for this question: we are only interested in where E can go, but these scenarios might come in handy for a different question, so it can be time well spent.

We are now in a position to answer the question. E can be built in years 5, 6, or 7, which is answer choice **b**.

This was admittedly an involved way of finding the answer. Alternatively, you can cross out choice **d** since E can't go in year 2. We also made an upfront deduction that E can't go in year 1 because of the DE block, so answer choice **c** is out. Years 5 and 6 are in all of the remaining answer choices, so they don't need to be tested. E can't be in year 3 since the DE block can't be placed, so choice **e** is out. The remaining hurdle is then to decide whether E can go in year 7, and it's straightforward to show a situation where it can, so the answer has to be **b**.

Question 4

The correct answer choice is **a**. To answer this question, start with the original diagram:

A = 3 or 7
D/E
F = 4 $\longrightarrow$ G–B
B–G $\longrightarrow$ F ≠ 4

	C					
1	2	3	4	5	6	7
~~D/E~~						

A must be built in years 3 or 7, and C must be built in year 2, so they are out. As part of a block, neither D nor E can fit into year 1. We are left with B, F, and G. At this point, we can eliminate answer choices **b**, **c**, and **e**, since they contain terminals other than B, F, and G. We have to choose between **a** and **d**.

To do this, draw a diagram where F is built in year 1:

F	C	A	E	D	B	G
1	2	3	4	5	6	7

Since none of the rules are violated, F can be in year 1, and the correct answer is **a**.

Question 5

The correct answer is choice **e**. To see this, we simply need to go through the same process we did for Question 3. We start with the new information that F is built in year 4, and end up with three scenarios:

G	C	A	F			B
1	2	3	4	5	6	7
				D/E	D/E	

G	C	A	F	B		
1	2	3	4	5	6	7
					D/E	D/E

G	C	B	F			A
1	2	3	4	5	6	7
				D/E	D/E	

For each of the scenarios, the order of D and E can be switched (yielding two sub-scenarios for each of our three scenarios). Therefore, there are six possible orders, and the answer is **e**.

Game 4

This is a standard sequencing game, so draw and label seven slots:

1	2	3	4	5	6	7

Now symbolize the first restriction:
H—J—M
Symbolize the second restriction: I—K—L or L—K—I

Symbolize the third restriction and its contrapositive:

J—N $\longrightarrow$ K—J
J—K $\longrightarrow$ N—J

Notice, however, that if Jack sits to the left of Nick, we know that the relative order must be K—J—N.

This information and the conjoined contrapositive can be symbolized:

J—N $\longrightarrow$ K—J—N
J—K $\longrightarrow$ N—J—K

And finally, symbolize the fourth restriction and its contrapositive:

N—J $\longrightarrow$ L—K
K—L $\longrightarrow$ J—N

Now we move on to the questions.

Question 1

The correct answer is choice **e**. This question is a standard "Test-the-Rules" question. The first restriction rules out choice **c**, since M is not to the right of J. The second restriction rules out also choice **d**, since K is not in between L and I. The third restriction rules out choice **b**, since J is to the left of N, but K is not to the left of J. The fourth restriction rules out choice **a**, since N is to the left of J, but L is not to the left of K.

Question 2

The correct answer is choice **b**. Start by filling the new information into the diagram, and seeing what follows:

$$\underline{}\ \underline{}\ \underline{}\ \underline{}\ \underline{}\ \underline{J}\ \underline{}$$
$$1\ \ 2\ \ 3\ \ 4\ \ 5\ \ 6\ \ 7$$

Looking at the first restriction, we see that M must be in seat 7:

$$\underline{}\ \underline{}\ \underline{}\ \underline{}\ \underline{}\ \underline{J}\ \underline{M}$$
$$1\ \ 2\ \ 3\ \ 4\ \ 5\ \ 6\ \ 7$$

Looking at the fourth restriction, and realizing that N must now be left of J, we see that L must be left of K. This means that, according to the second restriction, we have:

L—K—I
(H, N)
$$\underline{}\ \underline{}\ \underline{}\ \underline{}\ \underline{}\ \underline{J}\ \underline{M}$$
$$1\ \ 2\ \ 3\ \ 4\ \ 5\ \ 6\ \ 7$$

Also, H now must be left of J and M, and N must be to the left of J.

We now consider our list of possible letters for slot 5. L and K could not sit in slot 5, since if they did,

there would be no room for I in slot 5. And since there are no further restrictions on H and N, N, H, and I are our only options for seat 5—answer choice **b**.

Question 3

The correct answer is choice **c**. One approach is to take each answer choice in turn, and see whether a diagram could be constructed that doesn't violate the conditions. Choice **a** was already shown possible in the answer to Question 1. One possible arrangement accommodating choice **b** is: I, N, H, J, M, L, K. When you get to choice **c**, start the diagram by putting J in the second spot.

By the first restriction, the first spot must then be occupied by H:

$$\underline{H}\ \underline{J}\ \underline{}\ \underline{}\ \underline{}\ \underline{}\ \underline{}$$
$$1\ \ 2\ \ 3\ \ 4\ \ 5\ \ 6\ \ 7$$

Now check each restriction to see how to continue the diagram, and see if any restriction can't be met. Notice that N must now be to the right of J, so by the third restriction, K must be to the left of J. However, notice in the diagram that there is no room for K to the left of J. Therefore, putting J in the second spot is not possible. Circle your answer and move on.

Just for your information, there are possible diagrams for choices **d** and **e**. One possible sequence for choice **d** is I, K, H, J, M, N, L. One possible sequence for choice **e** is H, I, K, J, N, M, L.

Question 4

The correct answer is choice **c**. To see this, start with the leftmost spot, and check the restrictions to see if M could sit there. He cannot sit in seats 1 and 2 because that would not leave room for H and/or J, as required by the first restriction (you should immediately see this by your symbolic/visual representation of restriction 1).

What about seat 3? Try constructing a diagram in which Matt sits in seat 3:

$$\frac{}{1} \ \frac{}{2} \ \frac{M}{3} \ \frac{}{4} \ \frac{}{5} \ \frac{}{6} \ \frac{}{7}$$

By restriction 1, H must be in seat 1, and J in seat 2:

$$\frac{H}{1} \ \frac{J}{2} \ \frac{M}{3} \ \frac{}{4} \ \frac{}{5} \ \frac{}{6} \ \frac{}{7}$$

Now, look to the other restrictions to see how the diagram-filling must proceed. The third restriction says that if J is to the left of N, the order must be K—J—N. Notice in the diagram that N must be to the right of J—so the order must in fact be K—J—N. But notice again, in the diagram, that there is no room for K to the left of J, so it's not possible for Matt to sit in seat 3.

What about seat 4? Again, H and J must be somewhere to the left of M, in that order. There is now room to place K somewhere to the left of J as well:

$$\frac{}{1} \ \frac{}{2} \ \frac{}{3} \ \frac{M}{4} \ \frac{}{5} \ \frac{}{6} \ \frac{}{7}$$

H—J
K

(H—J and K are placed into spots 1–3.)

But now notice a new problem: K must be in between I and L, according to the third restriction—but there is no room for either I or L to the left of K, so this won't work.

But also notice that we don't need K to the left of J anymore. The only reason we needed that before was that N had to be the right of J, since there was no space to J's left if M was in seat 3. But now M is in seat 4, so we have space to place N to the left of J:

$$\frac{}{1} \ \frac{}{2} \ \frac{}{3} \ \frac{M}{4} \ \frac{}{5} \ \frac{}{6} \ \frac{}{7}$$

H//N—J

(H//N—J is placed into spots 1–3; remember, this symbolization means that H and N are to the left of J, but the relative order of H and N is unspecified.)

Restriction 1 is not violated, restriction 3 does not apply (since J is not to the left of N), and restrictions 2 and 4 (which applies because N is to the left of J) can be accommodated by filling in seats 5, 6, and 7 with the order L—K—I.

So Matt can sit in seat 4, but not in seats 1–3. Seat 4 is therefore the lowest numbered seat in which he could sit.

Question 5

The correct answer is choice **d**. Start by seeing what follows from the new information that Kate sits to the left of Lorna. According to the contrapositive of the fourth restriction, Jack must sit to the left of Nick. We also know that according to the first restriction, Helen must be to the left of Jack and Matt to the right of Jack.

We can summarize this deduced information:

$$H—J—M//N$$

Remember, this symbolization means that Jack is to the left of Nick, and to the left of Matt (though the order of Matt and Nick is unknown), and Helen is to the left of Jack.

We also know, from the information that Kate sits to the left of Lorna and the second restriction, that I—K—L. According to the third restriction, since Jack sits to the left of Nick, Kate must sit to the left of Jack: K—J

So we have three strings that need to be joined, K—J, I—K—L, and H—J—M//N. We can join H—J—M//N and K—J at the common point, J. Since both K and H appear to the left of J, we will have to choose one for the primary string and one for the secondary string. Since K also appears in I—K—L, we should choose K for the primary string, and therefore H for the secondary string:

$$K—J—M//N$$
$$←H⊣$$

Now we have to join I—K—L at the common element K. We can keep I on the primary string, but have to add L as another secondary string:

$$\vdash L \longrightarrow$$
$$I—K—J—M//N$$
$$\longleftarrow H \dashv$$

With this master joint sequence string put together, we can easily tackle the answer choices. There must be at least five people to the right of I (namely, K, L J, M and N), so I cannot sit in seat 3 (there are only seven seats), and choice **a** is incorrect. There must be at least four people to the left of M (namely, I, K, J, and H), so M cannot be in seat 4, and choice **b** is incorrect. Similar reasoning applies to N: there must be at least four people to the left of N (namely, J, K, I, and H), so N cannot be in seat 3, and choice **c** is incorrect. H could sit in seat 4 if I, K, and L preceded it—for example, we could imagine moving the letters on in the following way:

$$\vdash L$$
$$I—K———J—M//N$$
$$H \dashv$$

This gives us the sequence: I-K-L-H-J-M//N

So it is possible for H to be in seat 4, and **d** is the correct answer.

You should circle your choice and move on, but if you checked **e**, you would see that J cannot be in seat 3 because at least three people (namely I, K, and H) must sit to his left.

Game 5

An efficient approach to working through this selection game will make heavy use of formal logic. Symbolize the restrictions as conditionals, and symbolize their contrapositives as well. Then look for connections and further deductions that can be made.

The first restriction can be symbolized:

$$A \longrightarrow \neq C$$

This means that if A is chosen, C is not chosen. Its equivalent contrapositive is:

$$C \longrightarrow \neq A$$

The second restriction can be symbolized:

$$B \longrightarrow E$$
Its contrapositive is: $\neq E \longrightarrow \neq B$

The third restriction can be symbolized:

$$\neq A \longrightarrow (F \text{ or } G)$$
Its contrapositive is: $(\neq F \text{ and } \neq G) \longrightarrow A$

The fourth restriction can be symbolized:

$$(F \text{ and } G) \longrightarrow (\neq E \text{ and } D)$$
Its contrapositive is: $(E \text{ or } \neq D) \longrightarrow (\neq F \text{ or } \neq G)$

Now that you've collected all the symbolizations and contrapositives into one place, look for connections. The most obvious connection is that the third restriction and the contrapositive of the first restriction join up:

$$C \longrightarrow \neq A \longrightarrow (F \text{ or } G)$$

Also notice that the second restriction connects with the contrapositive of the fourth restriction:

$$B \longrightarrow E \longrightarrow (\neq F \text{ or } \neq G)$$

Restrictions three and four both deal with F and G, but they cannot be straightforwardly connected since one deals with F *or* G and one deals with F *and* G. Further connections between the conditionals will become apparent as more suppositions are introduced in the questions.

Question 1

The correct answer is choice **e**. This question is a standard "Test-the-Rules" question. The first restriction rules out choice **d**, since both A and C are chosen. The second restriction rules out choice **c**, since B is chosen, but E is not chosen. The third restriction rules out choice **a**, since A is not chosen, but neither is F nor G chosen. The fourth restriction rules out choice **b**, since both F and G are chosen, but D is not chosen.

Question 2

The correct answer is choice **d**. The right approach here, again, is to check each answer choice against the restrictions. This is a more sophisticated version of the "Test-the-Rules" question and tests your ability to draw connections between the rules.

Choice **a** is incorrect because it violates the third restriction: if A is not chosen, F or G (or both) must be chosen. Choice **b** is incorrect because it violates the contrapositive of the third restriction combined with the first restriction. That is, the first restriction says that if C is chosen, A cannot be chosen. But the contrapositive of the third restriction says that if neither F nor G are chosen, then A is chosen. If, as in this answer choice, it's both the case that C is chosen, and that neither F nor G are chosen, we are led to a contradiction concerning A. So this answer choice cannot be true.

Choice **c** is incorrect because according to the fourth restriction, if F and G are chosen, then E is not chosen (and D is chosen, but that is irrelevant here); according to the second restriction, if E is not chosen, then B is not chosen. But in choice **c**, B is chosen even though F and G are also chosen. Choice **e** is incorrect because it violates the contrapositive of the fourth restriction. Since D is not chosen, according to that restriction, either F is not chosen or G is not chosen. But this answer choice has both F and G being chosen.

Choice **d** is correct—one possible scenario is one in which A is chosen and nothing else is—this would not violate any restrictions.

Question 3

The correct answer is choice **b**. The first thing to do is to see if the new information provided, that neither F nor G is chosen, leads to a new deduction. According to the contrapositive of the third restriction, if it's the case that both F is not chosen and G is not chosen (i.e., that neither F nor G is chosen), then A is chosen. Are there any further deductions to be made? According to the first restriction, if A is chosen, then C is not chosen. Now look for any further deductions—none are readily apparent. Now, scan the answer choices to see if any of them contradict this newly deduced information, that C is not chosen, and that A is chosen. Choice **b** says that C is chosen (as well as E, though that is irrelevant)—and this contradicts our deduced information, so the statement in choice **b** cannot be true, and choice **b** is the correct answer to the question. If you've approached the question in this way, you should be confident in your answer and move on at this point. Of course, you could see if each answer choice represents a possible reading list if neither F nor G are chosen by coming up with a list of chosen books and testing them against each restriction to be sure the restrictions are not violated.

Again, this would be very time-consuming and is not recommended.

Question 4

The correct answer is choice **b**. Start by seeing if the new information can set off a chain of deductions. If C is chosen, then according to the first restriction, A is not chosen. And if A is not chosen, then according to the third restriction, either F or G must be chosen. But we also know that F is not chosen. So therefore G must be chosen. Now scan the answer choices to see if any of this information (that A is not chosen and G is chosen) appears—it does, in choice **b**. Circle your answer, and move on.

Question 5

The correct answer is choice **c**. Start by seeing if the new information can set off a set of deductions. According to the second restriction, if B is chosen, then E must be chosen. According to the contrapositive of the fourth restriction, if E is chosen (or if D is not chosen), then either F will not be chosen or G will not be chosen, but we also know that G is chosen, so we know that F is not chosen. Now, scan the answer choices to see if any of this information (that E is chosen and F is not chosen) appears—the fact that F is not chosen appears in choice **c**.

Game 6

This selection game is on the difficult side, since the entities to be selected from are characterized by combinations of characteristics (whether they are red or white, and whether they are antique or modern), rather than just being a list of named entities (A through F). This selection game uses a cross-group domain. So, create a two-by-two grid and place dots to represent the cars:

	A	M
r	• •	• • •
w	•	• • •

Now symbolize and incorporate the restrictions. The first restriction says that exactly two antique cars are selected:

	A	M
r	• •	• • •
w	•	• • •

ex. 2

The second restriction says that at least three and at most four red cars are selected:

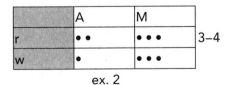

ex. 2

The third restriction can be symbolized:

$$wA \longrightarrow +2wM$$

The fourth restriction can be symbolized:

$$wA \text{ or } +2rM$$

We also want to add the information that at least five and at most seven cars must be selected:

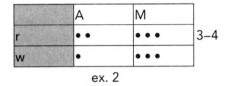

ex. 2

Select 5–7
$wA \longrightarrow +2wM$
wA or $+2rM$

Now we consider the conditions and start making deductions.

The first condition says that exactly two antiques are selected. Since there is only one white antique, that must mean that at the very least, one red antique must be selected (and in addition, either another red antique or the white antique). So, we can circle one red antique in our grid to remember that at least one red antique must be selected.

The second condition says that there are either three or four red cars selected. Looking at our grid again, we see that there are a total of five red cars, two of them antique and three of them modern. Since at least three red cars must be selected, and at most two of them can be antique (since there are only two antique red cars), that means that at least one red modern car must be selected. So circle a red modern car as well.

The grid now looks like:

	A	M
r	⊙ •	⊙ • •
w	•	• • •

ex. 2

Select 5–7

wA ⟶+2wM

wA or +2rM

Armed with this diagram, we can turn to the questions.

Question 1

The correct answer is choice **d**. This question is a standard "Test-the-Rules" question. The first restriction rules out choice **b**, since only one antique car is selected. The second restriction rules out choice **e**, since five red cars are selected. The third condition rules out choice **a**, since the white antique car is selected, but only one white modern car is selected. The fourth condition rules out choice **c**, since neither the white antique car is selected, nor are two red modern cars selected.

Question 2

The correct answer is choice **a**. Use the diagram to see what follows from the new information, that exactly one red antique car is selected (which means we cross out the second rA car):

	A	M
r	⊙✗	⊙ • •
w	•	• • •

ex. 2

select 5–7

wA ⟶+2wM

wA or +2rM

Exactly two cars must be selected in column A, so wA must be selected. But if wA is selected, then at least two wMs are selected:

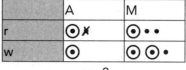

	A	M
r	⊙✗	⊙ • •
w	⊙	⊙ ⊙ •

ex. 2

select 5–7

wA ⟶+2wM

wA or +2rM

We also need at least three red cars, so we need to select at least one more rM:

	A	M
r	⊙✗	⊙ ⊙ •
w	⊙	⊙ ⊙ •

ex. 2

select 5–7

wA ⟶+2wM

wA or +2rM

Now, all the restrictions are satisfied. We have six cars selected, and the leeway to select one more car, an rM or a wM. Now look at the answer choices to see which statement must be true given this diagram.

Choice **b** is incorrect because five modern cars could be selected (e.g., three red and 2 white). Choice **c** is incorrect because according to the diagram, a fourth red car could be selected. Choice **d** is incorrect because four modern cars must be chosen, and in fact, five could be selected. Choice **e** is incorrect because the car show selection could include just three white cars. Therefore, choice **a**, that at least three white cars are selected, is correct.

Question 3

The correct answer is choice **d**. For this "except" question, the incorrect answers will yield an acceptable scenario or fail to produce a contradiction. We start with our original diagram, and apply the scenarios of each answer choice.

Choice **a** states that exactly 3 wM's are selected:

	A	M
r	⊙ •	⊙ • •
w	•	⊙ ⊙ ⊙

ex. 2

select 5–7
wA ⟶ +2wM
wA or +2rM

Now we apply the other restrictions to try to find a contradiction. We could select the other rA (since we need exactly two As) and another rM (so that the "wA or +2rM" restriction is satisfied):

	A	M
r	⊙ ⊙	⊙ ⊙ ✗
w	✗	⊙ ⊙ ⊙

ex. 2

select 5–7
wA ⟶ +2wM
wA or +2rM

With these restrictions satisfied, **a** could be true, and is definitively incorrect. What about choice **b**? All four white cars are selected. Since we have two As selected, the second rA cannot be selected, so we'll cross that out:

	A	M
r	⊙ ✗	⊙ • •
w	⊙	⊙ ⊙ ⊙

ex. 2

select 5–7
wA ⟶ +2wM
wA or +2rM

Now we apply the other restrictions to try to find a contradiction. One more rM must be selected to get three red cars:

	A	M
r	⊙ ✗	⊙ ⊙ ✗
w	⊙	⊙ ⊙ •

ex. 2

select 5–7
wA ⟶ +2wM
wA or +2rM

All restrictions are satisfied, so **b** is definitively incorrect. What about choice **c**, that exactly one white car is selected? Keep in mind that if you select a white car and reach a contradiction, you would need to check if selecting a different white car would also reach a contradiction.

In our first scenario, we select the wA and cross out all other white cars. However, the third restriction states that if the white antique car is selected, at least two white modern cars are selected. We have a contradiction here. Now we employ a second scenario, where we select a wM and cross out all other white cars. Since wA is not selected, 2 rAs must be selected to fulfill the first restriction that there must be exactly two antique cars. And since wA is not selected, another rM must be selected, to satisfy the "wA or +2rM" restriction:

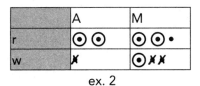

	A	M
r	⊙ ⊙	⊙ ⊙ •
w	✗	⊙ ✗ ✗

ex. 2

select 5–7
wA ⟶ +2wM
wA or +2rM

All other restrictions are satisfied in the second scenario, so **c** is incorrect. What about choice **d**, where exactly one red modern car is selected?

We start by crossing out the other two rMs from our original diagram. The first restriction states that exactly two antique cars are selected, and the second restriction states that at least three red cars must be selected. Therefore, we must also select the other rA.

	A	M
r	⊙ ⊙	⊙ ✗ ✗
w	•	• • •

ex. 2

select 5–7

wA ⟶ +2wM

wA or +2rM

However, this presents a contradiction with the fourth restriction, which states that either the white antique car or at least two red modern cars must be selected. So we have found our contradiction, and choice **d** is the correct answer.

You've found your correct answer and moved on. For your reference, here is how you would rule out choice **e**, in which five modern cars are selected—by looking at all scenarios with five modern cars. In the first scenario, you take the original diagram, then select the other two rMs, two wMs, and (in order to fulfill the second restriction where at most four red cars are selected) the wA:

	A	M
r	⊙ ✗	⊙ ⊙ ⊙
w	⊙	⊙ ⊙ ✗

ex. 2

select 5–7

wA ⟶ +2wM

wA or +2rM

This scenario fulfills all restrictions. In the other scenario, you take the original diagram, and then select only one other rM, all three wMs, and the other rA:

	A	M
r	⊙ ⊙	⊙ ⊙ ✗
w	✗	⊙ ⊙ ⊙

ex. 2

select 5–7

wA ⟶ +2wM

wA or +2rM

This scenario also fulfills all restrictions. In the last scenario, you take the original diagram, and then select only one other rM, all three wMs, and the wA:

	A	M
r	⊙ ✗	⊙ ⊙ ✗
w	⊙	⊙ ⊙ ⊙

ex. 2

select 5–7

wA ⟶ +2wM

wA or +2rM

Since this scenario also fulfills all restrictions, choice **e** is incorrect.

Question 4

The correct answer is choice **b**. Place the new information that wA is not selected (and therefore the other rA must be selected) into the original diagram:

	A	M
r	⊙ ⊙	⊙ • •
w	✗	• • •

ex. 2

select 5–7

wA ⟶ +2wM

wA or +2rM

Since wA is not selected, at least one more rM must be selected; and since there can be no more than four red cars in the show, the third rM should be crossed out. Finally, between one and three wMs could be selected to fulfill the requirement that five to seven cars appear in the show, and all the restrictions will be satisfied.

In our diagram, we'll include just one wM:

	A	M
r	⊙ ⊙	⊙ ⊙ ✗
w	✗	⊙ • •

ex. 2

select 5–7
wA ⟶+2wM
wA or +2rM

Now scan the answer choices for a statement that must be true given this diagram. The diagram shows that exactly four red cars must be selected, so the correct answer is choice **b**. Circle this choice and move on to the next question.

For your reference, choice **a**—exactly three modern cars are selected—is incorrect because you could have five modern cars in the show. Choice **c**—at most four modern cars are selected—is incorrect for the same reason as choice **a**. Choice **d**—at most three red cars are selected—is incorrect because in fact four red cars must be selected. Choice **e**—at least two white cars are selected—is incorrect because, as our diagram shows, you could have just one white car in the show.

Question 5

The correct answer is choice **c**. Since only five cars can be selected, wA cannot be selected. This is because if wA were selected, then at least two wM would need to be selected:

	A	M
r	⊙ •	⊙ • •
w	⊙	⊙ ⊙ •

ex. 2

select 5–7
wA ⟶+2wM
wA or +2rM

But then we would already have the maximum five cars selected, and we do not have at least three red cars as required by the second restriction. Therefore, the other rA must be selected:

	A	M
r	⊙ ⊙	⊙ • •
w	✗	• • •

ex. 2

select 5–7
wA ⟶+2wM
wA or +2rM

Since wA is not selected, another rM must be selected:

	A	M
r	⊙ ⊙	⊙ ⊙ •
w	✗	• • •

ex. 2

select 5–7
wA ⟶+2wM
wA or +2rM

We have our maximum of four red cars, so the fifth car must be a wM:

	A	M
r	⊙ ⊙	⊙ ⊙ ✗
w	✗	⊙ ✗ ✗

ex. 2

select 5–7
wA ⟶+2wM
wA or +2rM

Now we can just check each answer choice to see which represents an accurate part of this selection list. Choice **a** is incorrect because no wA is selected. Choice **b** is incorrect because exactly two rMs are selected. Choice **d** is incorrect because there is only one wM selected. Choice **e** is incorrect because there is only one white car selected (the wM). Choice **c** is correct, as there are two rMs and one wM selected.

Game 7

The first thing to do is to diagram the action of this matching game. Three features (g, f, and a) are to be matched with five houses (Q, R, S, T, and V). Each house must have at least one feature, but can have up to three features. A grid would be helpful here:

	Q	R	S	T	V
g					
f					
a					

Now consider and symbolize the restrictions with checks and ✗s. The information from the first two restrictions can be written directly into the diagram: Q has features g and f, and S has feature f. Also, some of the information from the third restriction can be added, namely that R does not have feature a.

	Q	R	S	T	V
g	✓				
f	✓		✓		
a		✗			

The rest of the restrictions cannot be written directly into the diagram without making some further deductions (by looking for connections between the restrictions). The third restriction says that Q and R share exactly two features, so R must have both g and f. Now consider the fifth restriction. Since T has one

more feature than R, and R has two features, T must have all three features.

	Q	R	S	T	V
g	✓	✓		✓	
f	✓	✓	✓	✓	
a		✗		✓	

The fourth restriction states that V must have at least one more feature than S. We can write in "+1" with an arrow to specifically indicate that V will have one more feature than S. We also therefore know that S must have at most two features, and V must have at least two. We can also write a "1" under the S column, and "2 or 3" under the V column to remind us of the number of features that can be added to V and S.

	Q	R	S	T	V
g	✓	✓		✓	
f	✓	✓	✓	✓	
a		✗		✓	

(1)——+1——(2 or 3)

Our diagram and deductions are now complete, and we move on to the questions.

Question 1

The correct answer is choice **b**. To answer this question, we need to refer to our finished diagram. Only two houses have no blanks: R and T. So the correct answer is two. Because you took the time upfront to make your deductions and diagram the results, you can be confident in your answer and move on to the next question.

Question 2

The correct answer is choice **c**. To answer this question, first see how the new information—that exactly four houses have alarm systems—fits into the diagram. Since there are only five houses, and R cannot have an alarm system, all the other houses must have an alarm system. Now see what other deductions can be made.

S has now maxed out its number of features, and the fourth restriction kicks so that V has all three features (one more than S's two features).

The entire diagram is now filled out.

	Q	R	S	T	V
g	✓	✓	✗	✓	✓
f	✓	✓	✓	✓	✓
a	✓	✗	✓	✓	✓

(1)———+1———(2 or 3)

We just count now. There are three houses with exactly three features, which is answer choice **c**.

Question 3

The correct answer is choice **c**. First, see what deductions can be made from the new information that every house with a fence but one also has an alarm system (note that this does NOT mean that every house with an alarm system also has a fence—the direction of the conditional is one way: if a house has a fence, then that house also has an alarm system).

First, what is the "but one" business? See if there is any house with a fence that you already know doesn't have an alarm system—there is, house R. So house R is the "one" in "but one," the exception to this new rule. Now, simply find any house that has a fence, and add in the information that it also has an alarm system (if not there already)—these will be houses Q and S. Now look for any house that does not have an alarm, to ensure that it doesn't also have a fence (the contrapositive of the new information)—there is one, R, but that is already covered by the exception in the new rule.

	Q	R	S	T	V
g	✓	✓		✓	
f	✓	✓	✓	✓	
a	✓	✗	✓	✓	

(1)———+1———(2 or 3)

Now see what further information can be deduced. Just as before, S is now maxed out at two features, and V must have all three features:

	Q	R	S	T	V
g	✓	✓	✗	✓	✓
f	✓	✓	✓	✓	✓
a	✓	✗	✓	✓	✓

(1)———+1———(2 or 3)

Now compare each answer choice to our filled-out grid. We are looking for a false statement, so the incorrect answers will be statements that must be true.

Choice **a** is incorrect because Q has an alarm system. Choice **b** is incorrect because V has a fence. Choice **d** is incorrect because R has a guard dog. Choice **e** is incorrect because T has a fence. Choice **c** is correct because S does not have a guard dog.

Question 4

The correct answer is choice **d**. Start by seeing what deductions can be made from the new information, that Houses R and S have exactly the same features. We already know R's features, so mirror those in S. Since S now has its max of two features, we know that V has all three features.

	Q	R	S	T	V
g	✓	✓	✓	✓	✓
f	✓	✓	✓	✓	✓
a		✗	✗	✓	✓

(1)———+1———(2 or 3)

Now see which houses could have an alarm system. Q may or may not have an alarm system (you could try both scenarios to see if any restriction is violated, but you can trust the diagram you have created). T and V definitely have alarm systems, and houses R and S definitely don't. So, the houses that could have an alarm system are houses Q, T, and V, which is choice **d**. Choices **a** and **b** are incorrect because they do not include Q and V. Choice **c** is incorrect because it includes S, but not T and V. You also know it's incorrect because it includes S but not R, and S and R now functionally equivalent, or interchangeable, since according to the question set-up they have exactly the same features. Choice **e** is incorrect because it includes R and S, but not V.

Question 5

The correct answer is choice **b**. Start by seeing what new deductions can be made from the information that V does not have g. We know that what happens in V is connected to what happens in S—and since there are two features in V, there must be only one feature in S (which must be f, as per the second condition).

	Q	R	S	T	V
g	✓	✓	✗	✓	✗
f	✓	✓	✓	✓	✓
a		✗	✗	✓	✓

(1)———+1———(2 or 3)

Now check each answer choice against our filled-out grid. Choice **a** is incorrect because R has two features, and S only has one feature. Choice **c** is incorrect because S has two features, and Q might have two features as well. Choice **d** is incorrect because T has three features while V only has two features. Choice **e** is incorrect because V and R both have two features. Choice **b** is the correct answer, since Q has two or more features, while S has only one feature.

Game 8

This hybrid game combines elements of matching (cargo or military to ships), sequencing (the sequence of ship arrival), and grouping (of ships into three groups, based on place of origin). To keep track of the volume of information and all the moving parts, a diagram will be necessary. We'll use matching diagram, where ships (D, E, F, G, H, and I), places of origin (P, S, or V), and ship-type (c or m) are matched to sequence spots (note that the grouping element and sequencing element have been subsumed under a matching scheme).

1	2	3	4	5	6

D E F G H I
P P P S S V
c m

Now symbolize the restrictions and start filling information into the diagram where possible.

The first restriction can be symbolized by 'F/H' in boxes 5 and 6. That is, the last two spots, 5 and 6, are taken by F or H. The second restriction says that of the four remaining spots (1 through 4), ship I must be in spot 1, and the rest of the spots are taken up by G, D, and E, in some unknown order. The third restriction gives us information for spot 2—that it is from Portland and a cargo ship (so we put P and c under 2). The fifth restriction says that spot 1 is a cargo ship (so we put a c under 1).

1	2	3	4	5	6
I	G/D/E	G/D/E	G/D/E	F/H	F/H
	P				
c	c				

P P S S V
c m

The fourth restriction says that at least two military ships are from Portland. We know from the third restriction that at least one Portland ship is a cargo ship (the ship in the second spot). Therefore, we can definitively deduce that the remaining two Portland ships are military. This means all other cargo ships (aside from the one in column 2) cannot be from Portland—so the cargo ship in column 1 must be from Vancouver or Seattle:

1	2	3	4	5	6
I	G/D/E	G/D/E	G/D/E	F/H	F/H
V/S	P				
c	c				

P P S S V
c m

2 remaining P's are m.
We can now turn to the questions.

Question 1

The correct answer is choice **d**. This question is a "Test-the-Rules" question. The first restriction rules out choice **a**, since F is not one of the last two ships, and choice **c**, since H is not one of the last two ships. The second restriction rules out choice **b** and choice **e**, since I is not first.

Question 2

The correct answer is choice **b**. We start by consulting the diagram we created, and scanning the answer choices to see if any, based on the diagram, must be false. Choice **a**—that D is from Portland—could be true, so it is incorrect. Choice **b**—that I is from Portland—cannot be true. Our diagram shows that Ship I must be from either Vancouver or Seattle. None of the other answer choices—that H is from Vancouver, F is from Seattle, and D is from Portland—can be proved false based on the information provided.

Question 3

The correct answer is choice **a**. First see what deductions can be made from the new information that four cargo ships arrive before all military ships. We know from the fourth restriction that there are at least two military ships—so the first four ships to arrive must be cargo ships, followed by two military ships. Furthermore, we know that at least two ships from Portland are military—so we can definitively deduce that these must be the two military ships from Portland. This information can be put into the diagram:

1	2	3	4	5	6
I	G/D/E	G/D/E	G/D/E	F/H	F/H
V/S	P	V/S	V/S	P	P
c	c	c	c	m	m

Now scan the answer choices to see which one of them must be true. Choice **a** states that H is from Portland, which is confirmed by the diagram. Circle your answer choice and move on to the next question.

For your reference, choice **b**—that F is from Seattle—is incorrect because F must be from Portland. Choice **c**—that I is from Vancouver—is incorrect because ship I could be from Seattle. And choices **d** and **e**—that D is from Portland or Vancouver, respectively—are incorrect because according to the information in our diagram, D could be from Portland (if it is second), Vancouver, or Seattle (if it is third or fourth).

This question is also a good example of how important it is to pay close attention to the wording of each question. You were asked for what *must be* true, not what *could be* true or must be *false*. If you dove into the answer choices without taking note of what you were being asked for, you could turn an easy, straightforward question into a time-consuming problem.

Question 4

The correct answer is choice **d**. Start by seeing what new deductions can be made from the additional information that ship E and ship F have two ships in between them, and that both E and F are from Seattle. We know from the set-up and diagram that E must be in spot 2, 3, or 4. If E is in spot 4, to maintain a separation of two ships, F would have to be in spot 1 (since there is no spot 7). But we know from the first restriction that F must be in spot 5 or 6, so E cannot be in spot 4.

What about spot 3? That would seem to work, as F would be in spot 6. What about spot 2? The third restriction states that the ship in spot 2 is a cargo ship from Portland. But the additional information specifies that E is from Seattle, so E cannot be in spot 2.

Therefore, E must be in spot 3, forcing F into spot 6. Fixing F in spot 6 will also fix H into spot 5, and fixing E in spot 3 leaves G and D either in 2 or 4.

Now consider the fact that E and F are both from Seattle. Since only two ships are from Seattle, this means that no other ships can be from Seattle, so I must be from Vancouver. And since there is only one ship from Vancouver, this must meant that the rest of the ships are from Portland. Draw all this in, along with the facts that the other Portland ships are military:

1	2	3	4	5	6
I	G/D	E	G/D	H	F
V	P	S	P	P	S
c	c		m	m		c m

Now, look at the answer choices. Any answer choice that must be true is incorrect. Choice **a** is incorrect, since the diagram shows that I is from Vancouver. Choice **b** is incorrect, since the diagram shows that H is from Portland. Choice **c** is incorrect, since the diagram shows that H is a military ship. Choice **e** is incorrect because regardless of sequence, the diagram shows that D is from Portland. Choice **d** is correct because if G in spot 4, it is a military ship, not a cargo ship.

Question 5

The correct answer is choice **d**. Since we know that the second ship is from Portland, and the first ship is either from Vancouver or Seattle, we know that the second, third, and fourth ships are all from Portland.

Then, consider the ships from Seattle. There must be two open spots next to one another for them. Spot 1 is adjacent to a ship from Portland, so there is no room there—therefore, the two Seattle ships must be in spots 5 and 6—this leaves the Vancouver ship in spot 1. Draw all this out, including the further information (from the fourth restriction) that the remaining Portland ships are military, and that the ships in spots 5 an 6 could be military or cargo.

1	2	3	4	5	6
I	G/D/E	G/D/E	G/D/E	F/H	F/H
V	P	P	P	S	S
c	c	m	m	c/m	c/m

Now consider the answer choices, looking for the answer choice that must be false. Choice **a** is incorrect because according to the diagram, the Seattle ships could both be either military or cargo. Choice **b** is incorrect for the same reason. Choice **c** is incorrect because there are in fact two Portland ships that are military. Choice **e** is incorrect because, again, the Vancouver ship is cargo. Choice **d** is correct because the Vancouver ship is a cargo ship.

C H A P T E R

Practice Set 2

Game 1

Six animals are selected for a new zoo exhibit. They are selected from four lions (A, B, C, D), four giraffes (H, I, J, K), and three tigers (X, Y, Z), according to the following conditions:

At least two lions are selected.
If H or J or both are selected, then both X and Y will be selected.
If Y is selected, then A is not selected.
If J is selected, then K is not selected.
If at least two tigers are selected, then exactly three lions will be selected.

1. Which one of the following could be a complete and accurate list of the animals selected for the exhibit?
   a. A, B, C, J, X, Z
   b. B, H, I, J, K, Y
   c. A, B, C, I, K, Y
   d. C, D, I, K, X, Y
   e. B, C, D, I, X, Y

2. If J is selected, then each of the following must be selected EXCEPT:
   a. B
   b. C
   c. D
   d. I
   e. Y

3. If the only tiger selected is Y, then which one of the following could be a partial, accurate list of the animals selected?
   a. H
   b. A, C
   c. B, D, I
   d. I, J, K
   e. B, D, H, K

4. If exactly one giraffe is selected, then which one of the following CANNOT be a true?
   a. Exactly one tiger is selected.
   b. Exactly two tigers are selected.
   c. Exactly two lions are selected.
   d. Exactly three lions are selected.
   e. Exactly four lions are selected.

5. Which one the following statements CANNOT be true?
   a. Exactly two tigers are selected.
   b. Exactly three tigers are selected.
   c. Exactly two giraffes are selected.
   d. Exactly three giraffes are selected.
   e. Exactly three lions are selected.

Game 2

A textbook is to be translated into at least one of seven languages—Arabic, Chinese, French, German, Hindi, Russian, and Spanish—according to the following conditions:

If it is translated into French, it is translated into German.
If it translated into Arabic or Chinese or both, it will not be translated into Russian.
If it is not translated into Arabic, it is translated into Hindi.
If it is translated into Spanish, it will not be translated into German.

1. Which one of the following could be a complete and accurate list of the languages into which the book is translated?
   a. Chinese, German
   b. Arabic, French, Spanish
   c. Chinese, French, German, Hindi
   d. Arabic, French, German, Spanish
   e. Arabic, Chinese, Russian, Spanish

2. If the book is translated into Russian, then what is the maximum number of languages into which the book could be translated?
   a. One
   b. Two
   c. Three
   d. Four
   e. Five

3. Which two languages CANNOT be a pair into both of which the book is translated?
   a. Spanish and French
   b. Russian and French
   c. German and Hindi
   d. Spanish and Hindi
   e. Arabic and Chinese

4. If the book is not translated into Hindi, which one of the following must be true?
   a. It is translated into Spanish
   b. It is translated into German
   c. It is not translated into French.
   d. It is not translated into German.
   e. It is not translated into Russian.

5. If the book is neither translated into Hindi nor German, then which one of the following could be an accurate, partial list of the languages into which it is translated?
   a. Chinese, French
   b. Spanish, Chinese –This choice does not correlate with the description of choice B in the Answer Key
   c. Russian, Arabic
   d. Spanish, Chinese, Russian
   e. Spanish, Arabic, French

Game 3

Three cheese platters are to be served at a party, each containing three types of cheeses. The cheeses are to be chosen from nine cheeses—American, Brie, Chevre, Dunlop, Evora, Feta, Gouda, Havarti, and Jarlsberg—and each of these nine cheeses will be served on exactly one platter, according to the following conditions:

The American and Chevre are not served on the same platter.
The Dunlop and Havarti are served on the same platter.
If the Evora and Gouda are served on the same platter, then the Jarlsberg and Havarti will not be served on the same platter.
The Chevre and Gouda are served on the same platter.

1. Which one of the following is an acceptable division of cheeses into platters?
   a. Platter 1: Dunlop, Havarti, Jarlsberg
      Platter 2: American, Brie, Evora
      Platter 3: Chevre, Feta, Gouda
   b. Platter 1: Dunlop, Havarti, Jarlsberg
      Platter 2: American, Brie, Feta
      Platter 3: Chevre, Evora, Gouda
   c. Platter 1: Evora, Feta, Jarlsberg
      Platter 2: American, Chevre Gouda
      Platter 3: Brie, Dunlop, Havarti
   d. Platter 1: Brie, Dunlop, Jarlsberg
      Platter 2: American, Evora, Feta
      Platter 3: Chevre, Gouda, Havarti
   e. Platter 1: Brie, Evora, Feta
      Platter 2: Chevre, Dunlop, Havarti
      Platter 3: American, Gouda, Jarlsberg

2. If the Jarlsberg is served on the same platter as the Dunlop, then which one of the following CANNOT be true?
   a. Feta is served on the same platter as Evora.
   b. Feta is served on the same platter as Brie.
   c. Brie is served on the same platter as Gouda.
   d. Brie is served on the same platter as American.
   e. American is served on the same platter as Evora.

3. If the American and the Evora are served on different platters, then which one of the following CANNOT be the list of cheeses on a single platter?
   a. American, Brie, Jarlsberg
   b. Evora, Feta, Jarlsberg
   c. Chevre, Gouda, Jarlsberg
   d. American, Dunlop, Havarti
   e. Dunlop, Harvarti, Jarlsberg

4. If the Feta and the Brie are served on the same platter, then which one of the following CANNOT be a pair of cheeses served on the same platter?
   a. American and Brie
   b. Gouda and Jarlsberg
   c. Dunlop and Jarlsberg
   d. Dunlop and Evora
   e. American and Feta

5. If the Evora and Feta are served on the same platter, then how many different ways can the platters be served?
   a. One
   b. Two
   c. Three
   d. Four
   e. Five

Game 4

Each of eight patients—A, B, C, D, E, F, G, and H—is assigned to exactly one of three wings in a hospital ward. The west wing is assigned three patients, the north wing is assigned two patients, and the south wing is assigned three patients, according the following restrictions:

Patient D is assigned to the north wing.
Patients E and G are assigned to the same wing.
If patient H is assigned to the west wing, then patient B is assigned to the south wing.
Patients B and G are not assigned to the same wing.

1. Which one of the following could be a complete and accurate assignment of patients to wings?
   a. West: A, G, E
      North: C, D
      South: B, F, H
   b. West: A, C, F
      North: D, G
      South: B, E, H
   c. West: A, C, H
      North: B, D
      South: E, F, G
   d. West: D, F, H
      North: C, G
      South: A, B, E
   e. West: B, E, G
      North: D, H
      South: A, C, F

2. Which one of the following statements must be true?
   a. Patients B and E are not assigned together.
   b. Patients D and E are not assigned together.
   c. Patients D and H are not assigned together.
   d. Patients B and D are not assigned together.
   e. Patients G and H are not assigned together.

3. If patient B is assigned to the west wing, then which one of the following could be true?
   a. Patient E is assigned to the west wing.
   b. Patient H is assigned to the west wing.
   c. Patient H is assigned to the south wing.
   d. Patient G is assigned to the west wing.
   e. Patient G is assigned to the north wing.

4. If patients A, C, and F are assigned to the same wing, then which one of the following pairs must be assigned to the south wing?
   a. Patients A and C
   b. Patients B and D
   c. Patients D and E
   d. Patients H and B
   e. Patients H and E

5. If patient G is in the south wing, then which one of the following CANNOT be true?
   a. Patients C and F are assigned together.
   b. Patients D and H are assigned together.
   c. Patients A and B are assigned together.
   d. Patients B and H are assigned together.
   e. Patients G and H are assigned together.

Game 5

Six horses—A, B, C, D, E, and F—are stabled in six horse stalls, numbered 1 through 6, with one horse per stall. They are stabled according to the following conditions:

Horse E is in a stall next to horse D.
Horse B is either in stall 1 or stall 2.
Horse A is in a higher-numbered stall than horse D, but in a lower-numbered stall than horse C.

1. If horse F is stabled in a lower-numbered stall than horse B, then which one of the following CANNOT be true?
   a. Horse E is in stall 3.
   b. Horse E is in stall 4.
   c. Horse A is in stall 4.
   d. Horse A is in stall 5.
   e. Horse C is in stall 6.

2. If horse C is in stall 5, then which one of the following must be true?
   a. Horse B is in stall 2.
   b. Horse A is in stall 3.
   c. Horse D is in stall 3.
   d. Horse E is in stall 2.
   e. Horse F is in stall 6.

3. Which one of the following could be the stall in which horse A is stabled?
   a. Stall 1
   b. Stall 2
   c. Stall 3
   d. Stall 4
   e. Stall 6

4. If there are four stalls in between the stall in which horse F is stabled and the stall in which horse C is stabled, then for how many stalls is it determined which horse is stabled there?
   a. One
   b. Two
   c. Three
   d. Four
   e. Five

5. If horse E is stabled next to horse F, then how many different sequences of horses in their stalls are possible?
   a. One
   b. Two
   c. Three
   d. Four
   e. Five

Game 6

A bus has eight seats, numbered 1 through 8, with odd-numbered seats on the left side, and increasing from 1 to 7 from front to back, and even-numbered seats on the right side, increasing from 2 to 8 from front to back. Seat 1 is across the aisle from seat 2, seat 3 across from 4, seat 5 across from 6, and seat 7 from 8. Eight passengers fill the bus, one to each seat. Each passenger is headed to Philadelphia or Boston (not both), and is a senior, adult, or youth. The passengers take seats according to the following conditions:

Seat 6 is taken by a youth headed for Philadelphia.
Seat 3 is taken by an adult headed for Boston.
Seniors only sit across the aisle from other seniors.
Exactly six passengers are headed for Philadelphia.
Every youth sits across from an adult.

1. Which one of the following could be a complete and accurate list of the passengers in seats 1, 2, 5, and 8, respectively?
   a. A senior headed for Boston, an adult headed for Philadelphia, an adult headed for Philadelphia, a youth headed for Philadelphia
   b. A senior headed for Philadelphia, a senior headed for Boston, a youth headed for Philadelphia, an adult headed for Philadelphia
   c. A senior headed for Boston, a senior headed for Boston, an adult headed for Boston, a youth headed for Boston
   d. A youth headed for Philadelphia, a youth headed for Boston, an adult headed for Boston, an adult headed for Philadelphia
   e. A youth headed for Philadelphia, an adult headed for Philadelphia, an adult headed for Boston, a senior headed for Philadelphia.

2. If there are exactly five adults on the bus, what is the maximum number of youths that could be on the bus?
   a. Zero
   b. One
   c. Two
   d. Three
   e. Four

3. If the right side of the bus has exactly three youths headed for Philadelphia, which one of the following must be true?
   a. There are exactly four adults on the bus.
   b. There are exactly three adults on the bus.
   c. There are at most two seniors on the bus.
   d. The left side of the bus has all adults.
   e. There are exactly two seniors on the bus.

4. Which one of the following statements could be true?
   a. Seat 5 is taken by a senior headed for Boston.
   b. Seat 4 is taken by a senior headed for Philadelphia.
   c. There are at least five seniors on the bus.
   d. There are exactly two youths headed for Boston on the bus.
   e. There are exactly three adults headed for Philadelphia on the bus.

5. If there are more youths than seniors on the bus, what is the maximum number of seniors that could be on the bus?
   a. Zero
   b. One
   c. Two
   d. Three
   e. Four

Game 7

A band tours five cities—Honolulu, Indianapolis, Jacksonville, Kansas City, and Las Vegas—one at a time. In each city, they play a concert which ends either with a new song or a classic song. The band tours according to the following conditions:

The second city toured is Honolulu.
The band ends with new songs in Las Vegas and Indianapolis (but not necessarily only those cities).
In the third city toured, the concert ends with a classic song.
Kansas City is toured before Jacksonville.

1. Which one of the following could be a complete and accurate list of the cities toured, from first to last?
   a. Las Vegas, Honolulu, Indianapolis, Kansas City, Jacksonville
   b. Indianapolis, Honolulu, Kansas City, Jacksonville, Las Vegas
   c. Las Vegas, Kansas City, Jacksonville, Honolulu, Indianapolis
   d. Las Vegas, Honolulu, Jacksonville, Kansas City, Indianapolis
   e. Kansas City, Honolulu, Las Vegas, Jacksonville, Indianapolis

2. If Indianapolis and Kansas City are adjacent on the tour schedule, then which one of the following must be true?
   a. Las Vegas is first.
   b. Las Vegas is second.
   c. Kansas City is first.
   d. Kansas City is second.
   e. Jacksonville is fourth.

3. If the concert in the first city toured ends with a classic song, then how many different sequences of cities toured could there be?
   a. One
   b. Two
   c. Three
   d. Four
   e. Five

4. If Indianapolis and Las Vegas are adjacent on the tour schedule, then which one of the following CANNOT be true?
   a. The concert in the fourth city toured ends with a classic song.
   b. The concert in the fifth city toured ends with a new song.
   c. The concert in the second city toured ends with a new song.
   d. The concert in the second city toured ends with a classic song.
   e. The concert in the first city toured ends with a new song.

5. Which one of the following CANNOT be true?
   a. The concerts in the fourth city and fifth city toured both end with new songs.
   b. The concerts in the fourth city and fifth city toured both end with classic songs.
   c. The concerts in the first city and second city toured both end with new songs.
   d. The concerts in the first city and third city toured both end with classic songs.
   e. The concerts in the second city and fourth city toured both end with classic songs.

Game 8

Six flights—L, M, N, O, P and Q—depart from an airport at different times. They depart from gates A, B, or C, according to the following restrictions:

No two consecutive departures are from the same gate.
M departs fifth.
N departs before P and Q.
The departure before flight N is from gate A.
Flight P departs before flight M.

1. Which one of the following could be the order
   of departing flights, from first to last?
   a. L, O, N, P, M, Q
   b. N, O, P, L, M, Q
   c. O, M, N, L, P, Q
   d. L, N, O, Q, M, P
   e. O, L, P, N, M, Q

2. If the first flight departs from Gate C, then
   which one of the following must be true?
   a. Flight N departs second.
   b. Flight O departs first.
   c. Flight P departs fourth.
   d. Flight L departs second.
   e. Flight O departs sixth.

3. Which one of the following is a complete and
   accurate list of the possible departures for flight
   P?
   a. Third, fourth
   b. First, third, fourth
   c. Third, fourth, sixth
   d. First, second, fifth
   e. First, second, fourth, fifth

4. If Flight Q departs third from Gate B, which
   one of the following must be true?
   a. The fourth flight departs from Gate C.
   b. The fourth flight departs from Gate A.
   c. The fifth flight departs from Gate A.
   d. The sixth flight departs from Gate C.
   e. The second flight departs from Gate C.

5. If the second departure is from Gate C, which
   one of the following CANNOT be true?
   a. Flight O departs before flights N and M.
   b. Flight P departs after flight Q.
   c. Flight L departs after flight M.
   d. Flights L and O depart before flight N.
   e. Flight Q departs after flight P.

Answer Explanations

Game 1

This selection game has a sub-group domain, so symbolize the entities:

> l: A B C D
> g: H I J K
> t: X Y Z

Since we are selecting exactly six entities, we will use six spaces, with the top-side reserved for specific entities (A, B, C, etc.), and the bottom for entity sub-group types (l, g, t).

— — — — — —

Now symbolize the rules. The first and fifth rule can be worked into the entity list:

> l: A B C D (2–4)   (ex.3)
> g: H I J K   ↑
> t: X Y Z   (2+)

The second, third, and fourth restrictions are:

> (H or J) → X and Y
> Contrapositive: (≠ X or ≠ Y) → (≠ H and ≠ J)
>
> Y → ≠ A
> Contrapositive: A → ≠ Y
>
> J → ≠ K
> Contrapositive: K → ≠ J

Now these restrictions can be combined to form a deduction chain:

> (H or J) → X and Y → ≠A

If we choose J in particular, we have:

> J → X and Y → ≠A
> J → ≠K

Since we must select an exact number of entities (six), numerical rules will likely have importance here. The first numerical restriction is that if two or three tigers are chosen, three lions are chosen. There are many particular ways to select one, two, or three tigers, so we could instead create three general scenarios.

As mentioned before, you need to be careful not to spend too much time on scenarios. They can be time-consuming, and might not even be fruitful if you can't determine much. You may find that using scenarios is intuitive and doesn't take much of your time. If not, you could go straight to the questions and uncover the mechanics of the game as you go along.

For this practice game, we will provide both types of answer explanations—with and without the use of up-front scenarios.

With that in mind, let's create some scenarios

Scenario 1: If three tigers are chosen, exactly three lions will be chosen:

> __ __ __ __ __ __
> t t t l l l

Can any other deductions be made? Indeed, the first scenario requires all three tigers to be selected, so we can go ahead and fill in X, Y, and Z there. Since Y is selected, the third restriction kicks in, and A (a lion) cannot be selected. So now we know what will fill the three l's here: B, C, and D. So, in this scenario, we have a complete list.

> S1
> X Y Z B C D
> t t t l l l

Scenario 2: If two tigers are chosen, exactly three lions are chosen, leaving one space for a giraffe:

— — — — — —
t t l l l g

Scenario 3: If one tiger is chosen, the fifth rule does not kick in, but we can make some other deductions about this scenario.

First, look for restrictions that deal with the tigers—X, Y and Z. The second restriction says that if H or J or both are selected, then two tigers (X and Y) must both be chosen. We note that since exactly one tiger is chosen, then at least one of X and Y won't be chosen. So the contrapositive of the second restriction kicks in, and we know that neither H nor J can be selected. Therefore, when choosing giraffes for the remaining five spots, we only have I and K to select from. And since we have one tiger and two giraffes to choose from, we know that at least three spaces must be lions, with the remaining spot going to either a giraffe or a lion:

— — — — — —
t l l l l/g g (g = I or K)

So we have our three scenarios, with varying levels of concrete information given:

S1
X̲ Y̲ Z̲ B̲ C̲ D̲
t t t l l l

S2
— — — — — —
t t l l l g

S3
— — — — — —
t l l l l/g g (g = I or K)

Question 1

The correct answer is choice **e**. This is a standard "Test-the-Rules" question. The first restriction rules out choice **b**, since only one of A, B, C, D is selected. The second restriction rules out choice **a**, since J is selected but Y is not. The third restriction rules out choice **c** since both Y and A are chosen. The fifth restriction rules out choice **d**, since X and Y are selected, but only two of A, B, C, D are selected.

Question 2

The correct answer is choice **d**. We already had some upfront deductions concerning J:

$J \rightarrow X$ and $Y \rightarrow \neq A$
$J \rightarrow \neq K$

l: A̶ B C D (2–4)   (ex.3)
g: H I J K̶   ↑
t: X̲ Y̲ Z   (2+)

Is there anything else that we can deduce here? It should be clear from the diagram that since two tigers have been selected, exactly three lions must be selected, and those lions must be B, C, and D (since A is out). So, we have a full selection list: J X Y B C D.

Look for an answer choice that doesn't appear on this list—I does not appear on this selection list, so choice **d** is correct.

Question 3

The correct answer is choice **c**. If the only tiger is Y, then we must be in the one-tiger scenario, scenario 3:

S3
Y̲ — — — — —
t l l l g g/l (g = I or K)

Since Y is selected, we know from the third restriction that A cannot be selected. We have seen this logic at work before: since A is out, the three remaining lions must be selected, B, C, and D, meaning the remaining spots must both be giraffes, I and K.

So we have: Y B C D I K

Look for an answer choice consistent with this list. Choices **a** and **e** are incorrect because H is not on this selection list. Choice **b** is incorrect because A is not on this selection list. Choice **d** is incorrect because J is not on this selection list. Choice **c** works because B, D, and I are all on the selection list.

To answer this question without the use of up-front scenarios, make deductions from the information that the only tiger is Y by cycling through the rules and applying them. Keep track of what's selected and what can't be selected on the diagram:

Y is the only tiger:

> l: A B C D (2–4)   (ex.3)
> g: H I J K   ↑
> t: X̶ Y̲ Z̶   (2+)

Now go through the rules and their contrapositives. The first rule does not apply. The contrapositive of the second rules applies: since X is not selected, neither H nor J can be selected:

> l: A B C D (2–4)   (ex.3)
> g: H̶ I J̶ K   ↑
> t: X̶ Y̲ Z̶   (2+)

The third rule indicates that A is not selected:

> l: A̶ B C D (2–4)   (ex.3)
> g: H̶ I J̶ K   ↑
> t: X̶ Y̲ Z̶   (2+)

This means that to get six animals, the remaining entities must all be selected. So again, we have the selection list: Y B C D I K.

Question 4

The correct answer is choice **c**. Consult the scenario diagrams to see which ones have one giraffe selected. Scenarios 2 and 3 both allow for one giraffe:

S2

> — — — — — —
> t   t   l   l   l   g

S3 (modified)

> — — — — — —
> t   l   l   l   l/g g   (g = I or K)

Now check each answer choice against these scenarios. Choice **a** is incorrect because exactly one tiger is selected in S3. Choice **b** is incorrect because exactly two tigers are selected in S2. Choice **c** is correct because S2 has three lions selected and S3 has four lions selected; it is not possible to select just two lions. Circle your answer choice and move on to the next question.

To answer the question without the use of up-front scenarios, eliminate answer choices by looking at the answers for the other questions, and then test each remaining answer choice to see if it could be true. The answer to Question 1 shows us that an acceptable selection list includes two tigers and three lions, so you can eliminate choices **b** and **d**. Questions 2 and 3 don't appear to be much help, so try each of the remaining answer choices to see if an acceptable scenario could be constructed around it. If exactly one tiger is selected, and exactly one giraffe is selected, then the remaining four animals must be the four lions:

> __ __ A̲ B̲ C̲ D̲
> t   g   l   l   l   l

There don't seem to be any contradictions, but see if you can fill it out without violating any contradictions. The first rule is satisfied. The second rule will be satisfied as long as neither H not J is selected (since two tigers, X and Y, cannot both be selected)—so let's select I for the giraffe:

$$\underline{} \quad \underline{I} \quad \underline{A} \quad \underline{B} \quad \underline{C} \quad \underline{D}$$
$$t \quad g \quad l \quad l \quad l \quad l$$

The third rule will be satisfied as long as Y is not selected (since A is selected)—so let's select Z for the tiger:

$$\underline{Z} \quad \underline{I} \quad \underline{A} \quad \underline{B} \quad \underline{C} \quad \underline{D}$$
$$t \quad g \quad l \quad l \quad l \quad l$$

If you continue checking the rules, you will see that none are violated—so having exactly one tiger is possible, and we can rule out choice **a**. You might also notice that since four lions are selected here, choice **e** is also ruled out. That leaves choice **c** as the correct answer. One can see that **c** is indeed the correct answer, since exactly one giraffe and exactly two lions means we need exactly three tigers—which would violate the fifth rule, since we would have at least two tigers, but not have exactly three lions.

Question 5

The correct answer is choice **d**. Test each answer choice against the scenario diagrams. Exactly two tigers are selected in S2, so choice **a** is incorrect. Exactly three tigers are selected in S1, so choice **b** is incorrect. Exactly two giraffes could be selected in S3, so choice **c** is incorrect. But in no scenario are three giraffes selected, so choice **d** is the correct answer.

To answer the question without the use of up-front scenarios, eliminate answer choices by looking at the answers for the other questions, and then test each remaining answer choice to see if it could be true. The answer to Question 1 eliminates choice **a**, since exactly two tigers are selected there. The answer to Question 2 eliminates choice **e**, since exactly three lions are selected there. The answer to Question 3 eliminates choice **c**, since exactly two giraffes are selected there. So we need to test choices **b** and **d**. If three tigers are selected, then by the fifth restriction, three lions are selected. The three tigers are X, Y, and

Z. Since Y is selected, A cannot be—so the three lions must be B, C, and D. This selection does not violate any of the rules, and so choice **b** can be eliminated. That leaves choice **d** as the correct answer. If you tested choice **d**, you would see that if three giraffes are selected, they would have to be H, I, and one of J and K (since by the fourth restriction, J and K cannot both be selected). This means that X and Y must also be selected (by the second restriction), leaving one spot.

But we need two lions, and have none so far—so it's not possible to have three giraffes.

Game 2

This selection game has a simple domain, so merely list the symbols for the entities:

F S R H A G C

Now, symbolize the rules:

F → G
Contrapositive: ≠G → ≠F

(A v C) → ≠R
Contrapositive: R → (≠A and ≠C)

≠A → H
Contrapositive: ≠H → A
Disjunctive form: A v H

S → ≠G
Contrapositive: G → ≠S

Now look for connections among rules. The first and fourth restrictions connect through G:

S → ≠G → ≠F
F → G → ≠S

The second and third rules connect up through A:

≠H → A → ≠R
R → (≠A and ≠C) → H

The other thing to keep in mind is that there is a disguised disjunction: any selection of languages must have either A or H or both.

We now turn to the questions.

Question 1

The correct answer is choice **c**. This is a standard "Test-the-Rules" question. The first restriction rules out choice **b**, since French is chosen, but German is not. The second restriction rules out choice **e**, since both Arabic and Russian are chosen. The third restriction rules out choice **a**, since neither Arabic nor Hindi are present. The fourth restriction rules out choice **d**, since both Spanish and German are chosen.

Question 2

The correct answer is choice **d**. If the book is translated into Russian, then we know from our deduction chain—R → (≠A and ≠C) → H—that A and C are not selected, and H is selected.

So we have:

$$\text{F S } \underline{R} \text{ H } \cancel{A} \text{ G } \cancel{C}$$

There are now two selected (R, H), and three left (F, S, G) to select from. Can we select all three. We know from the fourth restriction that G and S cannot be selected together. So the most we can select is one of those two (G or S) and F, in addition to R and H. Let's pick one to see if it works: G, F, R, H. This selection does not violate any of the restrictions, so it works, and the maximum number we can select is four, choice **d**.

Question 3

The correct answer is choice **a**. Your first instinct for a question like this should be to review your deductions to see if the correct answer is obvious. The S → ≠G → ≠F deduction chain immediately tells you that choice **a** cannot be true. If Spanish is selected, French cannot be.

None of the other answer choices present pairs that cannot be together.

Question 4

The correct answer is choice **e**. Look again at your deduction chains to see what follows from the book not being translated into Hindi. According to the ≠H → A → ≠R chain, the book must be translated into Arabic and not into Russian. Scan the answer choices—choice **e** is that the book is not translated into Russian.

Question 5

The correct answer is choice **b**. If the book is not translated into Hindi, then according to the deduction chain ≠H → A → ≠R, it is translated into Arabic and not translated into Russian. If the book is not translated into German, then according to the deduction chain S → ≠G → ≠F, it is also not translated into French.

So we have:

$$\cancel{F} \text{ S } \underline{R} \text{ H } \underline{A} \cancel{G} \text{ C}$$

Now check each answer choice against this selection diagram. Choices **a** and **e** are incorrect because they include French, which is crossed out. Choices **c** and **d** are ruled out because they include Russian, which is crossed out. Choice **b** includes Spanish and Chinese—two languages that could be selected according to the selection diagram. So **b** is the correct answer.

Game 3

For this grouping game, first diagram the game play. We have three groups of three:

1: _ _ _
2: _ _ _
3: _ _ _

Note that we label the groups 1, 2, and 3 for ease of reference in these answer explanations; when you are actually diagramming, you wouldn't need these labels.

Next, symbolize the restrictions.

~~AC~~
DH
EG → ~~JH~~
Contrapositive: JH → ~~EG~~
CG

Now see what deductions can be made. Since there are only three cheeses per plate, pairs DH and CG must appear on different plates (they are placed on 1 and 3 arbitrarily—remember that the numbers here mean nothing):

1: <u>D</u> <u>H</u> __
2: __ __ __
3: <u>C</u> <u>G</u> __

To get a handle on the game play, you might try to divide the game into scenarios. There may be a few ways to do this. One way would be to work with the contrapositive of the third restriction, dividing the game into two scenarios—one on which J and H go together, and one in which J and H do not go together.

In Scenario 1, J and H go together, so platter 1 is set:

1: <u>D</u> <u>H</u> <u>J</u>
2: __ __ __
3: <u>C</u> <u>G</u> __

Now apply the other restrictions. Since A does not go with C, A must appear in platter 2 According to the contrapositive of the third restriction, since J goes with H, E cannot go with G, and E must appear in platter 2 as well. The two remaining cheeses, F and B, are free for the remaining slots. So we have scenario 1:

S1
1: <u>D</u> <u>H</u> <u>J</u>
2: <u>A</u> <u>E</u> <u>F/B</u>
3: <u>C</u> <u>G</u> <u>F/B</u>

What about scenario 2, in which J and H do not go together? All we know here is that J is not in platter 1 and, by the first restriction, that A does not go in platter 3.

S2
1: <u>D</u> <u>H</u> __ (~~J~~)
2: __ __ __
3: <u>C</u> <u>G</u> __ (~~A~~)

Question 1
The correct answer is choice **a**. This is a standard "Test-the-Rules" question. The first restriction rules out choice **c**, since A and C are together. The second restriction rules out choice **d**, since D and H are not together. The third restriction rules out choice **b**, since E and G are together, but so are J and H. The fourth restriction rules out choice **e**, since C and G are not together.

Question 2
The correct answer is choice **b**. If J and D go together, then we must be in S1:

1: <u>D</u> <u>H</u> <u>J</u>
2: <u>A</u> <u>E</u> <u>F/B</u>
3: <u>C</u> <u>G</u> <u>F/B</u>

To answer this question without the use of up-front scenarios, start with the information that J and D go together:

1: <u>D</u> <u>H</u> <u>J</u>
2: __ __ __
3: <u>C</u> <u>G</u> __

Now apply the rules. The first rule forces A into platter 2 The second rule is satisfied. And the contrapositive of the third rule indicates that E and G cannot go together, which also forces E into platter 2. We don't know where to place F or B yet. They could go in either platter 2 or 3.

Now we have scenario 1:

1: <u>D</u> <u>H</u> <u>J</u>
2: <u>A</u> <u>E</u> <u>F/B</u>
3: <u>C</u> <u>G</u> <u>F/B</u>

F and E could be served on the same platter (platter 2), so **a** is incorrect B and G could go together in platter 3, so **c** is incorrect B and A could go together in platter 2, so **d** is incorrect A is served on the same platter as E, so **e** is incorrect. F and B could not be served on the same platter, since those two have to be distributed over platters 2 and 3. So **b** is the correct answer.

Question 3

The correct answer is choice **e**. If A and E are not together, then we must be in scenario 2:

1: <u>D</u> <u>H</u> _ (J̶)
2: _ _ _
3: <u>C</u> <u>G</u> _ (A̶)

Since the new information involves A, let's work with A. A must appear in platter 1 or platter 2, so draw out both possibilities:

S2.1
1: <u>D</u> <u>H</u> <u>A</u>
2: _ _ _
3: <u>C</u> <u>G</u> _

S2.2
1: <u>D</u> <u>H</u> _ (J̶)
2: <u>A</u> _ _
3: <u>C</u> <u>G</u> _

Now add in the information that A and E do not go together. For S2.1, this means that E will be in platter 2 or platter 3, which was known already, so there are no further restrictions on E. For S2.2, this means E will not appear on platter 2:

S2.2
1: <u>D</u> <u>H</u> _ (J̶)
2: <u>A</u> _ _ (E̶)
3: <u>C</u> <u>G</u> _

Now test each answer choice against these diagrams A, J, B could appear on platter 2 in S2.2, so **a** is incorrect J, E, F could appear on platter 2 of S2.1, so **b** is incorrect C, G, J could appear on platter 3 of S2.2, so **c** is incorrect D, H, A appears on platter 1 of S2.1, so **d** is incorrect. But D, H, J could neither appear in a platter in S2.1, nor appear in a platter in S2.2 (since J has been ruled out from platter 1, where we already have D and H), so **e** is the correct answer.

Answering this question without the aid of scenarios is more time-consuming: you need to try each set of three cheeses to see if they could all appear together on a platter. Since we start with the initial diagram, which incorporates all the information from the second and fourth rules, we only need to consider the first and third rules. If A, J, and B are on the same platter, we have:

1: <u>D</u> <u>H</u> _
2: <u>A</u> <u>J</u> <u>B</u>
3: <u>C</u> <u>G</u> _

The new restriction (A̶E̶) forces E into platter 1, and so F is left for platter 3:

1: <u>D</u> <u>H</u> <u>E</u>
2: <u>A</u> <u>J</u> <u>B</u>
3: <u>C</u> <u>G</u> <u>F</u>

We need to check that the first and third rules are satisfied. A and C are separated, so the first rule is satisfied, and since E and G are separated, the third rule does not apply. So this is an acceptable distribution, and choice **a** is incorrect.

What about choice **b**? If J, E, and F are on the same platter, we have:

1: <u>D</u> <u>H</u> _
2: <u>J</u> <u>E</u> <u>F</u>
3: <u>C</u> <u>G</u> _

The first rule forces A into platter 1, leaving B for platter 3 Since E and G are separated, the third rule does not apply, and this is an acceptable distribution—meaning that **b** is incorrect.

If C, G, and J go together, we have:

1: <u>D</u> <u>H</u> _
2: _ _ _
3: <u>C</u> <u>G</u> <u>J</u>

None of the rules—the first rule, the third rule, or the new rule—are triggered, so rather than waste time completely filling out the scenario, we can tentatively assume this is an acceptable distribution, and tentatively rule out choice **c**.

If D, H, and A go together, then we have:

1: <u>D</u> <u>H</u> <u>A</u>
2: _ _ _
3: <u>C</u> <u>G</u> _

Again, none of the rules are immediately triggered, so we tentatively assume this is an acceptable distribution, and tentatively rule out choice **d**.

Since we have only tentatively ruled out choices **c** and **d**, we must test choice **e** (if we had definitively ruled them out, then we could circle **e** and move on).

If D, H and J go together, we have:

1: <u>D</u> <u>H</u> <u>J</u>
2: _ _ _
3: <u>C</u> <u>G</u> _

Since J and H are together, the contrapositive of the third rule kicks in, and E and G must be separated—meaning that E is on platter 2:

1: <u>D</u> <u>H</u> <u>J</u>
2: <u>E</u> _ _
3: <u>C</u> <u>G</u> _

Now look at the first rule (A̶C̶) and the new rule (A̶E̶): A can neither go on platter 2 or platter 3 (and there is no room on platter 1) So this distribution is impossible and choice **e** is the correct answer.

Question 4

The correct answer is choice **c**. If F and B go together, then we cannot be in Scenario 1 (in which F and B are split over platters 2 and 3), and we must be in Scenario 2. Since F and B go together, there is only room for them on platter 2:

1: <u>D</u> <u>H</u> _ (J̶)
2: <u>F</u> <u>B</u> _
3: <u>C</u> <u>G</u> _ (A̶)

Since A could go with B in platter 2, **a** is incorrect. Since J could go with G in platter 3, **b** is incorrect. Since J cannot go with D (which is in platter 1), choice **c** is the correct answer. Since E could go with D in platter 1, **d** is incorrect. Since A could go with F in platter 2, **e** is incorrect.

This question is also easy to answer without the use of scenarios. Since F and B go together, we have:

1: <u>D</u> <u>H</u> _
2: <u>F</u> <u>B</u> _
3: <u>C</u> <u>G</u> _

Now try to apply the rules. The first means that A cannot be on platter 3:

1: <u>D</u> H _
2: <u>F</u> B _
3: <u>C</u> G _ (~~A~~)

If it's not immediately clear what other deductions can be made from the rules, start testing the answer choices. Choices **a** and **b** can be eliminated as above (there are no immediate rules triggered or contradictions). Now we test choice **c**. If J and D go together, then we have:

1: <u>D</u> H J
2: <u>F</u> B _
3: <u>C</u> G _ (~~A~~)

Since J and H are together, the contrapositive of the third rule kicks in, and E and G are separated, forcing E into platter 2, leaving room only on platter 3 for A—a situation ruled out by the diagram. This contradiction shows us that **c** is the correct answer choice.

Question 5

The correct answer is choice **d**. We want to know how many different groupings of cheeses onto platters there are, so long as E and F are served on the same platter and other restrictions are being met. Consult the scenarios/diagrams. If in S1, then there is one possible grouping (with E and F both on platter 2). If we are in S2, then we have:

1: <u>D</u> H _ (~~J~~)
2: <u>E</u> F _
3: <u>C</u> G _ (~~A~~)

Since A could be on platter 1 or platter 2, let's take each one at a time. If A is on platter 1, then J could either be on platter 2 or platter 3—so we have two possible groupings. And if A is on platter 2, then

J must be on platter 3, and B must be on platter 1—so we have 1 possible grouping. The total possible groupings for S2 are three, combined with the one possible grouping from S1; therefore, we have a grand total of four possible groupings, answer **d**.

We could also answer this question without the use of scenarios. Since E and F are together, we see that we must have:

1: <u>D</u> H _
2: <u>E</u> F _
3: <u>C</u> G _

Since E and G are not together, the third rule does not apply, and so we only need to consider the first rule (remember, the initial diagram already incorporates all the information from the second and fourth rules). The first rule means that A could only be on one of two platters (platter 1 and 2), and there are two unrestricted cheeses left. Therefore, there are four total assignments—two in which A is on platter 1 and two in which A is on platter 2.

Game 4

Start by drawing the diagram for this grouping game:

w: __ __ __
n: __ __
s: __ __ __

We know that D is in n, so draw that in directly.

w: __ __ __
n: <u>D</u> __
s: __ __ __

No we symbolize the other restrictions:

EG
H = w → B = s
Contrapositive: B ≠ s → H ≠ w
~~BG~~

You could create scenarios (perhaps one with EG in the west wing and one with EG in the south wing), but these questions can be answered by just applying the rules.

Question 1

The correct answer is choice **a**. The first restriction rules out choice **d**, since D is not in the north wing. The second restriction rules out choice **b**, since E and G are not assigned together. The third restriction rules out choice **c**, since H is in the west wing, but B is not in the south wing. The fourth restriction rules out choice **e**, since B and G are assigned together.

Question 2

The correct answer is choice **a**. Look for the choice that does not violate any rules, or leads to a contradiction. Can E and B be assigned together? By the second rule, E and G must be assigned together; but by the fourth rule, B and G cannot be together, and so if B can't be with G, B can't be with E either. So E and B cannot be assigned together, and the correct answer is choice **a**.

Question 3

The correct answer is choice **c**. We know that patient B is assigned to the west wing:

    w: <u>B</u> __ __
    n: <u>D</u> __
    s: __ __ __

Now, go through the rules. The contrapositive of the third rule can be applied, since B is not in the south wing, it means H is not in the west wing:

    w: <u>B</u> __ __ <s>H</s>
    n: <u>D</u> __
    s: __ __ __

The fourth rule can also be applied: G cannot be in the west wing because B is:

    w: <u>B</u> __ __ <s>H G</s>
    n: <u>D</u> __
    s: __ __ __

This means that the EG block (given by the second rule) must be in the south wing:

    w: <u>B</u> __ __ <s>H G</s>
    n: <u>D</u> __
    s: <u>E</u> <u>G</u> __

No other deductions are immediately apparent, so consider the answer choices. Choice **a** is incorrect because E is assigned to the south wing. Choice **b** is incorrect because H is barred from the west wing. Choices **d** and **e** are incorrect because G is assigned to south wing. Choice **c** is correct because H can be assigned to the north wing or south wing.

Question 4

The correct answer is choice **e**. If A, C, and F are assigned to the same wing, that wing must be either the west wing or the south wing. Try each to see if we can figure out which one it is. If A, C, and F are assigned to the south wing, we have:

    w: __ __ __
    n: <u>D</u> __
    s: <u>A</u> <u>C</u> <u>F</u>

Now see what follows from the rules. By the contrapositive of the third rule, since B is not in the south wing, H is not in the west wing—meaning that H is in the north wing, and the remaining three patients are in the west wing:

    w: <u>E</u> <u>G</u> <u>B</u>
    n: <u>D</u> <u>H</u>
    s: <u>A</u> <u>C</u> <u>F</u>

But this violates the fourth rule, which says that B and G cannot go together. So A, C and F must be in the west wing:

w: <u>A</u> <u>C</u> <u>F</u>
n: <u>D</u> __
s: __ __ __

This means that the EG block must be in the south wing:

w: <u>A</u> <u>C</u> <u>F</u>
n: <u>D</u> __
s: <u>E</u> <u>G</u> __

Since B cannot go with G (by the fourth restriction, B must be in the north wing), H is forced into the south wing:

w: <u>A</u> <u>C</u> <u>F</u>
n: <u>D</u> <u>B</u>
s: <u>E</u> <u>G</u> <u>H</u>

Choice **a** is incorrect because A and C are assigned to the west wing. Choice **b** is incorrect because D and B are assigned to the north wing. Choice **c** is incorrect because D is assigned to the north wing and E assigned to the south wing. Choice **d** is incorrect because H is assigned to the south wing and B is assigned to the north wing. Choice **e** is correct because both H and E are assigned to the south wing.

Question 5

The correct answer is choice **d**. If G is in the south wing, E must be in the south wing as well (because of the EG block given by the second restriction), and we have:

w: __ __ __
n: <u>D</u> __
s: <u>E</u> <u>G</u> __

By the fourth rule, B cannot be in the south wing:

w: __ __ __
n: <u>D</u> __
s: <u>E</u> <u>G</u> __ B̶

By the contrapositive of the third rule, this means that H is not in the west wing:

w: __ __ __ H̶
n: <u>D</u> __ __
s: <u>E</u> <u>G</u> __ B̶

This captures all the information in the rules, and no further deductions are immediately apparent, so test each of the answer choices to see if it could be true. As usual, when testing answer choices for questions like these, check each for a relatively immediate contradiction—and if none surfaces, tentatively rule that choice out and move on. There are no immediate contradictions for choices **a**, **b**, and **c**. It seems that F and C could be assigned together in the west wing, H and D together in the north wing, and B and A together in the west wing, without any immediately apparent problems. But H and B seem to present a problem. There is space for both of them only in the west wing, but H cannot be in the west wing—so H and B can't be assigned together, and choice **d** is the correct answer.

Game 5

We have six stalls for this sequencing game, numbered 1 through 6:

1 2 3 4 5 6

Now symbolize the restrictions:

E/D

E/D—A—C

This captures the first and third restrictions. Since the second restriction—which says that B must either be in 1 or 2—presents two scenarios, we could see what follows from each scenario.

If B is in stall 2, then we know that the E/D block cannot be to the left of B (since there is only one spot to the left of B). So E/D must be to the right of B, which means that the whole sequence E/D—A—C must fill the four spots to the right of B (stalls 3 through 6). And that means that the remaining horse (F) must be in stall one. So for scenario 1, we have:

S1

$$\underline{F} \quad \underline{B} \quad \underline{E/D} \quad \underline{A} \quad \underline{C}$$
$$1 \quad 2 \quad 3 \quad 4 \quad 5 \quad 6$$

If B is in stall 1, then E/D—A—C must be to the right of B, and F floats somewhere to the right of B as well (but not between E and D). So we have:

S2

$$\longleftarrow F \longrightarrow$$
$$\underline{B} \quad \underline{E/D—A—C}$$
$$1 \quad 2 \ 3 \ 4 \quad 5 \ 6$$

Question 1

The correct answer is choice **c**. If F is before B, then we must be in scenario 1:

$$\underline{F} \quad \underline{B} \quad \underline{E/D} \quad \underline{A} \quad \underline{C}$$
$$1 \quad 2 \quad 3 \ 4 \quad 5 \quad 6$$

E could be in stall 3 or 4, so choices **a** and **b** are incorrect. A must be in stall 5, and cannot be in stall 4, so choice **c** is the correct answer and **d** incorrect. C must be in stall 6, so **e** is incorrect.

Question 2

The correct answer is choice **e**. If C is in stall 5, then we must be in scenario 2, since in scenario 1, C is in stall 6. If C is in stall 5, then E/D—A—C must be in between B and F (that is, there is only room for E/D-A to the left of C).

So we have:

$$\underline{B} \quad \underline{E/D} \quad \underline{A} \quad \underline{C} \quad \underline{F}$$
$$1 \quad 2 \quad 3 \quad 4 \quad 5 \quad 6$$

B is not in stall 2, so **a** is incorrect. A is not in stall 3, so **b** is incorrect. D could be in stall 3, but could also be in stall 2, so it's not the case that D must be in stall 3; so **c** is incorrect. E could be in stall 2, but could also be in stall 3, so it's the case that E must be in stall 2; so **d** is incorrect. F must be in stall 6, so **e** is correct.

Question 3

The correct answer is choice **d**. Consult the diagrams of the two scenarios to see where A appears. In S1, A appears in stall 5. But stall 5 is not one of the answer choices. In S2, A is floating—but it cannot appear in stalls 2 or 3, because that would leave no room for E/D to its left. And it cannot appear in stall 6, because that would leave no room for C to its right. So it must appear in either stall 4 or 5. So **d** is the correct answer.

Question 4

The correct answer is choice **d**. If there are four stalls between F and C, then we must be in scenario 1 (scenario 2 does not allow for four stalls between F and C):

$$\underline{F} \quad \underline{B} \quad \underline{E/D} \quad \underline{A} \quad \underline{C}$$
$$1 \quad 2 \quad 3 \quad 4 \quad 5 \quad 6$$

The diagram shows that stalls 1, 2, 5, and 6 are all filled by a particular horse; stalls 3 and 4 are not set (although we know that E and D fill the two). So there are four stalls for which it is determined which horse is stabled there—answer choice **d**.

Question 5

The correct answer is choice **b**. If E and F are next to one another, then we must be in scenario 2 (in scenario 1, B, and maybe D, separates E from F):

$$\overset{\longleftarrow F \longrightarrow}{\underline{B \quad E/D\text{—}A\text{—}C}}$$
$$1 \quad 2\ 3\ 4 \quad 5\ 6$$

But E and F must also be next to one another, so we have a new block that includes E, F, and D:

$$\underline{B \quad E/F/D \quad A \quad C}$$
$$1 \quad 2\ 3\ 4 \quad 5 \quad 6$$

But for E to be both next to D and next to F, it must appear in the middle of the two. There are two ways to accomplish this, D-E-F and F-E-D:

$$B\ D\ E\ F\ A\ C \quad \text{or} \quad B\ F\ E\ D\ A\ C$$

So there are two possible sequences, choice **b**.

Game 6

This matching game is particularly spatial in character, so a diagram will be a necessity. Draw the numbered seats on the bus left to right, front to back:

$$7(\,,\,) \quad 5(\,,\,) \quad 3(\,,\,) \quad 1(\,,\,)$$
$$8(\,,\,) \quad 6(\,,\,) \quad 4(\,,\,) \quad 2(\,,\,)$$

Each (,) notation is there be filled with a letter (P or B) for the destination, and a letter (s, a, y) for the age-type.

Now symbolize the first two restrictions:

$$7(\,,\,) \quad 5(\,,\,) \quad 3(a,B) \quad 1(\,,\,)$$
$$8(\,,\,) \quad 6(y,P) \quad 4(\,,\,) \quad 2(\,,\,)$$

The third restriction can be symbolized:

This indicates that if a senior is sitting in any seat, another senior must be sitting right across from him or her.

The fourth restriction can be symbolized:

$$6\ P,\ 2\ B$$

The fifth restriction can be symbolized:

and

This indicates that wherever a youth sits, an adult must sit across from him or her.

Finally, see if any obvious deductions can be made. Since, according to the fifth restriction, every youth sits across from an adult, we see that seat 5 must be filled by an adult. This deduction should also be made obvious by comparing our spatial symbolization of the fifth restriction to the diagram.

$$7(\,,\,) \quad 5(a,\,) \quad 3(a,B) \quad 1(\,,\,)$$
$$8(\,,\,) \quad 6(y,P) \quad 4(\,,\,) \quad 2(\,,\,)$$

Question 1

The correct answer is choice **e**. This question is a "Test-the-Rules" question, but it requires more processing than usual. We usually approach questions like this rule-by-rule—that is, we check to see which answer choice(s) violates the first rule, and then which answer choice(s) violate the second rule, etc. But that approach will be difficult here, because understanding each answer choice requires assessing how it looks in the diagram first. So you want to go choice-by-choice rather than rule-by-rule.

Choice **a** is incorrect because it violates the third restriction, which says that seniors only sit across from seniors (and a senior in seat 1 would be sitting across from an adult in seat 2). Choice **b** is incorrect because it violates a combination of the fifth restriction, which says that every youth sits across from an adult, and the first restriction, which says that there is a youth in seat 6 (since a youth in seat 5 would be sitting across from a youth in seat 6). Choice **c** is incorrect because it violates the fourth restriction, which says that exactly six passengers are headed for Philadelphia (since the combination of these four passengers headed for Boston, with the passenger in seat 3 headed for Boston, amounts to a total of at least five passengers headed for Boston, leaving only three or less headed for Philadelphia). Choice **d** violates the fifth restriction, since it would have a youth sitting across from a youth in seats 1 and 2. Choice **e** does not violate any restrictions.

Question 2

The correct answer is choice **d**. Start with the restriction that will play the most important part given the question: the fifth restriction says that for every youth, an adult sits across the aisle. So we want to play with our diagram to maximize the number of youths, given exactly five adults. Have as many adults sitting across from empty seats as possible, rather than sitting across from other adults.

Looking at our diagram, we see that there are already two adults fixed (in seats 5 and 3). So we have to distribute three adults to maximize space for youths. To do this, put one adult in one of the seat 7/seat 8 combo, and put another in one of the seat 1/seat 2 combo. At this point, we have space for three more youths (one in the seat 7/seat 8 combo, one in the seat 1/seat 2 combo, and one across from seat 3). But we still have to distribute one more adult. Since anywhere we put that adult will result in him or her sitting across from another adult, we reduce our capacity for youths by one. So there will be two open spots for youths, not three.

Add those two spots to the youth already present in seat 6, and we see that the maximum number of youth is three, or answer choice **d**.

Question 3

The correct answer is choice **c**. First, note that the right side of the bus will have two more (y,P)'s:

$$7(\,,\,) \quad 5(a,\,) \quad 3(a,B) \quad 1(\,,\,)$$

$$8(\,,\,) \quad 6(y,P) \quad 4(\,,\,) \quad 2(\,,\,)$$
$$\text{2 more (y,P)'s}$$

Scan each answer choice to see if it you could make it false without violating a restriction. Since you don't want to waste time, check each choice very briefly, in the hopes that the correct answer will be apparent once you try to make it false.

Could there be more than four or less than four adults? It seems we could have five adults if the left side were all adults and there was one adult on the right. So we can tentatively rule out choice **a**. This would also tentatively rule out choice **b** (and, incidentally, choice **d**—but we won't need to get that far). Now, could there be more than two seniors on the bus? Each senior needs to sit across from another senior—and since there are three youths on the right side, there is only space for one row of seniors (that is, space for only two seniors). So choice **c** is the correct answer.

Note that you could tell choice **e** is incorrect simply by noticing that it logically entails choice **c**—and so it couldn't be the correct answer, otherwise there would be two correct answers. In any case, choice **e** is incorrect because we could fill all the open spots (not taken by the required youths) with adults.

Question 4

The correct answer is choice **e**. Take each statement, and test it against the diagram, restrictions, and further deductions to see if it could be true. Choice **a** is incorrect because as our diagram shows, seat 5 is taken by an adult. Choice **b** is incorrect because according to the third restriction, every senior must sit across from another senior, and this choice would have a senior in seat 4 sitting across from an adult in seat 3. Choice **c** is incorrect because there is only room for, at most, four seniors on the bus—the seat 5/seat 6 and seat 3/seat 4 across-the-aisle pairs each contain at least one non-senior, leaving just two fully open across-the-aisle pairs, the seat 7/seat 8 pair and the seat 1/seat 2 pair. These two fully open pairs can accommodate at most four seniors. Choice **d** is incorrect because if there were two youths headed for Boston, then there would be three total passengers headed for Boston (including the adult headed for Boston in seat 3), which would violate the fourth restriction (which implies that there are only two passengers headed for Boston). So choice **e** is the correct answer.

Since you have eliminated the other answer choices, you should just circle this and move on.

If you happened to test choice **e** before testing all the others, you would see that it is correct because it could be the case that there are exactly three adults headed for Philadelphia, or three (a,P)s. It's enough to see that choice **e** probably allows for an acceptable scenario by not immediately seeing any problems with it (and then eliminating the other answers), rather than coming up with a specific example—but here's one example of the bus containing exactly three adults headed for Philadelphia:

7(a,P)   5(a,P)   3(a,B)   1(s,P)
8(a,P)   6(y,P)   4(y,B)   2 (s,P)

Question 5

The correct answer is choice **c**. First, note that the number of seniors must be a multiple of 2 (including 0), since they come in across-the-aisle pairs, as per the fifth restriction. So choices **b** and **d** are incorrect. Next, since there are a total of eight people, and more youths than seniors, there can be at most three seniors (if there were four seniors, there could only be four youth). So choice **e** is incorrect. Now we must choose between choices **a** and **c**. Could there be two seniors? Yes, it's possible for there to be more youth than seniors when there are two seniors.

You have to arrive at this conclusion by trying to make this possibility work:

7(y,)   5(a,)   3(a,B)   1(s,)
8(a,)   6(y,P)   4(y,)   2 (s,)

This diagram shows two seniors, and three youth. If you examine the rules, none are violated by this arrangement (as long as we assign P to exactly five more passengers). So we have found our maximum possible number of seniors: two. Choice **a** is incorrect because this diagram shows that we can have at least two seniors and still meet the requirement that there be more youth than seniors.

Game 7

This is a hybrid game—a sequencing game with an element of matching—so draw a grid in which we match the cities and song-type to each number, 1 to 5:

1	2	3	4	5	
					H, I, J, K, L
					c/n

Now symbolize the restrictions and start filling in the grid. The first restriction can be written directly into the diagram. The second restriction can by symbolized by writing n next to L and I. The third restriction can also be written directly into the diagram. The fourth restriction can be symbolized K—J.

1	2	3	4	5	
J̶	H			K̶	I(n) , J, K, L(n)
		c			c/n

K—J

We have also written in that the first city is not J, and the last not K.

See if any further deductions can be made. Since the third city has a concert that ends with a classic song, that third city cannot be either Indianapolis or Las Vegas, since they have concerts ending with new songs:

1	2	3	4	5	
J̶	H	I̶ L̶		K̶	I(n) , J, K, L(n)
		c			c/n

K—J

Question 1

The correct answer is choice **b**. This is a standard "Test-the-Rules" question. The first restriction rules out choice **c**, since the second city toured is Kansas City, not Honolulu. The second and third restrictions together rule out choice **a**, since the third city, Indianapolis, ends with a new song, not a classic song. They also rule out choice **e**, since the third city toured is Las Vegas, which ends with a new song, not a classic song. The fourth restriction rules out choice **d**, since K is not before J.

Question 2

The correct answer is choice **a**. I and K are next to one another, and form a block. Try to see where you can fit I/K into the diagram:

1	2	3	4	5	
J̶	H	I̶ L̶		K̶	I(n) , J, K, L(n)
		c			c/n

K—J

The block clearly cannot go in spots 1 or 2 for lack of room. This means they must take up spots 3–4 or spots 4–5. But the block I/K couldn't take up spots 4–5 because there would be no room for J to the right of K (as the string K—J requires). So they must take up spots 3–4. But I cannot be in spot 3, so spot 3 must be K, spot 4 must be I, leaving only spot 5 for J, forcing L into spot 1:

1	2	3	4	5	
J̶ L	H	I̶ L̶ K	I	K̶ J	I(n) , J, K, L(n)
n		c	n		c/n

(We have also noted that spots 1 and 4 have an n, due the second restriction).

K—J

Since Las Vegas is in spot 1 on this grid, **a** is the correct answer choice. Choice **b** is incorrect because Las Vegas is not second, choice **c** is incorrect because Kansas City is not the first, choice **d** is incorrect because Kansas City is not the second, and choice **e** is incorrect because Jacksonville is not the fourth city toured.

Question 3

The correct answer is choice **b**. Work the information that spot 1 has a c into the diagram, and see what follows:

1	2	3	4	5	
J̶	H	I̶ L̶		K̶	I(n) , J, K, L(n)
c		c			c/n

K—J

Since spot 1 is a c, neither I nor l can be in spot 1—this leaves only K for spot 1:

1	2	3	4	5	
J̶ I̶ L̶ K	H	I̶ L̶		K̶	I(n) , J, K, L(n)
c		c			c/n

K—J

Since neither I nor L can be in spot 3, they must be in spots 4–5 (meaning that spots 4 and 5 have an n, given the second restriction).

This leaves J for spot 3:

1	2	3	4	5	
J̶ I̶ L̶ K	H	I̶ L̶ J	I/L	K̶ I/L	I(n) , J, K, L(n)
c		c	n	n	c/n

K—J

There is no restriction on the order of I and L here, so there are two possible different sequences—answer choice **b**.

Question 4

The correct answer is choice **a**. I and L are next to one another, and form a block. See where this block can fit into the diagram:

1	2	3	4	5	
J̶	H	I̶ L̶		K̶	I(n) , J, K, L(n)
		c			c/n

K—J

The block clearly cannot go in spots 1 or 2, for lack of room. This means they must take up spots 3–4 or spots 4–5. But neither I nor L can be in spot 3, so the block must take up spots 4–5:

1	2	3	4	5	
J̶	H	I̶ L̶	I/L	K̶ I/L	I(n) , J, K, L(n)
		c			c/n

K—J

This means that to preserve the K– J sequence, K must be in spot 1 and J in spot 3. And it also means that spots 4 and 5 have an n (because of the second restriction):

1	2	3	4	5	
J̶ K	H	I̶ L̶ J	I/L	K̶ L/I	I(n) , J, K, L(n)
		c	n	n	c/n

K—J

Now turn to the answer choices. The fourth spot has an n, and so it can't be the case that the fourth city toured has a concert that ends with a classic song, so **a** is the correct answer. The fifth spot has an n, so **b** is not correct. The second spot is open, and so could be filled with either c or n, and so **c** and **d** are incorrect. The first spot is also open, so it could have an n, and therefore choice **e** is incorrect.

Question 5

The correct answer is choice **b**. Take each answer choice in turn, and quickly test it to see if any contradictions emerge when you apply the rules. Keep in mind that information from previous questions might come in handy—look for scenarios you have already established to be acceptable. The diagram created for Question 5 rules out choice (a), since spots 4 and 5 have n there. The diagram for Question 4 rules out choice **d**. Now test choice **b**:

1	2	3	4	5	
J̶	H	I̶ L̶		K̶	I(n) , J, K, L(n)
		c	c	c	c/n

K—J

If spots 4 and 5 have c, then neither of those spots can have I or L (since they both carry an n with them). And since neither I nor L can be in spot 3, that leaves only spots 1 and 2—but spot 2 is already taken by H. So it can't be that spots 4 and 5 have c's, and therefore choice **b** is correct.

Game 8

This is a hybrid game with an element of sequencing (putting the six flights in order of departure) and matching (matching each flight to a gate). The best way to diagram this game is with a grid:

1	2	3	4	5	6	
						L, M, N, O, P, Q
						A/B/C

Now symbolize the restrictions and add whatever information you can into the diagram. The first restriction is difficult to symbolize, so circle it and make sure to keep it in mind. You may also want to write it below the diagram to remember it. The second restriction can be directly coded into the diagram.

1	2	3	4	5	6	
				M		L, M, N, O, P, Q
						A/B/C

No consec dep. from same gate
The third restriction can be symbolized:

N — P/Q

The fourth restriction is also difficult to symbolize, so circle it for now and keep it in mind. You may also want to write it below the diagram to remember it.

The fifth restriction can be symbolized:

P — M

Now look for connections between the restrictions and make deductions. Since P cannot be after M (in the fifth spot), we can note that P does not depart sixth (which captures all the information from the P—M restriction). And since N is before P, we note that P cannot depart first. Similarly, since N is before Q, we note that Q cannot depart first:

1	2	3	4	5	6	
P̶Q̶				M	P̶	L, M, N, O, P, Q
						A/B/C

No consec dep. from same gate
Gate before N is A
N — P/Q

Since there must be at least one departure before N (as per the fourth restriction), we know that N cannot be first. Since P and Q must come after N (as per the third restriction), we know that N needs two open spaces to its right. N cannot be in spot 6 (zero spaces to its right), or spot 5 (M is already there), or spot 4 (only one open spot to its right):

1	2	3	4	5	6	
P̶Q̶ N̶			N̶	M	P̶ N̶	L, M, N, O, P, Q
						A/B/C

No consec dep. from same gate
Gate before N is A
N — P/Q

Question 1

The correct answer is choice **a**. This question is a "Test-the-Rules" question. The second restriction rules out choice **c**, since M is the second departure. The third restriction rules out choice **e**, since N does not depart before P. The fourth restriction rules out choice **b**, since N is the first departure on this answer choice, but the restriction implies that there is at least one flight before N. The fifth restriction rules out choice **d**, since M departs before P.

Question 2

The correct answer is choice **c**. See what deductions can be made from the new information that the first flight departs from Gate C:

1	2	3	4	5	6	
P̶Q̶N̶			N̶	M	P̶N̶	L, M, N, O, P, Q
C						A/B/C

> No consec dep. from same gate
> Gate before N is A
> N—P/Q

Since there can be no consecutive departures from the same gate, the second flight must leave from Gate A or Gate B. Further, since the gate for the departure before N is gate A, spot 2 cannot have N—this only leaves spot 3 for N, which means that spot 2 is gate A:

1	2	3	4	5	6	
P̶Q̶N̶		N	N̶	M	P̶N̶	L, M, N, O, P, Q
C	A					A/B/C

> No consec dep. from same gate
> Gate before N is A
> N—P/Q

Since N is before both P and Q, P and Q must take spots 4 and 6. But P cannot be in spot 6, so P must be in spot 4 and Q in spot 6:

1	2	3	4	5	6	
P̶Q̶N̶		N	N̶P	M	P̶N̶Q	L, M, N, O, P, Q
C	A					A/B/C

> No consec dep. from same gate
> Gate before N is A
> N—P/Q

Now scan the answer choices to see which one is given to us in this diagram. Choice **a** is incorrect

because N departs third, not second. Choice **b** is incorrect because it is not specified when O departs—it could be first or second, according to this diagram. Choice **d** is incorrect because L's departure is not specified either—it could either be first or second. Choice **e** is incorrect because O does not depart sixth; rather, Q departs sixth. Choice **c** is correct because P departs fourth in this diagram.

Question 3

The correct answer is choice **a**. We've already done the necessary work, so take a look at the diagram.

1	2	3	4	5	6	
P̶Q̶N̶			N̶	M	P̶N̶	L, M, N, O, P, Q
						A/B/C

> No consec dep. from same gate
> Gate before N is A
> N—P/Q

This tells us that P cannot be first, fifth, or sixth—this eliminates choices **b**, **c**, **d**, and **e**. This only leaves answer choice **a**.

Question 4

The correct answer is choice **e**. See what deductions can be made from the new information that Q departs third from gate B:

1	2	3	4	5	6	
P̶Q̶N̶		Q	N̶	M	P̶N̶	L, M, N, O, P, Q
		B				A/B/C

> No consec dep. from same gate
> Gate before N is A
> N—P/Q

Since N has to come before Q, and N can't be in spot 1, N must be in spot 2. Further, since the gate for the departure before N is Gate A, the first flight must then be from Gate A:

1	2	3	4	5	6	
P̶Q̶N̶	N	Q	N̶	M	P̶N̶	L, M, N, O, P, Q
A	B					A/B/C

No consec dep. from same gate
Gate before N is A
N—P/Q

1	2	3	4	5	6	
P̶Q̶N̶			N̶	M	P̶N̶	L, M, N, O, P, Q
	C					A/B/C

No consec dep. from same gate
Gate before N is A
N—P/Q

Now, look at the rules again. Since no two consecutive departures can be from the same gate, the second flight must depart from Gate C (since it is flanked by A and B). This rule also indicates that spot 4 must be Gate A or C.

1	2	3	4	5	6	
P̶Q̶N̶	N	Q	N̶	M	P̶N̶	L, M, N, O, P, Q
A	C	B	A/C			A/B/C

No consec dep. from same gate
Gate before N is A
N—P/Q

Note that flight N has to depart second or third. But it cannot depart third, because the gate for the departure just before it is Gate C (and the fourth rule tells us that that gate must be A). So N must depart second, and flight 1 must depart from Gate A:

1	2	3	4	5	6	
P̶Q̶N̶	N		N̶	M	P̶N̶	L, M, N, O, P, Q
A	C					A/B/C

No consec dep. from same gate
Gate before N is A
N—P/Q

This also means that the gate for the third flight must be A or B:

1	2	3	4	5	6	
P̶Q̶N̶	N		N̶	M	P̶N̶	L, M, N, O, P, Q
A	C	A/B				A/B/C

No consec dep. from same gate
Gate before N is A

Now turn to the answer choices and see if any of them are given in this diagram. Choice **a** is incorrect because according to the diagram, the fourth flight can depart from gate A. Choice **b** is incorrect because according to the diagram, the fourth flight can also depart from gate C. Choice **c** is incorrect because according to the diagram the fifth flight can depart from any gate (depending on what gates are assigned to the fourth and sixth flights). Choice **d** is incorrect for the same reason: the sixth flight can depart from any gate, depending on what gate is assigned to the fifth flight.

Choice **e** is correct because according the diagram, the second flight in fact departs from Gate C.

Question 5

The correct answer is choice **d**. See what new deductions can be made from the new information that the second departure is from Gate C:

Now check the answer choices to see which could be true (the incorrect answer choices), and which can't be true (the correct answer choice). While you may not be certain about the choices that could be true, you will be certain about the choices that can't be true. Choice **a** is incorrect because O could depart before M and N. Choice **b** is incorrect because P could depart after Q. Choice **c** is incorrect because L could depart after M. Choice **d** is correct because it can't be the case that both L and O depart before N, since there is only one space before N. The diagram makes clear that **d** cannot be the case, and so **d** is the correct answer. Choice **e** is incorrect because, as with choice **b**, it seems that the diagram makes no restrictions on Q departing before or after P.

ADDITIONAL ONLINE PRACTICE

Whether you need help building basic skills or preparing for an exam, visit the LearningExpress Practice Center! On this site, you can access additional practice materials. Using the code below, you'll be able to log in and complete additional LSAT Logic Game practice. This online practice will also provide you with:

- **Immediate scoring**
- **Detailed answer explanations**
- **Personalized recommendations for further practice and study**

Log in to the LearningExpress Practice Center by using this URL: **www.learnatest.com/practice**

This is your Access Code: **7793**

Follow the steps online to redeem your access code. After you've used your access code to register with the site, you will be prompted to create a username and password. For easy reference, record them here:

Username: _____ **Password:** _____

With your username and password, you can log in and answer these practice questions as many times as you like. If you have any questions or problems, please contact LearningExpress customer service at 1-800-295-9556 ext. 2, or e-mail us at **customerservice@learningexpressllc.com.**

NOTES

NOTES